Power and Control
in the Television Worlds
of Joss Whedon

Power and Control
in the Television Worlds
of Joss Whedon

SHERRY GINN

McFarland & Company, Inc., Publishers
Jefferson, North Carolina, and London

An earlier version of Chapter 6 appeared as "Memory, Mind, and Mayhem: Neurological Tampering and Manipulation in *Dollhouse*" in *Slayage, The Journal of the Whedon Studies Association* 8.23 (Summer/Fall 2010). Special Issue: *Fantasy Is Not Their Purpose: Joss Whedon's* Dollhouse, eds. Cynthia Masson and Rhonda V. Wilcox. Used with permission.

LIBRARY OF CONGRESS CATALOGUING-IN-PUBLICATION DATA

Ginn, Sherry.
   Power and control in the television worlds of Joss Whedon / Sherry
   Ginn.
       p.   cm.
   Includes bibliographical references and index.

   ISBN 978-0-7864-5858-5
   softcover : acid free paper ∞

   1. Whedon, Joss, 1964– —Criticism and interpretation.
I. Title.
PN1992.4.W49G57   2012
791.45'72—dc23   2011049868

BRITISH LIBRARY CATALOGUING DATA ARE AVAILABLE

Front cover images: Nathan Fillion as Capt. Malcolm "Mal" Reynolds and Adam Baldwin as Jayne Cobb in *Serenity,* 2005, written and directed by Joss Whedon (Photofest); cover design by David K. Landis (Shake It Loose Graphics)

Manufactured in the United States of America

McFarland & Company, Inc., Publishers
  Box 611, Jefferson, North Carolina 28640
   www.mcfarlandpub.com

This one is for Mama,
Dorothy B. Ginn (1930–2009).
Love always.

Table of Contents

Acknowledgments ix
Preface: Exploring the Whedonverses 1

1. The Problem of Power and Control 9
2. Love and Sex as Methods of Control 23
3. Aggression and Violence as Methods of Control 43
4. Supernatural Methods of Control 62
5. Manipulating the Brain as a Method of Control 81
6. Manipulating Memory as a Method of Control 97
7. Exerting Control with Pharmaceutical Agents 114
8. Other Methods of Control 130

Epilogue: Final Remarks 144
Appendix A: Whedonverses Character List 145
Appendix B: Series Episode List 149
Chapter Notes 159
Works Cited 173
Index 183

Acknowledgments

I came to Whedon late, much later than everyone else I know, or so it seems. I never watched *Buffy* when the series was on air. Why? For a very practical reason — my cable lineup did not carry it. By the time the series was available I was immersed in other things and was not interested in watching a series where I would have to start somewhere in the middle. I also never watched *Firefly*. I cannot imagine how I missed it during its first run, but given its quick demise, perhaps I can be forgiven. All I know is that I heard about *Firefly* from someone at work, who was also a big *Buffy* fan. So when the Syfy channel began to air *Firefly*, I watched and that, as they say, is that. I could not wait for another week to pass, so I immediately ordered the DVD from Barnes and Noble and watched the remaining episodes in one sitting. I was so excited that I tried to find more stuff about the series. A short time later I presented a paper on *Firefly* at a conference and most likely embarrassed myself with my naïveté about all things Whedon. But I persevered and kept learning what I could, meeting people knowledgeable about Whedon, and *listening* to what they had to say.

Now just think. I had still not watched Buffy, but I kept listening to what the Whedonians had to say and I kept my mouth shut as much as is possible whenever someone started talking about *Buffy* or *Angel*. I felt like I could hold my own with *Firefly* and *Serenity*. I think I can recite the dialogue from them in my sleep (and probably do). And, then came *Dollhouse* and I got in on that series from the ground floor up (or should that be pods to penthouse up?). More papers later and more conversations and, yes, I finally started watching *Buffy*. I cannot remember who talked about "Buffy virgins" at Slayage 3, but I just knew she was talking about me. I do wish that I had gotten in on *Buffy* from the beginning, thinking of what fun (and agony) it would have been waiting for the next week's revelations. It is great fun now that Nikki Stafford is hosting the Buffy Re-Watch. I can read the recaps, read the commentary by guest posters, and then read the reactions and comments from the newbies as well as the longtime fans. It is so interesting and exciting to have my thoughts confirmed or challenged by what others have to say. And it is really awesome when someone posts a comment that makes me (and sometimes everyone else) sit up and take notice. *Buffy* is definitely still a very rich mine with many gems just waiting to be uncovered.

Sometime within the past year I finally watched *Angel*. I managed to rope my husband in on this task and he watched every episode with me, knowing that I was writing a book about the televisual world of Whedon. The great part about this was that he did not know much about the Whedonverses, although he has seen all of the *Firefly* episodes several times. I had the pleasure of listening to his comments and queries about the Angelverse; sometimes those comments were quite astute and made me rethink and question earlier assumptions, not only about *Angel*, but about *Buffy* and Whedon as well.

As everyone knows, Whedon's works involve someone or something trying to exert power over and control someone else, whether it is through fair means or foul. As my bookshelves and files grew heavier with all things Whedon, I continued to think about the issues of power and control: who's doing the controlling and how are they doing it? In some cases it is very obvious, e.g., the Watchers' Council controls the Slayer, his neurological chip controls Spike, Topher's mind wipes control the Actives. But, how do those work exactly? And what about the more subtle ways in which control is exerted, like with love or fear of the loss of love? As I presented papers at various conferences exploring these issues, I realized that a book-length treatment might be possible.

Since my first paper presentation on Whedon's women years ago to my last presentation on "Aggression and Violence in the Whedonverses" at PCA in 2011, I have met many nice people whose work I admire and who have now become good friends. Some of those people volunteered their time to read and critique the chapters in this book. I will thank them all here. I did not always take their advice, so any errors that remain in any given chapter are my own. Special thanks then go to Alyson R. Buckman, Tanya R. Cochran, K. Dale Koontz, Linda J. Jencson, David Lavery, Heather M. Porter, and Mary Alice Money. I would also like to thank Rhonda V. Wilcox for providing a copy of the episode guides for *Buffy* and *Firefly* so that I would not have to recreate them herein. To all the members of every audience at every venue who commented on my research I extend my heartfelt thanks as well.

As does everyone who writes about the Whedonverses, I have to extend thanks to all of the cast members of the various series as well as the crew members for their dedication to the cause. Of course, none of it would be possible without Joss Whedon, who delighted us with these tales and who drove us crazy when he was unable to give us more. (Dear Buddha, Please let me meet Adam Baldwin and bring me a new *Firefly* movie...)

I dedicated my first book to my father who died while I was writing it (one reason why it did not make its deadline). I told my mother I would dedicate the next one to her: here it is, Mom. I just wish that you were here to read it. Finally, a special thank you goes to my husband and partner, Larry Williamson. All of those weekends and nights when I was squirreled away in my study, writing: I will make it up to you. Thanks for being my rock, for always being there, and for not being too jealous of Jayne.

Preface:
Exploring the Whedonverses[1]

Shiny. Let's be bad guys.— Jayne Cobb, *Serenity*

What is it about the Whedonverses? What are the Whedonverses? Specifically they are the four television series created by Joss Whedon: *Buffy the Vampire Slayer*, *Angel*, *Firefly*, and *Dollhouse*. Like most fans, I will also include *Firefly*'s sequel motion picture, *Serenity*. One could also include the graphic novels *Fray* and *Buffy* Season 8 as well as the various graphic novels of the 'verse, the way we refer to the world of *Firefly* and *Serenity*. And can we forget *Dr. Horrible's Sing-Along Blog*?

Why do people like me love these programs? Why do we cover our walls with posters of the characters, buy mass quantities of merchandise, endlessly watch the episodes, and quote dialogue (even when no one around us realizes it)?

All of those are very good questions, with at least a dozen, if not more, different answers. One of the answers lies with the community of people who are fans of the various programs. It was as much the programs as the people I met at various conferences that kept me searching for more information and beginning my own serious study of these worlds. For those of you who are unfamiliar with the Whedonverses — yes, there are probably a few people reading this who are only familiar with one of Whedon's oeuvre, or even none (those are probably my family members reading this and wondering why I have been buried in my study for so long) — I will provide below a short synopsis of the four series that I will discuss in this book.

1

Buffy the Vampire Slayer (original air dates 10 March 1997 to 20 May 2003)

"In every generation there is a Chosen One. She alone will stand against the vampires, the demons, and the forces of darkness. She is the Slayer."[2] Buffy Summers is a vampire slayer, a post held by females in our world, but generally held by men in most treatments of vampire lore, beginning with Bram Stoker's *Dracula*.[3] Buffy is quite petite,[4] possesses superhuman strength, has the ability to heal quickly, and delivers it all with a quick, acerbic wit. Buffy would fit the characteristics of the new woman warrior

> whose capacity to fight for just causes matches or exceeds that of [her] male colleagues. [Such] glamorous, larger-than-life, yet disarmingly recognizable heroes battle evil on a daily basis and, without much fanfare, repeatedly save the world from untold horror [Early and Kennedy, 3].

When the series begins Buffy and her mother Joyce have moved to Sunnydale, California, to escape the unfortunate incidents that occurred at her previous high school.[5] Buffy quickly makes friends with a couple of misfits, Willow Rosenberg and Xander Harris, and they join her in her battles against the forces of darkness using their brains (Willow) and strength (Xander), although perhaps Xander is more important for his emotional support than for his muscles.

Along the way Buffy is joined by her Watcher, Rupert Giles, Willow's boyfriend, Oz, and Xander's girlfriend, Cordelia Chase. Oz leaves in Season Four and Willow becomes romantically involved with Tara Maclay, who dies tragically in Season Six. Willow develops another relationship in Season Seven with a Potential Slayer named Kennedy. Xander and Cordelia break up in Season Three, and he subsequently dates an ex-vengeance demon named Anya, before leaving her at the altar on their wedding day, in Season Six. Cordelia leaves Sunnydale after graduation and moves to Los Angeles where she joins Angel Investigations. Rupert Giles is very important to Buffy, not just as a Watcher but also as a father figure. Buffy falls deeply in love with a vampire named Angel in Season One. She loses her virginity to him in Season Two, the result of which was to activate a Gypsy curse that causes him to lose his soul.

For the remainder of that season Angelus tortures Buffy (psychologically) and her friends (both psychologically and physically). Buffy realizes that she has to destroy Angelus and does so, although she realizes that his soul has been returned prior to the staking. Angel eventually returns from the hell dimension and continues to help Buffy in her mission to fight the forces of darkness. However, he realizes that they can never be together as lovers and so he leaves her, moving to Los Angeles where he believes that he can "help the helpless and the hopeless." Buffy has a serious relationship with a young man named Riley Finn throughout Seasons Four and Five; however, it is not serious enough, for Riley realizes that she does not love him the way that he loves her. He leaves her to continue his work with The Initiative, a secret government organization created to also fight the forces of darkness.

Buffy is presented with a little sister beginning in Season Five, one who causes no end of annoyance to Buffy and her fans. Dawn is a very young 15 and spends most of two seasons whining and complaining that no one pays any attention to her. She eventually matures enough to realize her importance to the Slayer. Along the way Buffy fights against and with the vampire Spike. Beginning as an enemy, Spike eventually becomes an ally, falling in love with Buffy. She is unable to return his feelings for her, but she increasingly relies on his strength in her fight against the forces of darkness. Spike sacrifices himself to save Buffy and the rest of the world. In the course of the seven seasons, Buffy dies and is returned to life twice, once by human means and once by dark magick.

Angel (original air dates 5 October 1999 to 19 May 2004)

Angel has much for which he has to atone. As a human named Liam he was a scoundrel and wastrel. In 1743 he was turned into a vampire, called himself Angelus, and wreaked havoc across Europe with his sire, Darla, for 155 years. In 1898, she gave him a Gypsy girl for his birthday present. The murdered girl's family cursed him by restoring his soul,[6] thus forcing him to suffer guilt for his depredations. In the 20th century, Angel meets a demon named Whistler who tells him that he must go to Sunnydale to help the Slayer, but he eventually leaves when he realizes that his love for her can never be. Traveling to Los Angeles, he meets a half-demon named Doyle who tells him that the Powers That Be have a job for him to do in L.A., to help the helpless and the hopeless who have no one else to be their champion. Doyle has visions that provide Angel with information about those needing his help.

Doyle dies a heroic death about halfway through Season One. His parting gift to Cordelia, a big kiss, was actually his way of transferring the visions to her. However, Cordelia is completely human and the visions begin to have serious consequences for her health. Wesley Wyndam-Pryce, another cross-over from the Buffyverse, joins Angel Investigations, bringing his considerable knowledge of demons, vampires, and other creatures of darkness to the battle. By the end of Season One they are also joined by a streetwise vampire-killer named Gunn. Season Two brings two more characters to the team, the demon psychic Lorne and the brilliant human physicist (Wini)Fred Burkle. However, Angel Investigations is torn apart by fear and a decided unwillingness of the team members to confide in one another.

When Darla, Angel's sire and a vicious one at that, becomes pregnant, she looks for ways to destroy the child. Unable to do so, she gradually grows to love the baby so deeply that she stakes herself so that the child can live.[7] Angel names the boy Connor in honor of his Irish heritage. Angel is a doting and loving father, but his happiness is short-lived. Holtz, a man from Angelus' past, seeks to take his revenge on Angel, as it was Angelus who killed his wife and children many years earlier. Holtz has vowed to make Angel suffer as he has suffered. He convinces Wesley that there is a prophecy foretelling that Angel will kill the boy.

Rather than discuss the prophecy and his fears with Angel and the rest of the team, Wesley kidnaps Connor. Holtz takes the boy and escapes into a hell dimension where he is able to indoctrinate Connor with hatred for Angel. Connor, aged to his mid-teens, returns and begins his campaign for revenge, eventually casting Angel into the sea. Angel escapes, forgives his son, and gives him up in an act of love that ensures Connor will have a happy life with no memory of his horrible past. Cordelia has an affair with Connor that results in the birth of a demonic daughter who attempts to destroy the world. In Season Five, Spike joins the cast as a ghost, and one of the Powers That Be possesses Fred and also tries to destroy the world.

Throughout the first four seasons Angel has many battles with the international and interdimensional law firm Wolfram and Hart, the senior partners of which are actually demons. The law firm is especially interested in Angel because an ancient prophecy has deemed that Angel will play a key role in the Apocalypse, although the prophecy does not state on which side Angel will fight. The senior partners give the firm to Angel at the end of Season Four and he accepts the offer in return for their help with Connor.

Firefly (original air dates 20 September 2002 to 20 December 2002)

> After the earth was used up, we found a new solar system, and hundreds of new Earths were terra-formed and colonized. The central planets formed the Alliance and decided all the planets had to join under their rule. There was some disagreement on that point. After the War, many of the Independents who had fought and lost drifted to the edges of the system, far from Alliance control. Out here, people struggled to get by with the most basic technologies; a ship would bring you work, a gun would help you keep it. A captain's goal was simple: find a crew, find a job, and keep flying.[8]

This pretty much sums up the 14 short episodes of *Firefly*. Malcolm (Mal) Reynolds and his second-in-command, Zoe Washburne, are veterans of the War for Independence. They are all that is left of their platoon after the massacre, subsequent surrender, and abandonment after the Battle for Serenity Valley. Mal buys a spaceship, names her Serenity in honor and memory of the battle, and then hires a crew. That crew is quite diverse: a male pilot named Wash, who will eventually become Zoe's husband; a female engineer named Kaylee; a male hired gun named Jayne Cobb; and a bonafide (to use Mal's words) female Companion (with a capital C) named Inara. In the first episode he acquires three more crew: a male Shepherd (or preacher) named Book; a male doctor, Simon Tam; and the doctor's little sister, River.

Simon and River are on the run because River had been held captive and subjected to mind-altering experiments by the Government. Incredibly smart and gifted, River is more powerful than anyone knows; however, she is still a young girl and does not know what is wrong with her. Neither does her brother. For all of his ability as a physician Simon is unable to help River primarily because he does not know what the Alliance doctors did to her.

With only 14 episodes filmed we do not learn much about Mal's 'verse, but what we do learn is not necessarily pretty. The Alliance is the governing body, but its meddlesome actions are apparently serious enough to instigate a civil war which has ended by the time the series begins. Residing in the core of the 'verse confers some advantages, like timely supplies, but many people prefer to live on the outer planets despite the peril because they are far removed from the Alliance and its "meddling." River notes this in the sequel motion picture *Serenity*, saying, "People don't like to be meddled with. We tell them what to do, what to think, don't run, don't walk. We're in their homes and in their heads and we haven't the right. We're meddle-some."

Dollhouse (original air dates 13 February 2009 to 29 January 2010)

One premise underlying Joss Whedon's *Dollhouse* is fantasy fulfillment. Wealthy clients can obtain the services of male and/or female "Actives" who can be programmed to fulfill any and every fantasy imaginable. Although Actives can be and are used for various other purposes— such as infiltrating a religious cult and negotiating a kidnapping— generally the Actives are hired for sexual purposes. As Dr. Saunders tells Topher in the unaired "Pilot," we are "fulfilling the whims of the rich." Actives are screened phys-ically prior to and after any engagement for the express purpose of protecting both the client and the Active. Thus, clients can engage Actives sexually and be assured that the Actives will not be able to blackmail them later, get preg-nant and make paternity claims, or spread sexually transmitted diseases. Even better, the Active's memory of these encounters is erased. Most of the Dollhouse's clients are male, and the majority of the Actives are female.

Actives were men and women who have entered into a five-year period of (perhaps consensual) servitude to a chain of Dollhouses operated by the Rossum Corporation. Actives' autobiographical memories are erased and, whenever they are hired, the requested persona is downloaded into the Actives' supposedly empty minds. People with enough money can hire any Active for any type of encounter; most encounters include sexual relations, and Actives can be programmed to be passive or active, hetero- or homo-sexual, or any other type requested by the client.

The main character in *Dollhouse* is Echo, the Active of a young woman named Caroline, recruited by the Dollhouse after attempting to liberate research animals from one of the Rossum Corporation's laboratories. One result of the failed rescue attempt was the death of Caroline's lover. Rather than be arrested and perhaps incarcerated, Caroline eventually "decides" to join the Dollhouse. Other Actives that figured prominently in the storylines of the two seasons the program aired are Victor, Sierra, Mellie/November, and Dr. Saunders.[9] Characters that worked for the Dollhouse include Adelle DeWitt, Director of the Los Angeles Dollhouse; Topher Brink, the program-mer; and Boyd Langton, Echo's "handler." Also included in the cast was Paul

Ballard, an FBI agent intent upon exposing the Dollhouses for their sexual exploitation of people. Ballard is also determined to rescue Caroline, as he has fallen in love with her picture.

As we follow Echo's various assignments we begin to learn that all is not well within the Dollhouse. Someone is a mole, sabotaging Echo's programming. She begins to retain memories of her various Active personalities, eventually incorporating all of those personas as well as their memories, skills, and emotions into her own psyche. She discovers the secret behind the Dollhouses and makes it her goal to destroy the Rossum Corporation before they can implement their grand design, immortality for their clients. She fails to stop Rossum from implementing that plan, but does lead the resistance that will free humanity.

CHAPTER 1

The Problem
of Power and Control[1]

It's about power. Who's got it and who knows how to use it.—Buffy
Summers, "Lessons" [*Buffy* 7.1]

The Whedonverses—*Buffy the Vampire Slayer, Angel, Firefly/Serenity,*
and *Dollhouse*—contain myriad ways in which power can be wielded, and
how that power can be used to control the thoughts, emotions, and behavior
of people. Joss Whedon examined how power can corrupt those who use it,
from a rogue Slayer to an unbalanced girl, from a government bent on controlling its populace to two corporations intent upon restricting power to a
select and wealthy few. He also presented examples in which power does
not corrupt and the ways in which its corrupting influence can be avoided,
using the power of love — of friends and family — to let us know that love
can be a force of both good and evil. The purpose of this book is to explore
the ways in which power can be used for both positive and negative purposes,
and how control can refer not only to the influence one has over others, but
also to the control one can have over one's self.

Defining Power and Control

What is control? It is the power to direct or determine. It is a relation
of constraint of one entity (a thing or a person or a group) by another. It
means to exercise authoritative control or power over. It means to lessen the
intensity of, to temper or hold in restraint, to hold or keep within limits. It
means restraint, as in discipline in personal and social activities. It is the

activity of maintaining control over something. It means to operate, to handle and cause to function. It means dominance: the state that exists when one person or group has power over another. It means to manipulate: to control the self or others, or to influence skillfully, usually to one's advantage.

What, then, is power? For the purposes of this book it will be defined as "possession of controlling influence": that which controls influence can be said to be powerful or in power. One sociology textbook defines power as "the ability of individuals or groups to achieve goals, control events, and maintain influence over others despite opposition" (Benokraitis 140). There are many reasons for desiring power or to be powerful: to increase one's importance in one's own eyes or in the eyes of others; to provide safety and security to oneself, one's family and friends, one's group or nation; and to accumulate wealth and status (and even more power). This power can be used against friend and/or foe, or against an entire group or population of friends and/or foes. Among the many ways of obtaining power are to use brute strength and force, intelligence, love, fear, stealth and cunning, power-sharing, or raw talent. It can even be achieved by using artificial or unnatural means, via mind control, for example.

Mind control can be achieved in a variety of ways. Although love, sex, fear, and violence are effective methods of controlling someone, there are other more reliable ways to do so. Early forms of mind control included mesmerism, or "animal magnetism," which proposed that all beings were affected by the same magnetic force that affected celestial bodies (Mesmer). Often confused with mesmerism, hypnosis is an altered state of consciousness mediated by the power of suggestion.[2] Another method of control involves brain surgery, rendering the victim incapable of speaking or reasoning. One example of this is psychosurgery, such as prefrontal lobotomy, in which the reasoning section of the brain, the frontal lobes, is disconnected from the parts of the brain controlling more primitive emotions (Mashour, Walker, and Martuza). Surgery can also enhance the brain's functioning, change the ways in which the brain stores memories, or create false memories. Joss Whedon explored the issue of neurological mind control in each of the series to be discussed herein.

Science fiction and fantasy (SFF) and horror allow one to explore the ways in which the supernatural can be used to control behavior. For example, extraterrestrial beings, demons, witches, and other monsters may exert control over unsuspecting victims. Extraterrestrials would be expected to have a variety of methods at their disposal for controlling an unsuspecting population. Advanced technology which allows them to stop time, as in *The Day the Earth Stood Still*, hijack communication systems as in *Independence Day*, or invade and inhabit human hosts as in *The Puppetmasters*, can all lead to subjugation and conquest. Whedon does not, however, use extraterrestrial beings in any of the four series discussed herein. Even in *Firefly* and *Serenity* Whedon's monsters, quite scary enough, are all too human.

One of the most famous of the monsters who exerts control over unsuspecting victims is the vampire, who uses sheer strength of will and a dose of sexual attraction as well as hypnosis for control. The earliest depictions of vampires, such as in the 1922 German Expressionist film *Nosferatu*, showed the ugliness of the undead. Bela Lugosi brought sex appeal to Count Dracula on Broadway and in the 1931 American film, an aspect that has continued through to the present day, when we see fans swoon over vampires as diverse as Spike and Angel on *Buffy*,[3] Edward in *Twilight* (Meyer), Mick St. John on *Moonlight*, and Bill and Eric on *True Blood*. Some of these cinematic vampires use hypnotism to exert control over their victims; Whedon's vampires do not. Whedon does make use of other supernatural devices in *Buffy* and *Angel*, notably magick and witchcraft. These devices may have positive and negative effects, with the magick in *Buffy* being mostly negative. Nevertheless, each of these devices can be analyzed for their use in providing a source of power with which to control others and bend them to one's will.

As Buffy says in the Season Seven episode "Lessons"—"It's about power: who's got it and who knows how to use it." By the series' end Buffy is strong enough and secure enough to share her power (Brannon; Wilcox). Her power stems from the fact that she is the "Chosen One." As such, albeit mortal, she is stronger and tougher than the average teenage girl. As she steps into the role for which she was destined, Buffy must learn to control her emotions (as does any teen-ager) as well as her body, which has been turning on her for several years, as it matured from girl-child to woman to Slayer. She also has to learn to control her own mind, to exert discipline over her emotions and her body; and we saw how, all too often, both her emotions and her body got the better of her, and not just the emotional and sexual relationships with Spike and Angel. However, we could just as easily discuss the vampires' control of her: Angel using her emotional vulnerability for him and his for her; Angel and Spike both using large doses of sexiness, their own, and in the case of Spike the sex itself, sex that was sheer raw animal magnetism, as Buffy and Spike each initially denies any emotional attachment to the other. Given that *Buffy the Vampire Slayer* begins in the sheer hell of high school, it is no wonder that sex exerts a powerful influence on the protagonists of the story. After all, the reality of raging hormones, pheromones, and secondary sexual characteristics indicate subtly and not so subtly that these people are "of age." Who can forget Xander's comment that he is a teen-age boy — looking at linoleum makes him want to have sex ("Innocence" 2.14)?

Years of research as well as common knowledge indicate that this is the period of time when youth begin to explore their sexuality, acknowledging to themselves, if not to the world, that they may or may not be heterosexual (as if sexuality were a dichotomy!). This issue is certainly explored in *Buffy* as Willow Rosenberg confronts her sexuality; however, a discussion of that topic is beyond the scope of this essay. Although Willow does not use her sexuality as a weapon in *Buffy*, she certainly uses witchcraft, with both positive and negative consequences. The power afforded Willow by witchcraft becomes increasingly seductive (for example, in the episode "Tabula Rasa" [6.8]). That power allows her to help Buffy in her quest to rid Sunnydale of its demonic denizens. However, Willow is not strong enough psychologically (Humanitas) to withstand the corrupting influence of that power, as she seeks control over her lover and eventually her lover's murderer (more about this in chapters 3 and 4).

Locus of Control

Julian Rotter proposed the existence of a psychological dimension he termed locus of control, defined as "the extent to which people perceive outcomes as internally controllable by their own efforts and actions or as externally controlled by outside forces" (Meyers 55). Thus, people with an external locus of control perceive the world as largely uncontrollable and themselves as powerless. Such a person is more or less living on the whims of fate. People with an internal locus of control, on the other hand, perceive themselves to be the captains of their own fate, controlling their own destiny. For instance, research indicates that those with an internal locus of control are more likely to stop smoking, reach their goals, and make more money than those with an external locus of control (Meyers).

This issue of personal control can have serious consequences for both the individual and society. Those who feel that they have no control over their lives may develop a condition that psychologists refer to as learned helplessness (Seligman). People who develop this learned helplessness become passive, believing that their efforts will have no effect on the outcome of their actions. Such a belief may lead to depression and other psychological problems.

The various characters in the Whedonverses can be assessed by using this dimension of control. At various times in each series certain characters may display both an internal and an external locus of control, depending upon the circumstances in which the characters find themselves. As would be predicted by the theory, characters who are experiencing events that indicate they have control over their lives are generally happier than when they experience events that indicate they are out of control. Buffy provides a notable example of this. Season Five of *Buffy* ends with the Slayer sacrificing her life to save her sister and the rest of humanity ("The Gift" 5.22). Her death is a good one, and Buffy is at peace with her decision. However, Season Six finds her resurrected by her well-intentioned but incredibly selfish friends ("Bargaining" Part 1 [6.1] and 2 [6.2]). Buffy's fate has been stolen from her by Willow and the others. Although Buffy tries to hide her unhappiness from them, she is unable to, finally singing her pain to everyone ("Once More with Feeling" 6.7). Willow, Xander, and Dawn face the reality of their selfish act in bringing Buffy back from Heaven and begin their own downward spirals into helplessness and depression. There are many other examples of this duel between having power and being powerless in the Whedonverses. Before I discuss the ways in which power may be wielded, I would like to discuss the various ways in which the characters in the four series can be considered powerless.

The Powerless in the Whedonverses

Joss Whedon might have presented *Buffy the Vampire Slayer* as a series about power — who's got it and who wants it — but, in actuality, the characters are quite powerless in many respects. This is also true of the characters in *Angel*, *Firefly*, and *Dollhouse*. Characters in each series might possess some type of power or they might not, but even so, that power does not always work to the characters' advantage. In some cases the characters only possess power in one realm, Buffy's Slayer power, for example. In other cases, the characters have no power, such as the Actives in *Dollhouse*. Malcolm Reynolds' power in *Firefly* comes at the end of gun,[4] and Angel's was the result of the superior strength he possessed as a vampire.

When the series begins, Buffy Summers is a teenage girl already realizing that she has some power, in that she is beautiful. But she has no control over her life. She is the Slayer, the Chosen One. Being a Slayer does not necessarily give Buffy's life meaning as she is quite ambivalent about her role throughout the seven seasons (Bardi and Hamby 7). She cannot do what she wants to do when she wants to do it: she cannot go to the mall, she cannot go shopping, and she cannot go on a date. She always has to be training, she always has to be patrolling, and she always has to be putting her life on the line. And what kind of a life is that? In the early seasons of *Buffy*, she rebels against her Watcher, Giles. But by the time we arrive at Seasons Six and Seven, Buffy likes her power. She doesn't necessarily want to share it with anybody. As Anya notes, Buffy thinks that she is better than everyone else, and Buffy admits it ("Empty Places" 7.19). Nevertheless, Buffy eventually realizes that the best way to have any control over her own destiny and over her own life is to share her power with the Potentials.

Prior to the events that occur at the end of the series, however, we note that, except for her being a beautiful girl and the Slayer, Buffy is powerless. Being a Slayer might give her super strength and the ability to heal from injury quickly, but it does not give her much else. It does not help pay the mortgage after her mother's death. It does not get her a loan at the bank. Like most of us, Buffy has to get a job to pay her bills. Being the Slayer does not keep her sister out of trouble, nor does it keep a social worker from threatening to remove Dawn from Buffy's guardianship. It does not help her earn good grades in high school or college, and it does not prevent her from having to withdraw from her classes at UC-Sunnydale. It does not keep professors from humiliating her. It does not help with her love life; as a matter of fact, the only men who seem absolutely attracted to her, and to whom she is really attracted, are vampires.[5] Being powerless is also par for the course for the other Scoobies: Willow Rosenberg, Xander Harris, Cordelia Chase, and Oz. Rupert Giles is also powerless.

Willow Rosenberg was fairly powerless her entire life. Her mother views her as an experiment, either a psychological or an anthropological experiment in how to raise a child. She is a misfit who is best friends with another misfit. Although not physically abused, Willow could be considered a product of neglect. Willow's parents present as a type referred to as uninvolved.[6] Her parents, or I should say her mother given that we never see her father, seems to look at her through the lens of what a child should be (and perhaps what they think a parent should be).

Willow's intelligence has given her power in some respects, at least in the classroom, with her teachers. It certainly did not give her any power with her classmates, except in the sense that they might want to use her to help them pass their classes. So, her brain power gained her nothing with her peers. She was ridiculed by her peers, and she was definitely not cool, until she started dating Oz, who was not only smart but cool. Cordelia Chase understands about being smart: she is quite intelligent but chooses to hide it rather than risk alienating her friends, or those who want to be her friends. Willow finally acquires power through her use of magick, but it is intoxicating. She cannot control her use of the power; she becomes abusive. She eventually becomes more and more powerful, but the price that she has to pay is unbearable. She has to give up the magick in order to learn to control herself.

Xander's parents, if they paid any attention to him at all, did so in an abusive way. He and Willow would appear to have found in each other what they were not getting at home. Xander is afraid of becoming his parents, and this fear is so overwhelming that he leaves the woman he loves at the altar rather than marrying her and risking that fate ("Hell's Bells" 6.16). He feels like he is spiraling out of control throughout the seven seasons of *Buffy*. He is not the Slayer; he is not the most powerful witch ever. He is just the sidekick — there to lend support — until he finally realizes that being the sidekick is important ("Potential" 7.12). His power is that he will always be in the background, and that is okay. Nevertheless there are a few times throughout the series when Xander does gain power, if only temporarily. For example, when a magick spell cast by Ethan Rayne transforms Xander into a soldier ("Halloween" 2.6) Buffy has to stop him from shooting people. In the fan favorite episode "The Zeppo" (3.13) Xander has various adventures with zombies, beautiful women, and a bomb, concluding this night by losing his virginity to Faith. And, it is Xander who saves the world with his love of Willow after, in her anguish over Tara, she goes dark ("Grave" 6.22).

Cordelia Chase (Cordy to her friends [that would be us]), had a license plate reading "Queen C," and that pretty much summed things up for her. She was one of the popular people at Sunnydale High, a cheerleader, beautiful and wealthy. Her downfall comes not from dating Xander, although that certainly helped, but from her father's incarceration for tax fraud. Cordy is forced to get a job in high school ("The Prom" 3.20) and after graduation moves to Los Angeles to pursue an acting career. It is here that she meets Angel again and begins working for him. Prior to this event, she was living in a rundown roach-infested room, attending as many parties as possible for the free food ("City Of" *Angel* 1.1). More evidence of her powerlessness comes when she receives a part in a commercial and the director humiliates her by ignoring her and focusing on her considerable assets ("Belonging"

Angel 2.19). Certainly Cordy became less selfish and egocentric as *Angel* proceeded, although one could argue as to whether the visions she received from the Powers That Be made her more or less powerful. They certainly took a physical toll on her body (more about this in Chapter 5), eventually forcing her to choose between dying and continuing to receive the visions. Cordy chose to become demonic rather than lose the visions, which helped her in her work with Angel. Nevertheless, she was certainly powerless to stop what happened to Angel and Connor, or to herself for that matter.

Daniel Osbourne, or simply Oz, was Willow's boyfriend. He was super smart, very laid-back and cool, and played guitar in the band Dingoes Ate My Baby. Unfortunately, his cousin Jordy bites him and he becomes a werewolf ("Phases" 2.15). The Scoobies discover that they can contain Oz in a cage in the library and take turns guarding him during the full moon when he is potentially dangerous. The fact that Oz turns into a werewolf under the moon's influence would certainly indicate that he has no control over himself at that time. He also falls under the spell of a she-wolf and is powerless to stop the inevitable from happening. He mates with Veruca, she attempts to kill Willow, and Oz kills Veruca instead ("Wild at Heart" 4.6). This is the catalyst that forces Oz to leave Willow in an attempt to discover some way to control his monthly transformation.

Buffy's Watcher is Rupert Giles, a man of many dimensions, although the Scoobies prefer not to think of him as a man. Over the course of the seven seasons of Buffy, Giles becomes increasingly important to her, assuming the role of a father figure, given that her real father has virtually deserted her. One would think that Giles would be a man in control, given that he is Buffy's Watcher and, as such, is the one to control her education and training as the Slayer. In some respects he does have control over her actions; this reaches its climax when he is forced to inject Buffy with a serum that will deprive her of her powers for the "Cruciamentum," a test to which each Slayer is subjected on her 18th birthday ("Helpless" 3.12). Giles is fired as her Watcher by the end of the episode, and another is assigned to take his place.

Wesley Wyndam-Price never succeeds in winning Buffy's affection or respect. He is quite smart, very well-versed in the lore necessary to help a Slayer in her job. However, he has no experience in the field, and thus Buffy, Faith, Giles, and the Scoobies feel nothing but contempt for him (with the exception of Cordelia who finds him very attractive). Wesley is eventually fired by the Watcher's Council and he becomes a "rogue demon hunter," eventually landing in Los Angeles where he meets Angel and

Cordelia again ("Parting Gifts" *Angel* 1.10). For all of his intelligence and skill, however, he is unable to recognize a false prophecy, stealing Connor away from Angel. Although he admires and likes Angel, at the core of his being he could not control the tiny voice that suggested that Angel might just turn and kill the boy. Connor himself has no control over the man who plots against Angel, his biological father. Holtz controls the information fed to Connor, removing him from any influence that others might exert over the boy by exiling the two of them to a hell dimension beyond Angel's reach ("Sleep Tight" 3.16).

Angel was out of control when he was the human Liam. When he became a vampire he was even worse. When he got his conscience back, he could remember what he did during his 155 years of savagery and debauchery. He begins to try to atone and places himself in an environment where he can exercise control over himself. Angel's character can actually be analyzed in terms of the triad that composes his self, this triad being Liam, Angel, and Angelus. Liam was the man who lived in Galway, Ireland, who was turned by Darla in 1753 ("The Prodigal" 1.15). As a man Liam was a wastrel and a good-for-nothing layabout whose favorite pastimes were drinking and whoring. Liam was a great disappointment to his father, who recognized the evil nature of his son. Liam's murder of his father, his revenge he believes, actually confirms the father's assessment of his son's character (Buckman). Angelus killed his entire family. He then spent the next 155 years indulging in a reign of terror across Europe with his sire, Darla, and his "daughter," Drusilla, until regaining his soul in 1898 ("Darla" 2.7), at which time he became Angel.

The concept of the soul is very important to Angel's mythology. One definition states that "the soul, in some religions, spiritual traditions, and philosophies, is the ... eternal part of a living being, commonly held to be separable in existence from the body — the metaphysical part as distinct from the physical part."[7] Conscience is also a very important concept in the Whedonverses. It can be defined as "an ability or a faculty that distinguishes whether one's actions are right or wrong. In psychological terms conscience is often described as leading to feelings of remorse when a human does things that go against his/her moral values." Thus, Angel regains his soul and regrets his many acts of brutality; they weigh heavily upon his conscience. This can be contrasted with Liam, who had a soul but no conscience. One could actually argue that the Gypsy's curse was to give Angel/Liam a soul: even before he was a vampire one could argue that Liam was possessed by evil ("The Prodigal"; "Darla").

17

Soul is something one possesses whereas morality is learned, and conscience is something one chooses to exercise. The two are very much evident in William/Spike as well. William was apparently a very nice, shy and reserved young man, who was devoted to his mother. William possessed a soul and a conscience. Spike definitely did not have a soul, but one could argue that there were signs he had a conscience, given his ability to love both Drusilla and Buffy. He was concerned for their welfare, tried to protect them whenever possible, and he felt pain when Drusilla left him for a Chaos demon ("Lovers Walk" *Buffy* 3.8) and Buffy refused his love ("Fool for Love" 5.7). He was powerless to avoid love's emotional toll. For example, William was powerless in the battle for his mother; he could not control what was happening to her. It was fairly obvious that she had consumption (TB) and there was nothing that he could do to make her better, until he was turned by Drusilla ("Fool for Love"). As a vampire he could turn his mother and thus save her from the disease that was ravaging her body. He was horrified when confronted with the demonic version of his mother and her cruel taunts and hints of incest. It took him over 100 years to realize that it was the demon talking to him and not his mother.

Several authors (e.g., Stafford) have spoken of this issue, as to whether it was really the demon taunting William. After all, there is much discrepancy in the Buffyverse and the Angelverse as to how much of the person's character remains after the person becomes a vampire. Angelus would seem to be an argument against this conflict, and Spike would be an argument for. Consider that Liam was not a very nice person before he was turned. He had a soul, but no conscience. He cared for no one — taking what he wanted when and where he wanted it. Angelus had neither a soul nor a conscience. Angelus took great delight in torturing his victims before finally ending their suffering. Angel, on the other hand, had a soul and a conscience. Angel regretted his actions, both as Angelus and as Liam, and wished to atone. As a vampire Spike was merciless; but, there is evidence that Spike had a conscience, although he tried his best to squash any hints of it. Spike seemed to have a mission, and his mission was love. Whatever Angel was, the heart of Spike was love — the love of his mother, the love of Drusilla, and the love of Buffy, for whom he sacrificed himself. I disagree with those viewers who believe that Spike was selfish. I think that Spike was not being selfish, although the passion he was feeling was— passion is always selfish. One moment when passion took over, he attempted to rape Buffy — to make her hurt the way that he did[8] ("Seeing Red" 6.19). He was determined that she would acknowledge how she felt about him. To his credit, he was horrified at what he did, and he went away to atone for it.[9]

Violence against women and sexual exploitation are topics important to Joss Whedon, who has attempted to the raise the public's awareness of this issue.[10] Unfortunately, his attempt to expose and condemn sexual exploitation and violence via the most recent of his television series, *Dollhouse*, was met with dismay and resistance. Actives or Dolls have no control over their lives. They relinquish all power and control when they sign their five-year contracts with the Rossum Corporation, which then has control over the Actives as it wipes their memories, gives them drugs to control their behavior, and perhaps manipulates their brains as well. Such tampering with people also occurs (although to a somewhat lesser extent) in Whedon's short-lived space western *Firefly* and its sequel motion picture, *Serenity*.

Captain Malcolm Reynolds (Mal) is powerless in the 'verse in which he lives (*Firefly*, Vol. One). He and many others like him, called Browncoats, attempted to gain power by rebelling against the Alliance, but they lost. They were forced to surrender, and they know they were on the losing side. Now they are living on the fringes of society. Mal perhaps represents all of the people living on the outer planets who have no control over what happens to them, even though they technically live on Alliance-controlled worlds. The Alliance makes the rules, the Alliance makes the laws, the Alliance decides whether it will help them in even so basic a way as to send them supplies ("The Train Job" 1.2). The people living on the outer planets are at the mercy of bandits and criminals ("The Train Job"; "War Stories" 1.10), the terraforming of their planets (which created diseases such as Bowden's Malady, "The Train Job"), the climate ("Jaynestown" 1.7), and a lack of such basic necessities as medical care ("Safe" 1.5). Mal has no power other than what he is able to garner and he is kind of a folk hero as far as some people are concerned. As far as the Alliance is concerned he is a pirate, a thief. To his crew he is the Captain, so he does have control within that tiny microcosm of humanity, the crew of Serenity.

Serenity's crewmembers are also powerless in this 'verse. The only power Jayne Cobb has is what he gets from his guns and his muscles—he is not very smart. He needs someone to tell him what to do; if he does not have that, then he would live by his "chain of command,"[11] which is the chain he would beat someone with until they recognized his authority. River Tam lacks control for another reason: she has no control over her own mind and body because the Alliance tampered with her. She has been at the mercy of others since she was a little girl when, like all children, her parents had power over her ("Serenity" 1.1). Then she was sent to a special "school" that was actually an experimental laboratory where scientists were able to do whatever they wanted to her. By the time her brother, Simon, rescues her, Alliance scientists have implanted her with subliminal triggers so that they can access her whenever they wish (*Serenity*). That is a dangerous situation to consider: she is a very powerful weapon and the Alliance has remote control over her. Simon feels powerless because he does not know what they did to River and, hence, he does not know how to help her. He gradually begins to learn exactly WHAT they did to her brain, but that does not give him an inkling as to WHY they did it, or how he can reverse or even repair the damage ("Ariel" 1.9). For all of his brilliance he does not know how to fix her. In addition, he has lost all of his money rescuing River, so he is powerless with respect to what money could bring him. On Mal's ship he does not know where he stands. Jayne would like both Simon and River off the ship — he knows that having them aboard is dangerous. Simon does not know where he stands with the others members of the crew, except Kaylee, who is attracted to him.

This short discussion indicates the ways in which the various characters in the Whedonverses are both powerful and powerless. The remainder of the book will explore the ways in which these characters are able to exert power over each other as well as other beings in their respective worlds. Given that power and control are two sides of the same coin, it will also explore several ways in which these characters exert control over others' behavior.

Overview

I have divided this examination of power and control in the Whedonverses into chapters based upon the type of control that someone could exert over someone else. Thus, each chapter has a theme that will be explored by examining how Joss Whedon addressed the issue in the four series in question. Although these are the themes that I will address, Whedon did not necessarily explore each theme in each series, or devote an extensive amount of time to each theme in each series.

Chapter 2 will explore love and sex in all four series. Given that both love and sex are important in people's lives, and fans apparently are very interested in these themes, each was explored to a greater or lesser degree in the series. For example, sex was much more apparent in *Dollhouse* given that *Dollhouse* was a thinly disguised attempt to explore sexual victimization. Obviously that was not the only theme of *Dollhouse*, but sex was more observable in that series than in *Angel*, for example. After all, Cordelia notes that "nobody in this office will ever get any" ("Couplet" *Angel* 3.14), and hardly anyone ever did. Love, on the other hand, was an entirely different story, with characters falling into and out of it repeatedly, causing one to despair and wonder if true love could ever be found or would ever last.

Chapter 3 explores more negative actions — aggression and violence — both of which were explored in each series. Violence was inherently obvious in a show dealing with vampires, but it was not only the vampires who were violent. Buffy was violent and, in many respects, downright abusive to her avowed friends. As a matter of fact, the major characters in the Buffyverse and the Angelverse abused one another in a variety of ways, and it is sometimes hard to remember that these people are supposed to be heroes. Violence was endemic of Mal's life aboard Serenity, as it was for all of the people living on the fringes of the 'verse.

Chapter 4 will explore magick within the world of Buffy and Angel. Magick was a useful tool for the characters in each of these series, but as both noted, its use could also bring a host of problems. Magick became a thinly disguised metaphor for substance abuse in *Buffy*, with much debate as to whether Willow's use of magick could really be characterized as addictive. Although magick was not explored in *Firefly*, the issue of witchcraft was, and I will refer to that particular episode.[12]

Chapter 5 will explore the ways in which the human brain was manipulated to exert control over other people. The human brain is far more powerful than the biggest, fastest, most complex computer currently in operation. It is doubtful that anyone will be able to create something better than the human brain anytime soon, which is one of the reasons that neuroscience is so fascinating. In this chapter I will propose a theory as to why the Alliance scientists were attracted to River Tam when she was a young girl, and I will speculate as to what I think they did to her. I will also mention a few other instances of Whedon's examination of neuroscience in *Buffy*, *Angel*, and *Dollhouse*.

Chapter 6 will explore the ways in which human memory was manipulated in the Whedonverses. This was the basic issue underlying *Dollhouse*, the ability to provide wealthy clients with the type of fantasy they could only dream about prior to the development of memory-imprinting technology. I will discuss the various types of memory and then how and what the Rossum Corporation was attempting to do. I will also mention examples of memory manipulations to be found on the other three Whedon series.

Chapter 7 will explore the ways in which people can be manipulated with drugs. Although each series devoted time to this issue in various episodes throughout their broadcast run, drugs figure most prominently in *Firefly* and its sequel motion picture, *Serenity*. I will first provide a short lesson about drugs and their mechanism of action in the central nervous system, after which I will discuss the drugs portrayed in the various episodes of the four series.

What Is and Is Not Included

This book was written to appeal to both an academic and nonacademic reader. Every academic discipline has its own jargon, and psychology and neuroscience are certainly no exceptions to that fact. However, I have tried my best to keep the text jargon-free. I hate trying to read a book that is so dense as to be unreadable. My presumption is that the author wrote such a book either for their dissertation committee or their tenure and promotion committee, else why write that way? Needing an advanced degree in order to read someone's work seems a little pompous to me — remember I have a doctorate in experimental psychology (with a major in neuroscience) — and sometimes I cannot make heads or tails of what such people are talking about. I don't think it is necessary to proclaim your intellectual ability by such writing efforts. We have a name for that in psychology.

I will also not discuss power and control as it would be discussed in a sociology textbook. I am well aware that power is exerted via economic means — those who control wealth pretty much control everything else and have power over those who are not wealthy. Certainly people in the Whedonverses were not wealthy. We see Buffy struggle to pay her bills; Cordy constantly nag Angel to get some paying customers; Mal engage in piracy to feed his crew; and the Actives serve at the whim of wealthy clients. Not having money can leave one pretty much powerless.

I will also not discuss political power. Such power is typically not broached in the Whedonverses, with the exception of Mal's repudiation of the Alliance's power over him. Rather, I will discuss the ways in which individual people can be controlled by those with power over them and that might be by means of money or politics, but it might not.

CHAPTER 2

Love and Sex as Methods of Control[1]

I may be love's bitch, but at least I'm man enough to admit it.— Spike, "Lover's Walk" [*Buffy* 3.8]

Although the Joss Whedon television series discussed in this book are all about power and control — who's got it and who wants it — they are also all about love. Love of family, love of friends, sexual love, platonic love — Whedon explores them all. Love is a powerful emotion. It can make people engage in horrific behavior that they would never dream possible, and it can also incite noble types of behavior. Defining "love," while not impossible, is quite difficult; expressing love is much easier. Sometimes the expression is as simple as a tiny smile after saving the world. Sometimes the expression is so powerful it will demolish a building. However one defines the term (and there are numerous definitions), this chapter will present one theoretical perspective on love and discuss how that theory explains the various types of love displayed by Whedon's characters. In addition, this chapter will analyze the characters' sexuality and sexual behavior in terms of one theoretical perspective on sexual behavior.

The Triangular Theory of Love

Robert Sternberg[2] proposes that love consists of three components that combine to produce 7 types of love. The first component is *intimacy*, which "refers to those feelings in a relationship that promote closeness, bondedness, and connectedness" (6). According to Sternberg, intimacy consists of at least ten elements: a desire to promote the welfare and happiness of a loved one, giving and receiving emotional support, counting on the loved one in a time of need, holding them in high regard, enjoying a mutual understanding with them, sharing possessions and self with them, valuing them, and communicating intimately. Intimacy is the foundation of love and develops slowly, over time. It can be hard to achieve and even harder to maintain. As one becomes more involved with someone, a fear of losing self may occur. The task is to maintain the sense of intimacy while also maintaining a sense of autonomy.

The second component of love is *passion*, which involves "a state of intense longing for union with the other" (9). Sternberg states that passion consists of the expression of our needs and desires, one of which is sexual fulfillment, but that is not the only need that can be fulfilled passionately. For example, someone with a strong need for dominance could be aroused by someone who provides a convenient outlet for that need. Passion may dissipate as quickly as it arises.

The final component of love is *commitment*, which consists of both a short-term and a long-term aspect. Sternberg states that the "short-term aspect is the decision to love a certain other, whereas the long-term one is the commitment to maintain that love" (11). These two decisions do not necessarily occur at the same time, or within any given relationship. It is this component that keeps a relationship going.

Excluding nonlove, seven types of love can be combined using the aforementioned components. *Liking* consists only of intimacy. This is the type of love one feels for close friends and family members. The term liking is not used in a trivial sense. Sternberg uses the term liking to refer to the type of feeling you find in friendships: you feel close to the friend, but you feel no passion towards them and do not expect or desire a long-term commitment. *Infatuated love* consists only of passion. This is what most would consider "love at first sight." It consists of intense physical arousal, but it can dissipate as quickly as it arises. *Empty love* consists only of commitment. Love may sometimes devolve into this type of love, as in the case of couples who have been together for many years. In cultures wherein marriages are arranged, empty love may mark the beginning of a relationship. *Romantic love* consists of passion plus intimacy. Liking in combination with the arousal of physical attraction characterizes this type of love (20). Romantic love includes the feeling that you have met the person who is right for you and the feeling that you would like to fuse your spirit with theirs. *Companionate love* consists of intimacy and commitment. One could think of this type of love in terms of a committed friendship. Many relationships devolve into this type of love once physical attraction, which is a major source of passion, has waned (21). *Fatuous love* consists of passion plus commitment. We often read about this type of love in the tabloids, when two people meet, fall in love and marry after a whirlwind romance. Since intimacy takes some time to develop, the people who fall "head over heels in love" and rush to the altar wake one morning to realize that they do not even *like* their partner. As Sternberg notes, "The partners commit ... to one another on the basis of passion without the stabilizing element of intimate involvement" (22). Finally, a combination of all three components yields *consummate love*. Many people would consider this to be a complete love. Sternberg notes, however, that it is often like meeting your goal in a weight-loss program: it is easier to achieve than to maintain: "Like other things of value, [it] must be guarded carefully" (22).

As noted, love may be expressed sexually, although it is not necessary for all types of love. Nevertheless, humans are sexual beings and engage in sexual acts for a variety of reasons, including to obtain and hold power over someone, to express love, for recreation, in the place of intimacy, and for relaxation, to name a few. As would be expected, the characters in the Whedonverses may engage in sexual acts. However, it is surprising how few of his characters are actually sexually active.

An Evolutionary Explanation about Sex

Psychology is defined as the scientific study of behavior and mental processes. Explanations for these behaviors and mental processes arise from a number of perspectives, and one such perspective emphasizes evolution (Darwin *Origin*). Behaviors and mental processes that increase the probability of an organism's survival will be selected, meaning that the organism will survive to reproduce and the traits that aided in that survival will be transmitted to the next generation (Darwin *Descent*). One of the behaviors which evolutionary psychologists study centers on reproduction, attempting to explain the differing sexual behaviors displayed by men and women in terms of evolution.

According to evolutionary psychologists, men and women have different mating strategies. For example, some men and women display jealousy toward their partners. However, men and women display differences in the type of jealousy they exhibit toward their partners. Men are more likely to be jealous of *sexual* infidelity in their partners, whereas women are more likely to be jealous of *emotional* infidelity. In other words, men are more likely

25

to be jealous if their lovers engage in sexual activity with another person, and women are more likely to be jealous if their lovers develop an emotional attachment to another person (Buss, Larsen, Westen, and Semmelroth; Buunk, Angleitner, Oubaid, and Buss). Evolutionary psychologists propose that this jealousy stems from evolutionary forces that dictate mating strategies.

Although the data are admittedly largely theoretical, an individual woman is capable of producing about 65 children in her lifetime, assuming she could (or would want to) give birth every nine months. This assumes that she would give birth and be impregnated immediately (and one would wonder what kinds of men she would be encountering!). However, women do not reproduce that often. Even considering advances in modern medicine, the human body probably could not withstand the effort involved in reproducing that often. Men, on the other hand, can father thousands of children in their lifetimes, assuming a limitless supply of fertile women. Thus, evolutionary psychologists suggest that men and women have different strategies with respect to reproduction. Because men produce millions of sperm cells in each ejaculate, but only one is necessary for fertilization, it is in a man's evolutionary interests to impregnate as many females as possible. This ensures that some of his offspring will reach the age of maturity and his genes will be transmitted to future generations.

Men have little energy invested in their offspring. Women, on the other hand, usually only carry one offspring at a time, and it is in her best interests to ensure that that one offspring survives to maturity so that it can transmit her genes to future generations. Because women invest more energy in their offspring's survival, women are motivated in different ways than men. Men want to mate with as many women as possible, but women want to mate with one man who will help them raise and protect their offspring so that the offspring can reach maturity. Although any given woman might not know who the father of her child is, she will always know that her offspring is her own. Men can never reliably know that a woman's children are his, hence different reasons for jealousy (Buss). If she is sexually unfaithful, then her offspring might not be his, and he is raising a child not his own. If he is emotionally unfaithful, he might leave her, which would leave her and her child undefended, rendering them unsafe in an unsafe environment. She will also lose her mate's resources and his paternal investment (Buss).

Although this was a very brief description of evolutionary psychology and its tenets on human mate selection and reproduction, the theory can be used to explain many of the sexual relations depicted in the four Whedonverses. Likewise, Sternberg's triangular theory can explain many of the emotional relationships in these series. Each of the four series will be examined in turn for the ways in which the characters develop emotional and sexual relationships and how the two theories described above relate to various characters. It should be noted that Joss Whedon's explorations of sexuality are sometimes at odds with evolutionary theory. For example, Buffy loves Angel and he loves her even if they can never be together. Notwithstanding this fundamental truth, each has sexual, as well as emotional, relationships with other partners, as do the other characters. The characters on Whedon's series *Firefly* may or may not reflect evolutionary forces toward sexual selection, but their relationships can certainly be analyzed in terms of Sternberg's Triangular Theory. Whedon's controversial series *Dollhouse* explored sexuality more so than the other three series. Very rich clients were able to rent so-called Actives for (mostly) sexual encounters. These Actives were men and women who had entered into a five-year period of (perhaps consensual) servitude to the Rossum Corporation. Each Active's persona was wiped clean and, whenever hired, the requested persona would be downloaded into the supposedly empty receptacle. People with enough money could hire any Active for any type of encounter. Most encounters included sexual relations and Actives could be programmed to be passive or active, hetero- or homosexual, or any other type requested by the client. And yet, some of these programmable people were able to develop relationships with each other that can be considered in terms of Sternberg's theory. Each of the four series will be examined in turn and I will begin with *Buffy*.

Love and Sex on Buffy

The vampires on *Buffy* are emotional and sexual creatures. That is, each enjoys emotional and sexual relationships with other vampires (e.g., Angelus and Darla, Angelus and Drusilla, Drusilla and Spike) as well as the occasional human (Buffy with both Angel and Spike). These sexual relations are rather interesting in the sense that vampires engage in sexual acts with their "sires." Incest taboos are thus invoked, given that these relationships occur between parent and child. For example, Angelus engages in sexual intercourse with Drusilla, his "daughter," and she, in turn, enjoys sex with Spike, her "son." A number of people have proposed that Spike and Angel have engaged in sexual relations with each other (see, for example, Weber). Later Angel(us) has a child with his "mother," Darla ("Lullaby" *Angel* 3.9). These actions can be interpreted in a variety of ways. The simplest is that siring another vampire is not difficult; it happens on *Buffy* whenever a vampire bites a human.[3] There is no emotional involvement between the two: vampires must feed and they feed on humans. The consequence of feeding is siring another vampire. Other depictions of vampires do not illustrate siring in this way. For example, siring a new vampire takes more than just one bite on *True Blood* (*TB*), and on *TB*, the sire must take responsibility for the progeny and educate him/her in the ways of the "life." Furthermore, the emotional bonds between vampires and sires on *TB* is very strong, as evidenced by the relationships between Eric Northman and his sire, Godric, and between Eric and his "daughter," Pam. That is not to say that the vampires on *TB* do not have sex with their sires; some of them do, one notable example being Bill Compton and his sire Lorena. As on *Buffy*, *TB*'s vampires also enjoy sex with humans, although the vampires on *TB* do not physically change from one state into another as they do on *Buffy*.

One could argue that vampires would not care about an incest taboo for at least two reasons. One is that incest taboos arose to minimize inbreeding. Although early humans did not know about genetic mutations, they were probably aware that mating with close relatives led to problems with any offspring resulting from such a mating. Outbreeding would also confer advantages, such as the wealth a new bride would bring to her groom's family, or the skills a new groom would bring to his bride's family. Vampires do not breed sexually, and even if they did, they are not genetically related to their progeny (unless they "turn" their parents, children, or siblings). Thus, no genetic mutations would be transmitted to their offspring. One reason vampires have sex with their progeny is that they simply do not see their progeny as their children. But I would say that the primary reason vampires have sex with their progeny is simply that they are evil, and evil beings would not care what humans think of their actions. In fact, they might have sex with their progeny simply because so many humans would be disgusted by the act. Because Buffy loved Angel and Spike, fans tended to forget that the two were vampires and, thus, evil (Havens 89). Although both of these characters were redeemed, their actions were not always good.

One of the most popular *Star Trek* villains was Gul Dukat, the former Cardassian Prefect of Bajor, on *Deep Space Nine* (*DS9*). Prior to the events depicted on *DS9*, Dukat had brutally administered Cardassian law on the planet. During his administration, Bajoran people were housed in concentration camps and forced into labor. Bajoran women were forced into sexual slavery; Dukat himself had a Bajoran lover who bore him a mixed-species daughter, a fact he deviously hid by exiling the child and her mother. Dukat's popularity with fans increased over the course of *DS9*'s seven-year broadcast run. He flirted constantly with *DS9*'s second-in-command, the Bajoran Major Kira Nerys, who was a freedom fighter/terrorist during the occupation. Even though their races were bitter enemies and Kira would never forgive him for the brutality the Cardassians exhibited toward her people, many fans lobbied for a relationship to develop between the two. With time, fans also began to debate the degree of Dukat's evilness, with some claiming that since he had "only" killed a few million Bajorans, he was not really that evil (just as many debate who is more evil, Hitler or Stalin, by comparing the numbers of their victims). Such debates horrified the producers, who refused to redeem the character, and in the last three seasons, Dukat was written as a darker and darker character. The producers were intent upon reminding their viewers that evil is evil, and Dukat was evil (Erdmann).

Joss Whedon did the same thing with Spike on *Buffy*. Although we finally learn that Spike was called William the Bloody, not for his reign of brutality, but rather for his "bloody awful poetry" ("Fool for Love," *Buffy* 5.7), nevertheless he was a vampire and had killed countless human beings, as well as two Slayers, in his 100-odd years of vampirehood. Hence, Whedon's repeated reminders to the fans that Spike was a vampire, and he was dangerous, even if he did have a chip in his head. This reminder was particularly painful in the episode "Seeing Red" (*Buffy* 6.19) when Spike attempted to rape Buffy (see Chapter 3).

Nevertheless, Spike is a romantic at heart. As we watched Spike's actions over the course of *Buffy* we realized that his romantic feelings toward women were directed toward the wrong women. Prior to being sired by Drusilla we observed William writing lovesick poetry to a woman named Cecily in the episode "Fool for Love" (*Buffy* 5.7). She is horrified to learn that William's poems are about her, and finally tells him that she can never love him, that he is beneath her, a probable referral to his lower status in the very class-conscious Victorian society in which they lived.

Spike and Drusilla's relationship is characterized by passion and tenderness. He loves her passionately and their sexual relationship is apparently quite passionate as well (for example, "What's My Line?" *Buffy* 2.9). However, his feelings for Dru are also characterized by tenderness. Despite being a very deadly vampire, Dru is clearly insane, and Spike takes care of her. His actions and words indicate that he still believes in love, even if he is a vampire, and he also feels emotional pain, as evidenced by his complete devastation when Dru and Angelus become involved ("I Only Have Eyes For You" 2.19) and later when she leaves him for a chaos demon ("Lover's Walk" 3.8). As he gradually realizes that the emotion he is feeling for Buffy is love, his love becomes more and more intense and more and more passionate. When finally consummated in "Smashed" (*Buffy* 6.9), the building in which Buffy and Spike mate falls down around them, the destruction serving as Whedon's metaphor for the strength and violence of their passion. We continue to see this passion over the course of Season Six; generally, Spike's crypt looks demolished after a sexual encounter between the two ("Dead Things" *Buffy* 6.13). In this episode they joke about missing the bed, which is a lucky thing for the bed, and Spike tells Buffy that the rug is not new, "It just looks different when you're under it." Despite the violent nature of the sex between them, or perhaps because of it, Spike is a considerate lover, and Buffy apparently experiences complete satisfaction after her sexual encounters with him. Nevertheless, Buffy thinks that there is something wrong with their relationship. She believes that love should be more restrained, whereas Spike believes it should be a grand passion. I believe that part of the problem is that Buffy is only 21 years old and still has an adolescent's view of love. In addition she has had only three lovers prior to Spike (Angel, Parker, and Riley), and two of those (Angel and Parker) were sexual one-night stands. The encounter with Parker was completely about sex as far as he was concerned ("Harsh Light of Day" 4.3) whereas for Buffy the sex was only part of the encounter (see Naficy and Panchanathan). Buffy's introduction to sex was on her seventeenth birthday and left her confronting a monster, one of her unknowing making ("Innocence" [Part Two] 2.14). After all, if they had not had sex, then Angel would not have experienced a moment of "pure happiness," and he would not have lost his soul.[4] Buffy's guilt is enormous, especially considering the things that Angelus will do to her and the ones she loves (for example, "Becoming" [Part Two] 2.22). Because Buffy can never have sex with Angel again, their relationship centers on the love (for example, "Graduation Day" [Part Two] 3.22).

Yet Buffy clearly wanted a relationship that contained both the emotional and the physical aspects of love, hence her attempt to have a relationship with Parker and her eventual relationship with Riley. The encounter with Parker did not last long enough to even become a relationship, and Buffy was unwilling and unable to open up and disclose the emotional turmoil she was experiencing to Riley ("Buffy vs. Dracula" 5.1). He cannot touch the dark side of her soul, the part that contained the essence of what made her the Slayer. Riley eventually realizes this and, in effect, offers her the classic ultimatum: choose ("Into the Woods" 5.10). Circumstances keep them apart and when they next meet, she is having sex with Spike and Riley is married ("As You Were" 6.15).

Buffy is horrified to discover that she is shagging Spike.[5] Not only shagging, but loving it, as in "can't get enough of it and let's do it constantly," like in the front yard of her house, in the alley behind the Double Meat Palace ("Doublemeat Palace" 6.12), and in the Bronze ("Dead Things" 6.13), for example. Part of Buffy's problem is her belief that nice girls don't do IT, and they especially do not do IT unless they are "in love." Given her avowed hatred of Spike, how can she possibly do IT with him? And love IT? Prina Moldovano argues that Buffy's darkness will not be able to find pleasure or satisfaction in a non-aggressive sexual relationship, that is, one characterized by "normal" heterosexual behavior, the type that is increasingly referred to as vanilla. One could argue that Season Six of *Buffy* is about addiction: Will's addiction to magick and Buffy's addiction to Spike, and what the consequences of addiction are to one's self and one's friends. Buffy's addiction to Spike, if we call it that, certainly affects her friends ("Entropy" 6.18). They wonder how she could be attracted to Spike, given what they know of him. They worry that she really did come back [from the dead ("The Gift" 5.22)] wrong. Even Spike tells her that she is wrong when he realizes that she is the only human he cannot harm ("Smashed" 6.9); after all, the chip implanted in his head by the Initiative renders him unable to harm humans (see Chapter 5).

Spike, very much a romantic at heart despite his attempts to hide this aspect of his personality, has two relationships over the course of *Buffy* that I would characterize as romantic: the one with Drusilla and the one with Buffy.[6] One might argue that the relationship with Dru could not have intimacy given her madness, but he was gentle with her and appeared to have only her best interests in mind.[7] He was committed to her for many years, until his feelings for Buffy changed him. Buffy's feelings for Spike definitely changed over the course of the series: from enemies to reluctant allies to eventual lovers, Buffy comes to like Spike/William. Despite what Giles and the other Scoobies believed, Buffy came to know him as a friend and companion and his love for her increased in depth as well. Buffy's relationships with Riley and Angel could also be characterized as romantic love. Although Buffy and Angel declared their undying love for each other, neither was able to actually make a long-term commitment to the other, which was pretty much the norm on *Buffy* for any of the characters.

Willow Rosenberg's journey to sexual awareness begins with Xander Harris and ends with the Potential Slayer Kennedy. Willow and Xander are best friends, and she has always loved him. Their relationship illustrates companionate love although in the beginning Willow's unrequited love for Xander limits her ability to thoroughly enjoy his friendship. She believes that her love for him is real and that he is "the one." Xander, on the other hand, thinks of Willow only as a friend and he develops a crush on Buffy the minute he meets her. Xander's feelings for Buffy begin as an infatuation that gradually develops into a deep and abiding friendship (but see Chapter 3). Xander's love life is a running joke on *Buffy*. He is prone to infatuations[8] and almost all of his (short-lived) relationships are with demons, with the exception of Cordelia (and some of the Scoobies might say she's one also).[9] This tendency reaches its apex when he falls in love with Anya, an ex-vengeance demon. However, I would argue that Xander and Anya's love is more characteristic of romantic love: in addition to their easily observed (and equally as voiced) passion, they also exhibit increasing intimacy as their relationship progresses. Unfortunately, Xander is unable to commit to her in the end because of his fear of the future (see Chapter 3).

Although initially jealous, Willow befriends Buffy and eventually the two will consider themselves to be best (female) friends; Willow describes both Xander and Buffy as her best friends. Willow will eventually meet a young man who is smitten with her, one who loves her quirky looks and her brains equally. Oz is very cool and laid-back, and his persona belies his years. Although only about one year older than the Scoobies, Oz is very mature and appears to be the kind of man that women profess to want: sensitive and caring, kind and considerate. When Willow attempts to seduce Oz — she has decided that he is the one who will claim her virginity — he refuses, telling her that they will have sex when they are ready ("Amends" 3.10). They will not have sex just because she thinks that they should do it. They do eventually have sex ("Graduation Day" [Part One] 3.21) and then continue to do so, although Whedon does not make it a point in the series to cue us as to when.

I would characterize Willow's relationship with Oz as romantic love: they become increasingly intimate and passionate with time. The fact that Oz is a werewolf in no way lessens his attraction (to either Willow or the audience). He does not want to be a werewolf and fights to contain the animalistic part of himself ("Phases" 2.15). With the Scoobies' help, Oz is able to control himself until he meets Veruca, a female werewolf. The physical attraction between the two is intense and passionate, and Oz eventually succumbs to that attraction, breaking Willow's heart. Oz leaves Sunnydale in an attempt to discover a way to control the urge, promising Willow that he will return one day. Willow is depressed by Oz's betrayal of her with Veruca ("Wild at Heart" 4.6), but more so because he leaves without allowing her to help him with his problem. Oz reverts to a more stereotypical male, acting as if he does not need Willow's help (Jowett).

Willow's relationship with Tara Maclay, whom she meets during her first year of college, can also be characterized as romantic love. Willow's "gayness" was foreshadowed during the third season episode "The Wish" (3.9), in which we meet Vamp(ire) Willow, who is bisexual. Later Vamp Willow travels to real-time in "Doppelgängland" (3.16) and makes suggestive remarks to Willow (much as the Evil Kira did to her twin on *Deep Space Nine*). Unfortunately, like all of the relationships on *Buffy*, the one between Willow and Tara is doomed. Willow is a very powerful witch, but one who is also addicted to the power that the magick gives her (see Chapter 4). Magick allows her to be much more than the little geek girl everyone picked on. She is more powerful than anyone knows, but that power eventually gets the better of her. Her use of the magick frightens Tara and is a source of friction between the two. Much as an alcoholic does, Willow tries to hide her use of magick from Tara and even resorts to casting spells on Tara in order to make Tara forget their arguments over magick or her use of magick. When Tara finally discovers Willow's mind-rape, Tara leaves. Even then, Willow cannot admit that she is addicted to magick, although she finally realizes the extent of her problem when she erases everyone's memory during the episode "Tabula Rasa" (6.8). Tara and Willow do reconcile once Willow stops using magick, but the reconciliation is short-lived. Warren kills Tara and Willow almost destroys the world. Only Xander's love, coupled with Giles' spell, is able to break through and return Willow to her "normal" state.

Willow's guilt over Tara's death haunts her. Willow knows that she was unable to save Tara, but Tara might not have needed saving if Willow had not broken their bond. That is, if Willow had not abused magick, she and Tara would not have broken up, and it is possible that Tara would still be alive. Certainly they would have had more time together. Her guilt over the use of magick and her flaying of Warren also serves to shut Willow off from her friends ("Villains" 6.20). When Kennedy begins flirting with Willow, she does not recognize it for what it is. And, when Willow does realize what Kennedy is suggesting, she reacts negatively. She is horrified at the thought of becoming involved with someone else, especially so soon after Tara's death. Yet, it is Kennedy's flirtations and her refusal to let Willow succumb to Amy's spell that finally allows Willow to accept Tara's death and visit her grave ("The Killer in Me" 7.13).

Although this is by no means a complete discussion of all of the relationships depicted on *Buffy*, the ones discussed herein provide support for Sternberg's triangular theory of love. Each of the characters on the series were, at one time, intimately involved with someone and those relationships generally illustrated Sternberg's conception of romantic love, love characterized by both intimacy and passion. None of the relationships, however, contained the third ingredient, commitment. Whedon's characters also illustrated basic tenets of evolutionary theory, in which female characters were likely to develop emotional ties to their partners, with the physical aspects of the relationship reinforcing the emotional bond. Xander's reaction to Anya's sexual encounter with Spike was a perfect example of a male's jealousy at his mate having sex with another man, whereas Anya's jealousy of Xander's relationships with both Willow and Buffy provide evidence of her feelings about his emotional ties to other women.

Love and Sex on Angel

Realizing that he and Buffy can never be together, Angel relocates to Los Angeles where he is recruited by the demon-human hybrid Doyle, on behalf of the Powers That Be, to establish Angel Investigations and "help the helpless" ("City Of" *Angel* 1.1). Throughout the five seasons of *Angel* he is joined by various characters, both human and demon, in this mission, and as on *Buffy*, true love on *Angel* does not run truly or deeply. Also as on *Buffy*, not many people are having sex.

Because of the curse, Angel is unable to have sexual relations with those to whom he is attracted, and he is attracted to a number of females during the five seasons that the series is on the air. These include Kate Lockley ("Lonely Hearts" 1.2), Tamara Gorski ("Eternity 1.17), his sire, Darla, with whom he has a son named Connor (see earlier in this chapter and Chapter 3), and Cordelia Chase. Of these it is Cordy with whom he falls in love, only to be imprisoned by Connor and Justine before he can declare his feelings for her ("Tomorrow" 3.22). After Angel's rescue in Season Four and Cordy's subsequent return, she has forgotten her feelings for Angel and has a brief love affair with Connor. This entire storyline was deeply upsetting to the fans in addition to the actors who felt that Cordy was much too old to have an affair with Connor. After all, he was the equivalent of an 18-year-old boy and she was at least 23 years old. Of course, this is nothing compared to the 241-year-old Angel having sex with the 17-year-old Buffy ("Surprise" *Buffy* 2.13).[10] Angel is even able to resume his physical love affair with Buffy ("I Will Remember You" 1.8), but only for one night. The only way that Angel can continue to help Buffy in her fight against the forces of darkness is to once again become undead and immortal. Unfortunately for Angel, he is doomed to remember the day when he was human and able to let Buffy know how he felt about her while she will forget.

Other characters on *Angel* also fare poorly with respect to love. Both Wesley and Gunn are attracted to Fred, who eventually pursues a relationship with Gunn. Fred and Gunn are greatly at ease with each other, demonstrating the depth of their intimacy, until they discover who was responsible for her exile to Pylea. When Fred is determined to send Professor Seidel to Hell, Gunn kills the professor rather than letting Fred do the deed ("Supersymmetry" 4.5). He loves her so much that he does not want her to ever feel the guilt that would result from the knowledge that she killed a man. Unfortunately, this results in estrangement and they are never able to repair their relationship.

On the other hand, Wesley provides a perfect example of a relationship that contains only passion, when he begins having sex with Lilah Morgan. As matter of fact, his comment to her after they first have sex is priceless. Lilah tells him that the sex is just physical, and not to think about her when she is gone, to which Wesley replies that he "wasn't thinking about you when you were here" ("Tomorrow" 3.22).

Love and Sex on Firefly

As far as the relationships on *Firefly* are concerned, only Wash and Zoe appear to have a deep and abiding relationship. I would say that their relationship has all of the characteristics of consummate love. Zoe and Wash are married to each other and are sexually faithful, yet Zoe wishes to have a child, whereas Wash does not ("Heart of Gold" 1.13). Although Inara, as a Companion, has sexual relationships with her clients, she does not necessarily have emotional attachments to them. She is in love with Mal, who loves her also, but is unhappy that she is a Companion and having sexual encounters with male and female clients. Mal has only one sexual encounter during the time period of the series.[11] Despite her words, which indicate that she has no problem with his sexual encounter with Nandi, the encounter leaves Inara in tears when she learns of it ("Heart of Gold" 1.13). Mal's encounter with the former Companion Nandi would be a fitting example of infatuation. His relationship with Inara, on the other hand, provides a perfect example of how intimacy takes a long time to develop, as Inara acknowledges in "The Train Job" (1.3) when she tells Shepherd Book that she does not know if she will ever know the Captain. Inara and Mal's feelings for each other, although never spoken, are nevertheless acknowledged in the spin-off motion picture, *Serenity*. Kaylee and Simon share an infatuation with each other that is eventually consummated on *Serenity*. Their time together aboard the ship also allows them to become more intimate, leading to the richer relationship of romantic love.

Perhaps because of its early cancellation, *Firefly* was never able to depict the sexual relationships one would have expected of a group of mostly single adults traveling throughout space. However, there were a couple of notable exceptions. One occurred in the aforementioned episode "Heart of Gold." In this episode, Inara's old friend Nandi asks for help, and Inara in turn asks for Mal's. It seems that Nandi runs a whorehouse and one of her girls has gotten herself into trouble with one of the locals. Petaline is pregnant and one of the locals, named Rance Burgess, claims the child. Mal is reluctant to help, but eventually agrees. Upon meeting Nandi and her whores,[12] who are both male and female, we realize that they were not forced into prostitution, nor do they apologize for their way of life. The women and men who work in this "whorehouse" have a close bond to one another; in Marleen Barr's words these people have formed their own community. They may be bonded by their sex work, but they are bonded nonetheless. As this episode progresses we learn that Chari, one of the whores, will betray them by giving to Rance Burgess information about both Petaline and the crew's attempt to help protect her and her fellow whores. In a particularly disturbing scene, Rance addresses the men who will help him take his child. He tells the men that Chari knows her place and then he commands her to get down on her knees, apparently to fellate him while his men watch. After Nandi dies and Rance is killed, Petaline ejects the traitor from their house. She is no longer one of them and is cast out of their community.

As Barr notes, women who take charge of their sexuality and reproduction appear to be strange. They are scary: who knows what they might do next with all of that power? Indeed, when Mal makes a comment about "whose baby is it?" Nandi replies that she "reckons it's Petaline's," pointing out to Mal the one truth about childbearing that can never be refuted: women know who their children are. It took a DNA test for Rance to confirm that the child was his; Petaline never had any doubt that the child was hers.

Reproduction also surfaces in this episode when Zoe and Wash discuss having children. Wash states that he does not want to bring children into the "world," since it is a crazy place and who knows what could happen.[13] Zoe, however, tells Wash that she wants children regardless of the danger or the uncertainly. As a matter of fact she tells him, "You and me, we would have one beautiful baby." Zoe is the strong one in the relationship; Zoe is the Warrior Woman. But Zoe also wants to bear children with the man she loves even knowing that life is uncertain and unsafe. Certainly she would epitomize women who fought for the right to have choices in their lives; after all, she fought in a war to preserve her freedom. No one can tell her that she does not have the right to bear a child if and when she wants to.

Sexuality is implicit and explicit in this episode: implicit because the setting is a whorehouse, explicit because Mal finally has sex with a woman, in this case Nandi.[14] However, Nandi does not realize until afterwards that Mal and Inara have unrequited feelings for each other. As Inara confronts the obvious fact that Mal and Nandi have spent the night having sexual intercourse, Inara tells Mal the one good thing about the Companions is that they are not puritanical about sex. Thus, it is immaterial whether he is embarrassed about being caught having sexual relations with someone. Later, we see the abject misery Inara suffers after this confrontation, hiding in an empty room and crying. Even though she knows that Mal has the right to have sex with other women, she is hurt because he did so. Inara has sex with other people all the time: it is her profession. Of course, that does not stop Mal from being upset about it, and he actively and passively tries to prevent her encounters (e.g., Whedon, Matthews, and Conrad, *Better Days*).

Inara's sensuality is freely expressed. In this 'verse, Companions enjoy a very high status, although Inara's is somewhat less so because of her mysterious past (Greco). They spend many years in training for their role; apparently it is not unlike the role of the Japanese Geisha or the Greek Hetaera (Aberdein; Davidson "Whores"). Unfortunately, we do not learn nearly enough about this Guild to be able to determine what its exact function and role in this 'verse is. But, we know that Companions are trained to interact with both male and female clients, a detail that is very convincingly portrayed in the episode "War Stories" (1.10). Inara requests that everyone on board the Serenity behave with decorum when her client, the Councilor, visits. When the Councilor arrives and she is female, everyone reacts with shock, apparently not considering the fact that a female Companion would entertain a female client. Kaylee points out that she knew Inara entertained women, but had just never seen it before. Jayne reacts with a typical "I'll be in my bunk." Later we are given a glimpse of Inara and the Councilor as Inara gives her a massage. The Councilor is happy for the respite from her hectic life and career and makes a comment to the effect that sex is not necessary, to which Inara replies, "Let's just enjoy ourselves," and then kisses the Councilor passionately. This is one of the few overtly sexual scenes between two women in science-fiction television. As a matter of fact, Joss Whedon is one of the few writers to have depicted a sexual relationship between two women (the other was J. Michael Straczynski on *Babylon 5*).[15]

Love and Sex in Dollhouse

Whedon's controversial series *Dollhouse* explored sexuality in a way that startled many of his longtime fans. The main character in *Dollhouse* is Echo, the Active of a young woman named Caroline. Echo/Caroline was recruited by the Dollhouse after attempting to liberate research animals from one of the Rossum Corporation's laboratories. One result of the failed rescue attempt was the death of Caroline's lover. Rather than be arrested and perhaps incarcerated, Caroline eventually "decides" to join the Dollhouse. Caroline's encounters during the course of Season One of *Dollhouse* are both sexual and nonsexual. Specifically, Echo has five sexual encounters, although three of them occur mostly off camera: Richard, Mac (twice), Joel, and the unnamed client with the penchant for S&M ("A Spy in the House of Love" 1.9). Her other encounters include working as a hostage negotiator, a thief, the adult persona of an abused child, and a cult member, among others. Eventually we learn that Echo was imprinted with quite a number of different personas (36 she says in one episode; 38 in another). Seven of these were lesbian ("Meet Jane Doe" 2.7). By the series' end she has incorporated all of those various personas into her own. Caroline/Echo's relationship with FBI agent (and later Dollhouse handler) Paul Ballard does become increasingly intimate as she begins to integrate her various Active personalities into a new composite character. He does feel passion for her and she for him, but he is unable to act upon that passion, given his inability to understand how she can willingly give consent to such passion. The two are completely committed to each by the end of the series. After his death, his persona is downloaded into her consciousness. Wanting to be one with your beloved assumes a whole new meaning in their relationship.

The relationships held by the characters on *Dollhouse* are much harder to evaluate given the fact that the entire series is about fantasy and the distortion of memory. Nevertheless, several relationships might fit the taxonomy proposed by Sternberg. Victor and Sierra begin their relationship with passion, his physiological reaction to Sierra being easily observed despite their programming ("True Believer" 1.5). Topher's analysis reveals that Victor's erections are exclusive to Sierra, and to prevent further attachment, both Victor and Sierra's memories are scrubbed again. Nevertheless, they continue to bond with one another. Sierra's mannerisms when in Victor's presence indicate that she reciprocates his feelings for her: she smiles at him, makes room for him at her table, goes out of her way to speak to him, et cetera. Eventually they escape the Dollhouse, have a child together, separate and reunite ("Epitaph Two: The Return" 2.13). Quite interestingly we do not, at least during Season One, observe Sierra engage in sexual encounters with clients. All of her encounters reinforce Echo's assignments; usually Sierra is brought in to complete a (nonsexual) assignment that Echo has been unable to finish. Unfortunately, Sierra's sojourn in the Dollhouse is fraught with danger. We learn very early in Season One that Sierra has been raped several times by her handler, Hearn ("Needs" 1.8). Although she does not consciously remember the encounter, she reacts violently to touch. This example of procedural memory, the unconscious memory of actions, leads to the discovery of the rape (see Chapter 6). Later we learn that Sierra did not volunteer to become an Active; rather she was forced into servitude by a rejected lover named Nolan, who repeatedly uses her afterwards ("Belonging" 2.4). Obviously Nolan's abuse of Sierra speaks volumes to his motivations rather than to hers.

Another Active who was used in several ways during the course of the series is Mellie/November. As Mellie, she is planted in Paul Ballard's apartment building and programmed to fall in love with him. She is to keep him occupied and, if possible, make him fall in love with her. She is clearly enamored of him when we first meet her in the series. We almost feel sorry for a woman who appears to lurk at the door of her apartment waiting for her neighbor to come home. Mellie and Paul do become friends, and they eventually become lovers ("Man on the Street" 1.6). It is only later that we learn that Mellie is not only an Active, she is also a sleeper Active who can be triggered to engage a particular mission without endangering the primary imprint. In Mellie's case, she has been programmed to kill, perhaps Ballard himself, and she does kill Hearn after Boyd exposes Hearn's rape of Sierra. Ballard cares for Mellie, enough to bargain for her release from the Dollhouse when he finally discovers its location.

Given that the majority of the Active's clients are male, it seems that evolutionary psychology's predictions that men want to have sex with as many women as possible is supported by their actions with these people. One question raised by this is, if men desire variety, why is Echo the most requested Active? That is a reasonable question. Of course, we do not know if Echo is most requested, repeatedly. Over the course of Season One we do learn that two men have requested Echo more than once: Mac and Joel.

Given what we know of Mac, he is definitely seeking sexual adventure. Given how handsome he is, one might wonder why he needs to hire a woman, but considering that a Dollhouse encounter is risk-free, it may be well worth the money, especially when you can order the exact woman of your dreams. But considering what happened on *Buffy* when Warren was able to create the woman of his dreams, a fantasy might get old if it were to become a reality ("I Was Made to Love You" *Buffy* 5.15). Joel Mynor apparently thinks so as well. Although he requests Echo multiple times, apparently he does so only on his anniversary. We do not know if it is possible to "engage" an Active permanently, as it was possible to hire a Companion exclusively on *Firefly*, but Joel is apparently happy enough to engage Echo's services once a year. Echo is extremely beautiful, as are all the Actives, but she is also different. It may be that that something that makes her different appeals to her clients and that is why they request her more often than the others. Whatever it is that she has, it appeals to both men and women.

So, what about the male Actives and their male and female clients? Female clients hire male Actives for the same reasons as their male counterparts: variety, power, fantasy, et cetera. Victor provides an example of a female client engaging a male Active. Although referred to earlier, we do not learn until later in Season One that "Miss Lonely-hearts" is actually Adelle DeWitt, the Los Angeles Dollhouse's Director. Adelle has created an elaborate cover for herself; it is quite impossible for anyone to know that she is attached to one of the Actives. After all, Miss Lonely-hearts has engaged Victor eight times prior to events in "A Spy in the House of Love" (1.9). The encounter is definitely sexual, but also emotional: it is obvious that Adelle loves "Roger" and we are left to wonder about this Roger and their relationship. That she is emotional is obvious from her remarks, but that she knows that she is "cheating" is clear as well. She tells him that she does not have to hide anything from him. In a "normal" relationship (one that contains intimacy) this would mean that she trusts him enough to be able to tell him anything. In this fake relationship she does not have to hide anything from him because he will never remember it. As they lie in bed, Adelle tells him that "everyone has a first date and the object is to hide one's flaws. Then you are in a relationship and the object is to hide your disappointment. Then you are married, and the object is to hide your sins." We certainly wonder what disappointments and sins Adelle is hiding. She cries uncontrollably as she leaves him and, upon returning to the Dollhouse, tells them to destroy the Miss Lonely-hearts persona, as it will no longer be used.

Clients who hire female and male Actives for homosexual encounters would be using their Actives for the same reasons as their heterosexual peers: variety, power, fantasy, et cetera. At first glance one would think that evolutionary theory would have a rather difficult time dealing with homosexuality. Buss argues that homosexuals' sexual activity is more predicted by their gender than by their sexual orientation. Technically homosexuality is defined as sexual relations with a member of the same sex. Nevertheless, the actual numbers of people who have sexual relations with members of their own sex *exclusively* are apparently rather small. In addition, many homosexuals who marry or partner with other homosexuals want children, either through adoption or natural childbirth, with or without a surrogate. Those who wish for a biological child want one of their own or their partner's. They are still fulfilling their reproductive destiny according to evolutionary psychology. Examining the sexual activity of homosexuals in contemporary society shows that gay men engage in sexual activity with a variety of partners. Lesbians are much less likely to have multiple partners.

Given the stigmas with which homosexuals must live in contemporary society it is no wonder that such relationships are rarely depicted on television. As with many social revolutionary ideas, science-fiction provides a means of exploring this aspect of sexuality, but surprisingly, Whedon did not explore this aspect of sexuality in *Dollhouse*. Yes, we learn in Season Two that Echo has been programmed for both homosexual and heterosexual encounters; however, we do not see any of these. Unlike *Firefly*, in which Inara does engage a female client ("War Stories" *FF* 1.10), Echo's on-screen sexual encounters are heterosexual, as are those of the other Actives. As indicated above, we do learn that Echo was imprinted with quite a number of different personas of which seven were lesbian ("Meet Jane Doe" 2.7). Given the controversy surrounding *Dollhouse*'s obvious depictions of prostitution and sexual slavery, FOX-TV might have balked at adding fuel to the fire with open portrayals of homosexual sexual activity.

Conclusions

Love and sex, two ways to exert control over other people: neither seems to work very well in the Whedonverses. Cordy puts it very well in the *Angel* episode "Couplet" (3.14): "Nobody in this office will ever get any [sex]." The sexual couplings are short-lived, which might explain the broody, moody people who are always carrying on in a cranky manner.[16]

In addition, the love affairs never seem to run smoothly either. Just as it is a kiss of death to become involved with any actor who is a star of a show,[17] you should not get involved with anyone in the Whedonverses either. You are doomed to a life of loneliness, even though you are young and good-looking. Of the various character dyads on the four shows, only one could be considered to illustrate consummate love, and look what happened to poor Wash. We could say that Echo and Paul achieved consummate love — what could be more committed than carrying your lover's persona around inside your head? Angel and Buffy pledged "forever," but look what happened there. He fell in love with Cordy and Buffy fell in and out of love with Riley and (I say) Spike as well. I would classify those relationships as romantic love, having the components of passion and intimacy.

As a matter of fact, I would classify the majority of the relationships depicted on the various series as romantic. The key romantic relationships in the four series are also characterized by equality (Hook). One character's strength does not diminish one's partner's, with each member of any couple displaying a combination of strength and weakness. Unfortunately, even that does not help true love flow smoothly in any of the relationships in the Whedonverses. In addition to those of Buffy and Angel noted above, these include: Xander and Anya, Willow and Oz, Willow and Tara, Angel and Darla, and Spike and Drusilla. Xander's relationship with Cordy, and Wesley's relationship with Lilah contained only passion, with both partners feeling mostly contempt for the other, even while acknowledging the passion (even though in the case of Cordy and Xander it was not consummated). And despite the fact that Faith has sexual encounters with Xander, Riley (while in Buffy's skin), and Robin, all of them were about the passion, with no attempts at intimacy. Kaylee's relationship with Simon becomes more passionate as the series progresses, eventually being consummated in *Serenity*. Fred and Gunn also began their relationship with intimacy, but were unable to fulfill the promise that their love and friendship predicted. At the end of *Dollhouse* we are left with the image of Sierra/Priya and Victor/Tony reuniting, with the hope that their love will endure the trying times ahead. And, at the end of *Serenity*, we are left with the hope that Mal and Inara, having finally realized their feelings for each other, will eventually say it out loud.

Love is a powerful emotion. Love makes the world go round. Love makes your head swim. Love leaves you breathless. Love makes you sing. Love makes you cry. Love breaks your heart. And that can make you damn mad.

CHAPTER 3

Aggression and Violence as Methods of Control[1]

What do you tell a woman who has two black eyes? Nothing you haven't already told her twice.— Wesley Wyndam-Pryce, "Billy" [*Angel* 3.6]

Given his self-professed feminist perspective, it comes as no surprise that Joss Whedon addressed aggression and violence in his various television series. The number of times these issues were addressed was dependent upon the length of time that a particular series was on the air, with *Buffy the Vampire Slayer* providing the most examples of such violence and *Firefly* the least. Nevertheless, each series explored these issues in unique, sometimes unexpected ways. In this chapter I will discuss the issues of aggression and violence, including domestic violence, introducing the reader to ways in which such actions are defined, categorized, and cataloged from a psychological and feminist perspective. These perspectives will be illustrated with examples from various episodes from the four Whedon series.

A Short Lesson on Aggression

Psychologists define aggression as "any behavior intended to harm another person who is motivated to avoid the harm" (Baumeister and Bushman 290), a definition which includes three key features. First, aggression is a behavior, something that can be observed, rather than an emotion or a thought. Second, aggression is intentional rather than accidental and the intent is to cause harm to others. Third, the intended victim wants to avoid the harm. A variety of acts that one might consider aggressive then are not included in this definition; examples include suicide, battle play, and sado-masochistic sex play (290).

Aggression may be expressed in several ways. One way is physically as when we hit, slap, punch, shoot or stab someone. Another way is verbally as when we scream, swear, yell, or call someone names. We can express our aggression directly, meaning that the victim is physically present. Thus we can slap their face (physical aggression) or yell at them for lying to us (verbal aggression). We can also express our aggression indirectly, meaning that the victim is absent. Thus we can kill someone's pet (physical aggression) or we can spread rumors about them (verbal aggression). Research data indicate that men are more likely than women to engage in direct aggression, whereas women are more likely to use indirect aggression (291). We can also displace our aggression onto a more convenient, and usually weaker, target, such as when we kick the cat after a hard day at work.

Psychologists also make a distinction between whether aggressive acts are hostile (reactive) or proactive (instrumental). Hostile aggression is "hot." It is impulsive, the type of aggression where you want to harm someone now because you are so angry you cannot think of doing anything else. Proactive aggression, on the other hand is, "cold." It is premeditated and calculated and fits into the old saying, "Revenge is a dish best served cold."

Violence, according to psychologists, is "aggression that has as its goal extreme physical harm, such as injury or death" (291). Pushing someone out of the way in order to get onto the train faster is an act of aggression but not one of violence. Intentionally stabbing someone to take their place in line would be both aggressive and violent. Four crimes are classified by the FBI as violent: homicide, aggravated assault, forcible rape, and robbery. It is important to note that all violent acts are aggressive, but the converse is not true. Aggressive acts that "try to cause extreme physical harm are [considered to be] violent" (291).

Domestic or intimate partner violence is the type of violence that occurs between people who have close relationships with each other, generally in the home or family unit. Contained within the term are several forms of violence, including physical, sexual, and psychological or emotional violence and abuse. The National Coalition Against Domestic Violence (NCADV) defines *battering* as "a pattern of behavior used to establish power and control over another person through fear and intimidation, often including the threat or use of violence. Battering happens when one person believes he or she is entitled to control another."

Domestic violence and emotional abuse are behaviors used by one person in a relationship to control the other. Partners may be married or not married; heterosexual, gay, or lesbian; living together, separated or dating. Examples of abuse[2] include: name-calling or putdowns, keeping a partner from contacting their family or friends, withholding money, stopping a partner from getting or keeping a job, actual or threatened physical harm, sexual assault, stalking, and intimidation. Violence can be criminal and includes physical assault (hitting, pushing, shoving, etc.), sexual abuse (unwanted or forced sexual activity), and stalking. Although emotional, psychological and financial abuse are not criminal behaviors, they are forms of abuse and can lead to criminal violence (domesticviolence.org).

Whereas both men and women victimize their loved ones, 85 percent of victims are women. The statistics with respect to domestic violence are staggering (NCADV). One in every four women will experience domestic violence in her lifetime and young women, aged 20–24, are at the greatest risk of nonfatal partner violence. Almost one-third of female homicide victims in the U.S. are killed by an intimate partner. Domestic violence does not discriminate: such violence occurs in every socioeconomic stratum, religious and cultural group, every country of the world, and in both heterosexual and homosexual relationships. Risk factors[3] that predict violence include low income and education, witnessing such violence as a child, substance abuse, and unemployment (Duffy, Kirsh, and Atwater, 287).

The statistics on domestic violence should not be surprising given the level of violence observed in both men and women in the United States and other countries of the world. Although men are generally more aggressive than women, both physically and verbally, women can be just as aggressive as can men when the aggression is considered from a relational perspective. The definition of relational violence is intentionally harming someone's relationships with other people. Examples include excluding people from your circle of friends, talking about someone behind their back, and withholding affection in order to get what you want.

Aggression and Violence on Buffy the Vampire Slayer

Buffy allowed for much discussion of both interpersonal aggression and violence outside of the inherent violence in a show that depicts a beautiful, young woman engaged in battling monsters in every episode. Buffy's job as the Slayer is inherently violent; however, Buffy and her sidekicks, the Scoobies, are aggressive and violent toward each other in addition to the denizens of the dark from whom they are supposed to protect Sunnydale. That behavior is illustrative of relational aggression.

All of the Scoobies are verbally abusive towards one another at various times throughout the series. Xander, the product of an abusive home, is especially abusive toward Buffy and her choice of sexual partners. Partly this is a result of Xander's unrequited feelings toward Buffy: he wishes that she wanted him as much as he wants her. However, Buffy's feelings for Xander are platonic (see Chapter 2). Yet, if you really cared for someone, could you talk to them the way Xander talks to Buffy? Of course, the answer is yes. Xander has spent his life living in a home where his parents constantly degrade each other. It is the only life that he has ever known; the only way that he has ever observed a man and woman talk to each other. Regardless of whether he knew that it was wrong, and regardless of how his friendship with Willow had grounded him throughout his life, his primary reference for learning how men and women in intimate relationships communicate with each other was his parents.

Just consider the relationships that he has throughout the seven seasons of Buffy. Xander dates Cordy and Anya, and he has sex with Faith and Anya. Faith is quite abusive toward Xander before, during, and after their sexual encounter. Cordy and Xander are verbally abusive toward each other before, during, and after their short-lived relationship. Cordy is especially virulent given that her attraction to Xander marked her as "unpopular." It is rather ironic that Xander becomes less verbally abusive and more stable in his relationships with women once he begins dating a reformed demon. Nevertheless, his fear of becoming like his father results in his jilting Anya on their wedding day. Not only does he jilt her, but he becomes slightly more abusive toward her, especially when he discovers that she had sex with Spike, simply for solace she tells him ("Entropy" 6.18). As he berates Anya for that encounter, she notes that it is okay for Xander to leave her at the altar, but not okay for her to seek comfort where she can.

Xander was also the target of bullying when younger. The anger experienced as a result of such victimization begins to express itself as Xander grows up, with the result that he becomes somewhat of a bully. Cordelia is also a bully; she is rich and beautiful and people want to be part of her social group. She takes delight in tormenting "the little people." She is especially abusive to Willow throughout the first season of Buffy, often making snide remarks about Willow's clothes, for example, asking Willow if her mother dresses her ("Welcome of the Hellmouth" 1.1). Cordelia continues to abuse Willow, even after becoming a member of the Scoobies. Although involved in a relationship with Xander, Cordy abuses him as well. The abuse is mutual.

It is difficult to obtain reliable statistics about the issue of dating violence in teenagers. Many teenagers are so unsure of how to date and what such relationships mean that they do not understand what limits they should place on a dating partner. The Alabama Coalition Against Domestic Violence reports that *one in three* teens has experienced violence in a dating relationship (acadv.org/dating.html). The fact that a third of teens are reporting this level of violence makes it hard to understand why Joss Whedon did not address the issue more often on *Buffy*. It would certainly have been a service to young men and women and would have provided a forum for reaching large numbers of young people. Nevertheless the issue was broached several times.

The first instance was a stand-alone episode and concerned a young woman being abused by her boyfriend ("Beauty and the Beasts" 3.4). The young man, who is afraid of losing his girlfriend, concocts a potion that will allow him to keep her. Unfortunately, it makes him even more violent than normal, and by the end of the episode he kills her. This episode is especially good for showing the typical stages of an abusive relationship: (1) tension building, or the escalation to the violence; (2) the explosion or the violence itself; and, (3) the honeymoon phase, which includes remorse, apologies, and an attempt to place blame on someone other than the abuser (usually the victim) or something external to the situation, such as a hard day at work (*www.breakthecycle.org*).

Another abusive male character on the series is Warren Mears whose violent actions toward women are observed several times. Warren is so determined to have a girlfriend who will do anything he wants that he creates her ("I Was Made to Love You" 5.15). This robot is named April and she is designed to satisfy Warren's every whim. Unfortunately, she is so perfectly programmed that Warren grows bored with her and abandons her. He actually falls in love with a real woman named Katrina, who breaks up with Warren when she discovers what he has done. Warren is determined to have Katrina and uses a mind-control spell to make her love him again ("Dead Things," 6.13). When she awakens from the spell, she accuses Warren and the other members of the Trio, Jonathan and Andrew, of rape. Enraged, Warren kills her and then uses the same mind-control spell to make Buffy think that she killed Katrina. Warren's final action in the series is to shoot and wound Buffy. A stray bullet kills Tara, unleashing the full power of Willow's magick (see Chapter 4). Warren's actions toward women indicate a deep hatred for them and a desire to harm them, both physically and sexually. One could argue that his actions stem from the bullying he received as a child, although Xander, too, was bullied as a child, and he did not grow up to kill women.

Another character desiring a perfect mate and family is Ted Buchanan, although Ted himself is the robot ("Ted" 2.11). Apparently the real Ted created a replica of himself that would possess all of the characteristics a perfect man should have. He then sets out to find a family; he has had four wives up to this point in time. Ted becomes enamored of Joyce Summers and intends that she will be his next wife, and Buffy will be his new daughter. Buffy does not feel comfortable around Ted, but everyone, including Angel, tells her to give Ted a chance, that Joyce deserves happiness. However, Buffy kills Ted after he hits her. Since he is a robot, he cannot die, and he returns to the house. He and Buffy fight again, and Buffy discovers that Ted is a robot. When he hits Joyce, Buffy destroys him once and for all. There are certainly other instances of abuse in Buffy[4]; however, I will conclude this section by mentioning two very prominent instances. The first involves Willow and Tara, and the second involves Buffy and Spike.

Whedon's decision to have Willow explore her sexuality and begin a relationship with another woman was not without risks. Many fans were outraged that Willow "became" a lesbian and eventually chose Tara over Oz. Others were ecstatic that Whedon would choose to have two openly gay characters on the series, who were not only openly gay but openly sexual as well. The decision to have that relationship become increasingly abusive was distressing to many of these same fans. Willow's addiction to magick becomes stronger with the passage of time (see Chapter 4) and, like many addicts, she goes to great lengths to hide her use from her friends. Tara becomes increasingly suspicious and begins to question Willow about the number of spells she is casting. Willow dismisses Tara's fears, but eventually promises Tara that she will stop. Unable to do so, Willow casts a spell on Tara, causing Tara to forget their argument and Willow's inability to stop using magick ("Tabula Rasa" 6.8). Tara discovers Willow's treachery and moves out of the house. Willow is devastated and does not understand why Tara is so upset over a little spell. Willow does not understand that she has, in effect, mind-raped Tara, and not only that, if Tara and Willow had sex after the spell was cast, then Willow raped Tara as well, given that Tara was unable to consent to the sex (the definition of rape). Tara asks Willow how she could treat her that way given what happened to her prior to the events in this episode. Tara is referring not only to the mind-rape effected by Glory ("Tough Love" 5.19), but also to the abuse she suffered at the hands of her family throughout her childhood ("Family" 5.6), when she was told that she was literally a demon and she believed it.

Finally one of the most abusive relationships on the series involved

Spike and Buffy. When they first meet, they are mortal enemies. Spike is a vampire, intent upon adding another Slayer kill to his belt; he has already killed two. Buffy is a Slayer and, thus, she is sworn to kill him. Nevertheless, the two are drawn to each other and their relationship eventually evolves from that of enemies to reluctant allies to lovers to comrades-in-arms and friends. Buffy increasingly relies on Spike for help as the series progresses and Spike realizes that he will do anything for her, even die. As the relationship evolves, the abusive parts of it become less so and the relationship becomes more egalitarian and mutually respectful. If Buffy cannot stand the fact that Spike is a vampire, she becomes increasingly aware that he is a man as well. Not only does he possess a soul, but I contend that his soul was much purer than Angel's from the very beginning. Yet that does not stop Spike and Buffy from physically and verbally abusing each other, especially during Season Six when their relationship becomes sexual. Their sex play is quite violent; however, Spike cannot really hurt Buffy, nor can she hurt him. Depictions of this violent sex play are problematic in one sense: they suggest that violence is normal in a relationship. These scenes may be misunderstood by any viewer who thinks that violence should be part of the sex act.[5] Interestingly as Buffy and Spike's relationship changes to one of friendship and comradeship (i.e., as they become more intimate with each other and their love changes from romantic to companionate, see Chapter 2), they become much less abusive towards each other, both verbally and physically.

Aggression and Violence on Angel

Given that *Angel* is a continuation of the world created in *Buffy the Vampire Slayer*, *Angel*'s episodes will reflect the themes underlying that series along with the theme of redemption, as Angel seeks to find meaning in life and atone for the sins of Angelus.[6] Aggression and violence obviously figure prominently in most episodes and the series explored violence against women repeatedly.

The series opens with an episode ("City Of" 1.1) that focuses on violence against women, although in this case it is vampires preying upon women, from the young women in the bar in the opening act, to the waitress named Tina who is attempting to escape someone named Russell, to Cordelia Chase, who also encounters Russell. Angel saves the young women and tries to protect Tina from Russell but fails. For all her ditzy antics, Cordy is very demon savvy from her years as a member of the Scooby gang and so she recognizes

Russell for what he is. Not only that, but Cordy knows a few tricks that help her keep away from Russell until Angel arrives to save her. Angel's solution to the Russell problem is to kill him, thereby saving any future victims from the vampire's violence. Cordy attaches herself to Angel, realizing that she can work for him and thereby earn money (and have enough to eat) while pursuing her acting career.

Unfortunately for Cordy she is not always quite able to take care of herself and finds herself in peril far too many times. She is menaced by a ghost in the episode "Rm w/a Vu" (1.5), and manages to hold her own against the ghost until it proves too powerful and she must wait to be rescued by Angel and Doyle. Later, she meets who she thinks is a very nice man, invites him to her apartment, and into her bed. The next morning he is gone, but he has left a present — Cordy is pregnant, having been impregnated by a demon ("Expecting" 1.12). The babies apparently have the power to control their "mothers" and Cordy becomes content with the idea that she is carrying demon babies. She will be impregnated again ("Epiphany" 2.16) against her will, but this time it will be violent and painful. She gets pregnant again in Season Four, giving birth to Jasmine, an entity which has possessed her ("Inside Out" 4.17). Cordy will die as a result of this birth. None of Cordy's pregnancies occurred by her choice. Rather, the demons which impregnated her did so without her knowledge or consent, which is the definition of rape.

Cordelia suffers from what can only be termed a mind-rape in the episode "That Vision Thing" (3.2). Her visions have become increasingly difficult and now they are downright violent. Not only that, but they begin to manifest themselves physically. One vision results in deep, gouging claw marks on her body. The second manifests as boils, and the third as fire. By this time Cordy understandably does not want to have the visions anymore. It turns out that Lilah Morgan, of Wolfram and Hart, has hired a telepathic demon to induce visions with physical manifestations. The purpose of this rape/torture is to force Angel to rescue someone from a Hell dimension for Lilah. Although it appears that Cordy is not traumatized by these forced pregnancies, or the other instances of abuse she has endured, she will seek her revenge several episodes later.

The episode "Billy" (3.6) allows the writers to explore what they term "primordial misogyny," the hatred that men have for women that has existed from the beginning of time. Billy likes to watch men beat women. He incites the violence by touch and is completely contemptuous of women, telling Cordy: "I don't hate women. I mean, sure you're all whores who sell yourselves for money or prestige, but men are just as bad. Maybe even worse.

They're willing to throw away careers or families or even lives for what's under your skirt." This episode begins with Lilah Morgan, Billy's lawyer at Wolfram and Hart, being severely beaten by her colleague, Gavin Park. However, the truly horrific parts of the episode occur when the men of Angel Investigations are contaminated by contact with Billy's blood. They, too, succumb to this primordial misogyny. Wesley hits Fred and then stalks her throughout the Hyperion, telling her exactly what he will do to her when he catches her. When Gunn comes to help her, he, too, is infected and begins to stalk her. Cordy decides to pursue Billy and kill him. She goes to Lilah and demands help, telling her:

> You know that guy that you hired to hack into my visions? What he did to me? You know what it felt like? I was cut, torn up, my face disfigured, and burning with pain every second not knowing if it was going to end or just get worse till I died.... It's not the pain. It's the helplessness, the certainty that there is nothing you can do to stop it, that your life can be thrown away in an instant by someone else. He doesn't care. He'll beat you down till you stay down 'cause he doesn't even think of you as alive. No woman should ever have to go through that. And no woman strong enough to wear the mantle of "vicious bitch" would *ever* put up with it.

When Angel goes to help Cordelia, he also is infected, although he is able to resist the rage more so than the others. It is Lilah who kills Billy, although her motives for doing so are a mystery. Has she done it to be heroic, as Stephanie Romanov says (Stafford 208), to reclaim her power, or simply to take her revenge on yet another man who has abused her?

There are a number of other examples of violence against women on *Angel.* One particularly creepy example occurs in the episode "I Fall to Pieces" (1.4). A young woman named Melissa has a stalker, a neurosurgeon, who is able to detach various body parts and send them off to engage with Melissa. For example he can detach his eyes and spy on her. In one particularly unpleasant scene he disengages his hands and has them crawl into her apartment, into her bed, and up over her body. Dr. Meltzer is obsessed with Melissa and intends to possess her, attacking Angel when Angel interferes with his plans. Angel does eventually save Melissa from the doctor and she becomes Angel Investigations' first paying customer.

The episode "Untouched" (2.4) is particularly poignant and concerns a young woman named Bethany, a victim of child sexual abuse at the hands of her father. Bethany is now a grown woman who has no idea of how to act around men. Bethany is frequently promiscuous and offers herself to Angel after he rescues her from a pair of rapists, who in actuality have been hired by Lilah Morgan. It seems that Bethany's rage over her abuse has manifested itself as telekinesis. Lilah plans to use the threat of violence to awaken Bethany's ability, and she has befriended the girl in order to gain her loyalty. Fortunately, Angel intervenes and manages to convince Bethany that she is not worthless. Angel acknowledges that Bethany has power and tells her she can use it. She does use her power against her father, but stops herself from killing him. Another daughter who is helped by Angel Investigations is Virginia Bryce ("Guise Will Be Guise" 2.6). Virginia's father ostensibly hires Angel and crew to protect his daughter from his business partners. In actuality, Bryce just wants the gang to keep Virginia safe until his birthday, when he will sacrifice her to increase his power.

Angel encounters a female demon named Jhiera of the Oden Tal in the episode "She" (1.13). Jhiera is part of an "Underground Railroad" organization that attempts to keep women of the Oden Tal from having their Ko removed. The Ko is part of the female's body — a series of ridges running down the female's back — that contains her physical and sexual power (Holder, Mariotte, and Hart 123). When this part of the female is removed she is unable to express her sexuality and thus becomes subservient to the males of her species. It is the way that male Oden Tal control the females of their species. This episode is a very thinly disguised condemnation of the practice of female genital circumcision (also referred to as mutilation). Women in certain middle–Eastern and African countries are subjected to this type of surgery either in childhood or at puberty (Gruenbaum). Depending upon the country, the entire labia majora and minora (i.e., outer and inner vulvar lips) may be removed along with the clitoris. Such surgery renders the female unable to experience sexual pleasure. The surgery can be very dangerous; it is not uncommon for girls to die from the procedure.

Each of these episodes show the ways in which women can be abused and the ways in which they might respond. Women who have been victimized display a variety of symptoms, referred to as Battered Women's Syndrome (Walker).[7] Common psychological reactions, according to Browne, include shock, denial, confusion, withdrawal, psychological numbing and fear, chronic fatigue and anxiety, insomnia and other sleep disturbances, eating disorders, depression and suicide. Ruminating thoughts are common; examples include focusing on what the *victim* did wrong or what the *victim* could have done differently, to have avoided the abuse. Walker's feminist perspective on women-battering declares that violence against women is both a cause and an effect of the power differential that exists between men and women in our society. The fact that men have power over women means that they can do to them what they will. Angel's pre-vampire persona Liam had the power of his social position and that allowed him to get away with much. As Angelus, he had the power of his vampire status. Billy had the power of his wealth and family name along with a team of high-powered lawyers to resolve any pesky little problems arising from his abuse; plus he committed his abuse by using telepathy to make others his puppets rather than actively committing violence with his own hands, rendering himself blameless, at least in his own eyes. Russell's power arose from his vampire power. The demons that attacked Cordy had the power they possessed as demons. Bethany's abuser was her father.

Each of the women in the episodes mentioned above responded to her abuse in a variety of ways. Cordy appeared to be fine, but seemed to grow quieter and less cheerful as well as less elitist. Bethany acted out her abuse with antisocial behavior that included sexual promiscuity, even attempting to seduce Angel. Lilah denied anything had happened. Fred also showed clear signs of post-traumatic stress disorder following her return from slavery in Pylea, which was exacerbated when Wesley and Gunn began stalking her in "Billy."

Although never actually explored on *Buffy* or *Angel*, it is my belief that Liam and Angelus (and Spike) were probably rapists.[8] We have a tendency to think of rapists as being the men who jump out of the darkness and threaten to kill or maim their victims using some type of weapon. This is rarely the case. According to the program "No Safe Place,"[9]

> Sexual assault is defined as any unwanted sexual act including forced sexual contact and sexual touching.... Rape is defined as sexual intercourse without the consent of both parties.... Three-fourths of rapes are committed by a man the woman knows. Studies show that a rapist can be anyone — a date, a boyfriend, a father, a grandfather, an uncle, a neighbor, a friend, a brother, a son.... A 10-year government study that looked at more than a million cases of rape in the United States showed that 88 percent of rape victims are between the ages of 12–28. Prison psychologists say that while some rapists are calculating and planning, often stalking their victims, many rapists tend to be random — often looking for unlocked doors, or open windows, for example. They seize opportunities in an impulsive act.

Liam was certainly a wastrel before being turned by Darla. Jenny Calendar reminds him of this fact in the episode "Amends" (*Buffy* 3.10) when she says: "What a man you were! A drunken, whoring layabout and a terrible disappointment to your parents.... You were a worthless being before you were ever a monster." Given the few flashbacks we see of Angel prior to his transformation, he freely enjoys the women of the town and looks to enjoy his family's servants as well, a sure sign that he is abusing his power as the son of the house.[10] He freely admits torturing people prior to killing them as the vampire Angelus; rape would not be a form of torture a vampire would abstain from using. We were horrified when Spike attempts to rape Buffy. I contend that Angelus probably raped women and more, as did Spike. Knowing this could be one reason why Buffy is so frightened of Dawn's schoolgirl crush on Spike. Angel is certainly aware of the depths of his depravity as both a man and a vampire, when he tells Buffy that "it's not the demon in me that needs killing.... It's the man" ("Amends"). It is not my intention to suggest that Angel is incapable of redemption. Angel's actions do not necessarily include rape or sexual assault, but they might. Debating a particular character's evilness would be a pointless argument, as I mention in Chapter 2 when discussing Gul Dukat and Spike. As a psychologist I must admit to the possibility of change — it comes with the territory. Perhaps this is part of Whedon's message with respect to the violence on *Angel*: many of the characters engage in aggressive and violent behavior, but they are not necessarily doomed for all time.

Aggression and Violence on Firefly *and* Serenity

The 'verse was a very violent place, or at least, violence was a way of life on the Border planets, although violence was not unheard of in the heart of the Alliance either. Four episodes were particularly striking for their depictions or threats of aggression and violence toward women, although the series depicted many instances of violence against men as well. The film *Serenity* also provided numerous examples of aggression and violence.

The Reavers are the bogeymen of the 'verse, but at least there is a reason for their madness (see Chapter 6). Other people encountered by Mal and his crew do not have that excuse for their actions— they simply use violence as a means toward an end, that end being power. The most malevolent example of this is Adelai Niska, the psychopath who hires Mal and company to steal a shipment of drugs in the episode "The Train Job" (1.2). Niska delights in torturing people and in letting people see the results of that torture. He tells Mal in "The Train Job" that the dead man hanging in the next room — his wife's nephew — will solidify his reputation. Later, when Mal and Wash are captured by Niska ("War Stories" 1.10) we will see just how much Niska loves getting his hands dirty when he takes over Mal's torture. Mal is disgusted by Niska and his ilk, having had his fill of death and destruction during the war. Not to say that Mal will not get his hands dirty, we have seen much evidence of that, but Mal has a code of conduct and it does not allow him to abuse most people in such a fashion. Unfortunately Mal can be verbally abusive to the men and women who travel on Serenity.

In the episode "Shindig" (1.4) Mal and the crew visit Persephone, one of the central planets. Mal is particularly cruel to Kaylee upon first arriving. She sees a beautiful dress in a shop window and wishes that she could have something that pretty. Mal asks her why she wants something so frilly and then says it would be just like a sheep prancing around on its hind legs. Although the insult escapes Jayne, both Zoe and Wash are angry with Mal for hurting Kaylee's feelings, and this could be construed as an example of verbal aggression. Later, Mal will buy the dress for Kaylee and escort her to the ball as a way of apology (and a legitimate way to attend the ball and make his smuggling connection). Other women at the ball insult her taste in clothes, but Kaylee is a hit with the men because, not only is she pretty, she can talk about the types of things men apparently like to talk about, such as engines. At the ball, Inara's date, Atherton Wing, is verbally abusive to her, reminding her that she is a Companion and remarking that everyone at the ball wishes they could bed her. Mal takes offense and inadvertently challenges Atherton to a duel, which is apparently a very common way in which to defend one's honor on Persephone. Mal does fight the duel, which is to the death, but Mal refuses to kill Atherton, although he is quite happy to thrust his sword into Atherton a number of times. Mal does not hesitate to call Inara a "whore" and make disparaging remarks about her role as a Companion; however, he will not let others insult her. In many respects Mal acts as if only he has the right to insult her, a very possessive and controlling attitude to have toward someone who travels with you by choice. Later, Inara will leave Serenity because of the problems she has with her feelings toward Mal. In her essay "Terror Management Aboard Serenity," Wind Goodfriend argues that Mal's abuse of Inara is an "ill-designed effort to make them more like equals" (198). Mal feels inferior to Inara and thus calls her "whore" to make himself feel better.

Mal has no problems with Zoe, his second-in-command. Having served with Zoe in combat during the failed War for Independence, Mal is aware that Zoe can hold her own in any fight. Indeed, we observe that in several episodes of *Firefly* (e.g., "The Train Job" 1.2). Mal might consider Zoe to be more like one of the guys, rather than as a woman. After all, Zoe is not very "girly." The people who do rely on Mal, the ones who cannot necessarily take care of themselves without his help, seem to be the most likely victims of his verbal abuse. This is especially true of Kaylee and Inara, less so of River, especially as Mal and the rest of Serenity's crew come to realize just how formidable River is.

Mal is also verbally abusive toward a couple of the men who fly with him. Wash is essential to the crew as the pilot of the ship. Mal tolerates Wash because he is such a great pilot and he is Zoe's husband, both of which factors keep Mal from being too verbally abusive toward Wash. Jayne Cobb is also essential to the crew. He is a mercenary who is not scared of a fight. As a matter of fact, Jayne is generally not scared of anything. However, Jayne is not very bright so, although Mal is sometimes abusive to Jayne, Jayne generally doesn't get it, and the insults fly over his head. On the other hand, there is Shepherd Book. Mal's faith in God was destroyed during the War for Independence, and Book's presence on board Serenity is a constant reminder of what Mal lost. Nevertheless, Book is the one character, other than Zoe, that Mal relies upon for advice (not that he necessarily takes it). Book's past is mysterious and some of the things that he knows hint at violence.[11] Although Book has renounced that past and is apparently looking for absolution, Mal comes to rely more and more on Book's advice as time passes. Finally, there is Simon Tam who bears the brunt of Mal's abuse occasionally, and it has been suggested that Simon is a feminized man.[12] Simon is perhaps symbolic of all things that Mal hates about the Alliance: civilization, status, position, and wealth.[13] Mal does harbor some admiration for Simon because Simon gave up all of those privileges for River. However, Mal does not want Simon to forget that it is he, Mal, who now provides for River and Simon. He wants Simon to remain in his debt.

And Simon and River certainly need help, as evidenced by what happens in the episode "Safe" (1.5). Simon is kidnapped by a group of settlers in need of a doctor. River begins tracking Simon and is, thus, captured as well. River is placed in the care of a woman named Doralee, and while there she learns why a young girl named Ruby does not speak. The trauma of watching her mother kill her sister, and try to kill her, has rendered Ruby speechless. River discovers this by linking telepathically with Ruby. When Doralee realizes that River can read minds, she accuses River of being a witch. River is questioned by the leader of these people, the Patron, and she discovers via telepathy that he became Patron by killing his rival. The Patron declares that River is a witch and that she must be put to the fire. Women living in this community apparently know their place, and there are mechanisms designed to reinforce appropriate rules of behavior. Luckily, Mal and the crew arrive in time to rescue River and Simon.

A third example of violence against women occurs in the unaired episode "Heart of Gold" (1.13). Mal and the crew of Serenity are asked to help an old friend of Inara's, named Nandi, who operates a brothel. One of the local men, Rance Burgess, has claimed the baby of a prostitute named Petaline. Burgess is not a very nice man. He is abusive toward his wife, telling an off-color story in front of her and not acknowledging her presence. However, she is complicit in the plan to take the child, more than likely because a son will increase her status with her husband and her peers. Later in the episode, Burgess sexually abuses one of prostitutes, even though she has come to him to betray her companions. Chari gives information to Burgess about Petaline as well as the crew's plan to protect Nandi's house against Burgess' attempt to take Petaline's child by force. After Burgess learns what he needs to know from Chari, he addresses the men who will help him take the child. He tells them that Chari knows her place and commands her to get down on her knees, apparently to fellate him while the men watch and cheer.

Finally, the episode "Objects in Space" (1.14) provides one of the most chilling scenes in the entire short-lived series, when the bounty hunter Jubal Early threatens Kaylee with rape. Early's words to Kaylee are soft-spoken. He does not touch her in any way in the episode; he simply tells her that there are a number of things he can do to her and her soft body. Kaylee has been called the "heart" of Serenity (Whedon); she is sweet and kind, and also freely sexual. However, Kaylee does not know how to take care of herself: witness her actions in "The Train Job" when she could not even pull the trigger on a gun when Niska's men were threatening to board Serenity. Up until this point in time in *Firefly*, Kaylee has always had Mal or Jayne or Zoe to take care of her. Women might have some power in the 'verse — witness Inara's power as a Companion and Zoe's as a soldier — but certainly women have not received complete equality with men. As these few examples illustrate, women are still threatened by men in the 'verse.

Although Whedon explores violence against women in *Firefly*, this aspect of aggression is less evident in the sequel motion picture *Serenity*. One could note that the violence in the early part of the film is hostile or reactive. For example, Mal and the crew engage in violent behavior when chased by the Reavers early in the film. The Reavers attack while the crew is on one of their jobs. Mal tries to help as many of the townspeople as possible before the crew heads for Serenity. They must escape or they will face a fate that is beyond comprehension given that the Reavers rape, eat, and kill their victims (and hopefully they do not do it in that order). However, when they travel to Maidenhead to rendezvous with their contacts, River is triggered by a subliminal message and becomes overly aggressive. As she fights in the bar at Maidenhead, she is able to effortlessly engage the entire clientele. She even renders Jayne unfit to fight with a well-aimed blow to the genitals. The trigger, however, is simply an attempt by the Alliance to learn her whereabouts, although it certainly gives Mal even more information about this supposedly fragile girl who travels in his ship. From this point onwards the violence becomes even more reactive on Mal's part, as he tries to stay one step ahead of, and keep River from being captured by, the Operative, whose methods are cold and calculating, and thus more characteristic of instrumental or proactive aggression. Mal eventually stops reacting and begins to go on the offensive. It is this switch in tactics and his engagement of the Operative, using his own methods, that eventually works in Mal's favor. He also has the powerful River Tam on his side. River has been remade as a weapon (see Chapter 5); she becomes increasingly aware of this aspect of herself as the film proceeds. She begins to be less fearful, especially when she learns what was done to her and what secret she holds. Her actions become much more proactive and the scene in which she has vanquished the Reavers and is calculating whether to take on the Alliance soldiers is stunning in its simplicity: the bluish cast to the lighting, one eye peeking from beneath her hair, the drip-drip of blood falling from the battleaxe she holds in her hand. Mal seems to have changed by the end of the film *Serenity*, finding a new reason for life and love. Perhaps future adventures of the crew will find him less aggressive toward the crew ... well, maybe except for Jayne.[14]

Aggression and Violence on Dollhouse

Although the major theme of *Dollhouse* appeared to be sex for hire, the series was about much more, with the sex serving as a "red herring" for the real purpose underlying the use of memory manipulation (see Chapter 6). Given the variety of sexual behaviors practiced by men and women, we would expect to see a variety of practices on the *Dollhouse*. In actuality the majority of episodes did not contain sexual encounters between the Actives and clients, although a number of them did depict aggression and violence. As mentioned in the Preface, Echo is the major character in this series and the "A" story of each episode revolves around her. She is abused in various ways throughout the series as are the other major Actives: Sierra, Victor, November, and Whiskey. Abuse is both physical and sexual on *Dollhouse*. One could argue that the entire series was predicated upon the sexual abuse of women.[15]

The episode "The Target" (1.2) finds Echo engaged by a client named Richard, who appears to be the usual charming, rich man who makes up the client base of the Dollhouse. After an apparently satisfying sexual encounter, he makes Echo get dressed and then tells her that she is his target, his prey. He chases her through the forest; he is armed and has a tracking scope, but she is weaponless. She eventually finds a ranger's cabin, where she drinks water from a canteen, only to learn that Richard has killed the ranger and drugged the water. Echo eventually escapes, killing Richard in the process. We learn that Richard was not his real name and that he was apparently hired to "test" Echo by the escaped Active, Alpha.

Alpha is obsessed with Echo and has been ever since she joined the Dollhouse. Alpha himself had a psychotic break and escaped prior to events in the series. He has incorporated all of his Dollhouse personas into one composite being and that event has increased his madness above his pre–Dollhouse pathological state. Part of the reason for Alpha's break was Echo's entry into the Dollhouse. Alpha wanted Echo for himself but he also wanted her to be "Number One," the Active chosen most often by clients. At the time of Echo's entry into the Dollhouse, an Active named Whiskey (Claire) was Number One. Alpha cut Whiskey's face so that she would no longer be requested and Echo could take her place ("Omega" 1.12). Catherine Coker poses an interesting question in her essay "Exploitation of Bodies and Minds in Season One of *Dollhouse*" as to whether the original (male) Dr. Saunders raped Alpha. Such an act might explain Alpha's rage against the doctor and the doctor's murder.

Another instance of Echo's abuse occurs in the episode "Vows" (2.1) when she weds a British businessman named Martin Klar. This marriage is actually an assignment for Echo to gather evidence of his arms-dealing. Paul Ballard is following her to ensure her safety, but Klar obtains pictures of Echo meeting with Ballard. Upon confronting Echo with the pictures, Klar hits her several times. Apparently these blows to the head serve as a further stimulus for Echo's retrieval of her previously imprinted memories. Ballard also strikes Echo, although he claims that he is trying to shock her into remembering, not only her former imprints, but their skills as well (see Chapter 6). This episode continues the notion that Dollhouse clients have complete control over the Actives, doing whatever they want to them, without fear of consequences. Even Ballard abuses Echo when it suits his agenda, thereby suggesting that violence against women is sometimes necessary, especially when it serves the perceived greater good.

The more general theme of violence against women occurs in the episode "Belle Chose" (2.3). Echo is hired by a college professor[16] to enact his fantasy of the sexy, young co-ed trading her favors for a grade. This example of sexual harassment is all too real to many college-educated women.[17] Another example of violence against women is illustrated in the same episode with the Active named Victor. Victor is imprinted with the memories of a young man named Terry, who just happens to be the nephew of a highly valued Dollhouse patron. As Topher maps Terry's brain he realizes that Terry is a psychopath. Terry kidnaps women and injects them with a paralyzing drug. This renders the women helpless and Terry is able to play with them as he wishes, apparently re-enacting scenes from his own life with his little sister, big sister, mother, and aunt Sheila before killing the women, whereupon he begins collecting a new set of women to re-enact the scenes all over again. Terry denigrates the unwilling woman he casts as "Aunt Sheila," referring to her as a whore, before killing her. He is on a quest to replace "Aunt Sheila" when he is injured in the accident. Victor is imprinted with Terry's persona in an attempt to discover if there are any other victims and where Terry has hidden them. Events go horribly wrong and Echo ends up with the Terry imprint. Thus this episode ends with a woman imprinted with a man's persona abusing other women. The victims of Terry's violence are rescued, but the episode ends with the viewer realizing that Echo still retains some of the psychopathology characteristic of Terry's personality.

However, in my opinion, the most serious violence occurring on *Dollhouse* centered on the Active Sierra. We learn in "Man on the Street" (1.6) that Sierra has been raped by her Handler, Joe Hearn. Her memory of the rape is a perfect example of procedural/implicit memory (see Chapter 6). When Boyd discovers that Hearn is the rapist, rather than the Active who is in love with Sierra, Hearn claims that he was only doing what came naturally; after all, the Handlers are placed in a position of continuously being around these docile little Dolls in various stages of undress. He is the type of man who thinks that women are "asking for it," a comment that many rapists and pedophiles also make about the individuals they molest.

Later, in the episode "Belonging" (2.4) we will learn that Sierra was placed in the Dollhouse against her will. Priya Tsetsang would not submit to the advances of a man named Nolan who desired her. Enraged that she rejected him, Nolan fed Priya drugs that induced a psychotic break (see Chapter 7), and she was confined to a mental institution. It is this psychotic patient who is "recruited" by the Dollhouse. As with all of the Actives, her true personality is wiped, and the personas with which she is imprinted are not averse to engaging Nolan sexually. He eventually demands that Sierra be given to him permanently; a request to which Adelle DeWitt does not have to accede once Sierra kills Nolan. Nolan possesses many of the characteristics of an abuser: he wants and desires exclusivity with a woman to the extent that he attempts to possess her, and he is extremely jealous of anyone who shows interest in the object of his affections. He becomes violent when the loved one wishes to leave. Priya's actions also reflect the lengths to which some women will go in order to leave an abusive relationship.[18]

Conclusion[19]

The examples that I have discussed in this chapter are by no means all of the instances through which Whedon examined the issues of violence and aggression. The various characters in each of the series might or might not display verbal or physical aggression and violence. In some instances the aggressive acts directly targeted a victim and sometimes the aggressive acts were more covert. Violence might have a reason for its occurrence, or it might not. In any case, Whedon's message illustrates that these types of abuse occur, but reinforces the fact that they do not have to continue.

CHAPTER 4

Supernatural Methods of Control

Patron: The girl is a witch.
Mal: Yeah. But she's our witch. [Mal cocks his gun]. So cut her the hell
down.—"Safe" [*Firefly* 1.5]

Although *Buffy* and *Angel* both dealt with matters of the supernatural, including magick and witchcraft, the exact ways in which these terms were used in these series needs to be clarified. I will first attempt to define the terms and then present historical information about them (although a complete discussion is beyond the scope of this book). Given that the supernatural is not broached in either *Firefly* or *Dollhouse*, those series will not be discussed in this chapter, with one exception on *Firefly*. The majority of the chapter will discuss the ways in which supernatural agents, such as witchcraft and magick, were used on both *Buffy* and *Angel*.

Defining the Terminology

Attempting to determine someone's religious beliefs is problematical for a variety of reasons, but it appears that the five major religions practiced in the world are Christianity (33 percent), Islam (21 percent), no religion (16 percent), Hinduism (14 percent), and Chinese traditional and Buddhism (6 percent each).[1] About one million people worldwide consider themselves to be pagan, which is defined (not very well) as "an adherent of a polytheistic religion in antiquity, especially when viewed in contrast to an adherent of a monotheistic religion."[2] Paganism itself is not a religion, but rather an umbrella term and encompasses a variety of different religious beliefs, such as Druidism, Satanism, and Religious Witchcraft.[3] A pagan is also defined as someone who practices a religion other than one of the three monotheistic religions of Christianity, Judaism, or Islam. One modern pagan religion is Wicca. According to the Celtic Connection's website,[4] Wicca "draws from the Old Traditions of Witchcraft ... [However,] Witchcraft and Wicca, while similar in many respects, are not the same. One can be a Witch, without being a Wiccan, just as a person can be a Christian, without being a Baptist. Wicca is a recognized religion, while Witchcraft itself is not considered a religion. Thus, Wicca might best be described as a modern religion, based on ancient Witchcraft traditions." Witchcraft, on the other hand, is defined as "the art or power of bringing magical or preternatural power to bear or the act or practice of attempting to do so."[5] Even today witchcraft has a bad reputation, with witches believed to be those men and women who worship Satan.[6] Magick is

> the alleged art and science of causing change in accordance with the will by non-physical means. Magick is associated with all kinds of paranormal and occult phenomena, including but not limited to: ESP, astral projection, psychic healing, the cabala, and chakras. Magick uses various symbols, such as the pentagram, as well as a variety of symbolic ritual behaviors aimed at achieving powers which allow one to contravene the laws of physics, chemistry, etc. Magick should not be confused with magic, which is the art of conjuring and legerdemain.[7]

Finally, demons are defined as evil spirits or devils.[8] They have existed throughout history in the mythology of numerous groups of people; in the Christian tradition they are generally considered to be fallen angels, cast out of Heaven after following Lucifer, later referred to as Satan, when he rebelled against God. William Kent states that the science concerning demons is demonology and notes that it is a very ancient study associated with incantations and other magical properties.

Using these various definitions, we can argue that Whedon created a supernatural tool for use by the Slayer and her companions by combining witchcraft, magick, and Wicca. This combination is clearly represented by Buffy's best friend, Willow Rosenberg.[9] However, this is not the case in the Angelverse, where Angel and his gang make use of magick and witchcraft without wrapping such usage under the umbrella of Wicca.

In many respects, the ways in which magick and witchcraft are used varied in the two series. It is true that both are used in the fight against the forces of darkness, nevertheless the dichotomy between good and evil is more pronounced in the Buffyverse than in the Angelverse. Buffy's enemies are the denizens of the dark, vampires and other demons, whose *raison d'être* is to wreak havoc on the world of the living and wrestle the world away from human beings. Buffy's role as the Slayer is to stand *alone* against the forces of darkness (Wilcox, in Wilcox and Lavery), but along the way Buffy acquires a group of people who become "family." These people not only provide her emotional support (sometimes) but they are also there with her "fighting the good fight." The Scoobies have assets that allow them to aid Buffy in her fight: Xander's heart, Giles' knowledge, and Willow's computer skills. With time, Willow learns about witchcraft, joins a coven and embraces Wicca, and becomes adept in the use of magick. All of these help Buffy in her fight, but the power that Willow acquires from her supernatural abilities seduces her.

In the Angelverse, Angel will also fight against demons and other vampires. Nevertheless, the demons we encounter in the Angelverse are not necessarily evil like those in the Buffyverse. Sometimes they are the victims of other demons, as in the episode "Hero" (1.8) when a group of demons called the Scourge declare that only pureblood demons can be allowed to live.[10] Angel then becomes a champion of those who are oppressed, whether they are oppressed by humans or demons, and he does not care whether his clients are human or demon. Like Buffy, Angel is joined in his fight by a group of people with attributes that contribute to the mission, such as Wesley's knowledge of the occult, Gunn's street-smarts, and Cordy's visions. Unfortunately for Angel, there are any number of Higher Beings and demons who desire power and they manipulate Angel and his colleagues via the use of magick.

The Troubled History of Witches and Magick

Barstow uses the term witchcraze or mass panic to characterize outbreaks that resulted in the mass killing of people (i.e., of six to eight at a time) during the 16th and 17th centuries in Europe. The true numbers of those killed are difficult to determine, but one of the best estimates is that over 100,000 people were killed between 1450 and 1750, the height of the craze (Cawthorne). Barstow's analysis of the records of those who were accused and those who were executed shows that the vast majority of the accused were women, the numbers ranged from 40 percent in Russia to 95 percent in Basel (179–181). When numbers are available, they indicate that women were more likely to be executed than were men.[11]

A long tradition held that women were more likely to be witches than were men. Women were believed to be closer to nature than men, given their roles as child bearers and mothers. Women were also believed to have knowledge of herbs and potions which allowed them to care for their families in a time when one was more likely to die from a doctor's treatment than from the illness the doctor was treating. That some women would be more knowledgeable than other women was accepted and these women were considered to be healers in their communities. However, during the time when life was hard and the future uncertain, superstitious people looked for reasons for their misery and frequently "found" it in the prosperity of their neighbors. In addition, women who were widowed or never married, or who had no other male protectors such as a brother or father, were frequently targeted by their neighbors. It should come as no surprise to learn that those convicted of witchcraft lost all of their worldly possessions. Indeed, people who were accused of witchcraft, tried and then executed were required to pay their torturer as well as their executioner along with others involved in the proceedings (Cawthorne). There is considerable evidence to support the contention that some of the victims of the craze were targeted for their money, land, or other possessions (Cawthorne).

If women were witches, then their master had to be male, and the belief was that this master was Satan, whom the witches were thought to worship. As a matter of fact, several hundred years ago witches were believed to be in league with the Devil in an attempt to destroy all of Christendom (Martin). Thus, the witchcraze of the 16th and 17th centuries was an attempt by the Church to destroy the Devil's minions on Earth and keep him from gaining control of humankind. One could also argue that the persecutions were rooted in attempts by early Christian church fathers to strengthen the financial and political power of the church, noting that these persecutions began at a time when the Catholic Church was seen as increasingly corrupt, and Reformation "fever" was in the air (Cawthorne). The persecutions also allowed for ecclesiastical control of the spiritual life of the general population.

Torture was used to extract confessions under the belief that Satan would not be able to retain his hold over the individual believed to be possessed by this demon. In addition, those who conducted the hearings believed that the torture and execution would free the possessed soul so that it would not suffer in the flames of Hell for all eternity. Nevertheless, the torture that was used would put some contemporary Hollywood horror-meisters to shame and descriptions of it should not be read by the faint of heart.[12] Some executioners took pity on their victims and killed them prior to lighting the fire; other victims were not so lucky.

Although the largest numbers of those killed were in Europe, particularly in the Holy Roman Empire, the craze did reach the Colonies, with the hysteria reaching its climax in Salem, Massachusetts (Boyer and Nissenbaum). Religious leaders in New England during the time of the Puritans believed that women were more likely than men to be witches because women were weaker than men, not because they were more evil. Being weaker meant that they were more susceptible to sinful impulses, and "all women inherited the insidious blend of weakness and power from their mother Eve" (Godbeer 131). Women in Puritan society were considered "helpmeets" to their husbands. Women who did not have husbands or did not fulfill their proscribed role in Puritan society were violating the gendered hierarchy.

The fact that *Buffy*'s Willow and Tara are lesbians violates gendered notions of women and conceptions of female sexuality in contemporary American society. Consider that the men in Tara's family kept their women "in line" by claiming they were demons ("Family" 5.6); this strategy served to keep Maclay women from realizing the power they possessed as witches. Nevertheless, Tara learned about magick and witchcraft from her mother, and probably other female members of the family, in a time-honored tradition, as magick is traditionally transferred orally, with knowledge learned apprentice-style.

According to Jong, "During the long centuries when women were the semislaves of society, they were naturally drawn to witchcraft as cure for their powerlessness, a means of manipulating a world that otherwise painfully manipulated *them*" (69). Furthermore, says Jong (169),

> Witchcraft, then, served many purposes. It was a way of projecting the evils of society outward and seeming to expunge them, a way of intimidating women, a way of keeping health care in the hands of upper-class males, and a way of preserving ecclesiastical power in times of social unrest. Whether *originally* it had represented an ancient fertility cult or not, it came in time to have so many other *secondary* uses that society could hardly get by without it.

Barstow contends that the witchcraze was another manifestation of the violence against women that has persisted since the beginning of history. But, surely if women had the power foretold by witchcraft, they would not be at the mercy of men's violent impulses (see Chapter 3). They would be able to use the power afforded by their magick to control these impulses, taming the "demons" that direct the forces of violence.

Magick and Witchcraft in the Buffyverse

Generally magick and witchcraft are used synonymously on *Buffy*, as is Wicca and witchcraft although, as indicated above, the three are not equivalent. Nevertheless, in a series predicated upon the existence of vampires and demons, and one that breaks with traditional views of these denizens of the dark, it would be expected that the series would also make its own rules with respect to the use of magick and witchcraft. A number of characters used these tools throughout the series, and I will present these before discussing *Buffy*'s major practitioner of magic and witchcraft, Willow Rosenberg.

We first encounter the use of witchcraft in Season One's episode "The Witch" (1.3). Amy Madison's mother has cast a spell upon her daughter and changed places with her. It turns out that Catherine Madison wants to relive her glory days as a cheerleader at Sunnydale High School. As various students try out for the squad, those who are likely to be chosen suffer a number of serious accidents until Giles and Buffy find Catherine's spell book. They reverse the spell and inadvertently trap Catherine in the cheerleading trophy she won for Sunnydale High. Amy has inherited her mother's power and will continue to use magick throughout the series, gradually using her powers more and more malevolently as time passes. In Season Two's "Bewitched, Bothered and Bewildered" (2.16), Xander blackmails Amy into casting a love spell on Cordelia who, despite her attraction to him, will not admit it. Unfortunately, the spell backfires and every woman in Sunnydale *except Cordelia* becomes enamored of Xander. Amy turns Buffy into a rat, perhaps a foreshadowing of future events, to keep her from Xander, knowing that Xander has a major crush on Buffy.

Amy and Willow, who have been friends for many years, eventually join a coven and continue to learn about and practice witchcraft. Things take a nasty turn when two demons incite the townspeople of Sunnydale, including Buffy and Willow's mothers, to begin a campaign to rid the town of all supernatural influences. Under the demons' spell the mothers, along with the townspeople, plan to emulate the time-honored tradition of burning witches, with Buffy, Willow, and Amy as their targets. Amy turns herself into a rat to escape, but is then unable to reverse the spell. Amy remains in her rat form until Season Six when Willow finally realizes that she is powerful enough to reverse the spell. Amy understandably wants to make up for lost time and entices Willow to enter into some of her escapades. One of these is to introduce Willow to a warlock named Rack ("Wrecked" 6.10), who peddles dark magick. Willow quickly becomes addicted to the dark magick and almost kills Dawn after getting high on Rack's energy (see below).

Amy becomes increasingly dark during the remainder of Seasons Six and Seven, apparently seeking revenge on Willow for not de-rating her earlier. One could imagine that Amy would be rather angry at the cavalier way in which Willow reverses the spell; after all, Willow is powerful enough to bring Buffy back from the dead but she is not powerful enough to bring Amy back from "rathood?" We learned in "The Witch" that Amy's mother is willing to do anything to her daughter in order to relive her youth; her behavior toward her daughter is abusive. Like Willow and Xander, Amy had an unpleasant childhood. Unfortunately, the abuse she suffered at the hands of her mother is reflected in her own behavior as she ages, repeating the cycle of violence observed in many abusive families (see Chapter 3). Amy's evil and abusive actions apparently continue into the Season Eight comics (Whedon et al.). Other instances of magick and witchcraft occurring during the series include actions by Cordelia and Anya, Giles' former friend and fellow warlock Ethan Rayne, and the Troika.

After Cordelia and Oz discover Willow and Xander kissing in "Lover's Walk," an episode that also involves a magick spell (3.7), Cordelia wishes that Buffy had never come to Sunnydale ("The Wish" 3.8). Cordelia is horrified to learn that her wish has come true, via the powers of Anyanka, a vengeance demon. In this terrifying version of Sunnydale, the Master rose, Xander and Willow were vamped, and Cordelia will be killed. Luckily she is able to tell Giles what has happened before she dies and Giles destroys Anyanka's necklace, the source of her power. Unfortunately for Anyanka, she loses her job as vengeance demon and is rendered mortal, as a teenager named Anya.

Giles' former friend and colleague (and perhaps more) Ethan Rayne is one of the men on *Buffy* who practice magick. Rayne's magick is generally of the dark variety and most of his spells seem to directly or indirectly affect Giles, which just might give us a clue as to the depth of their previous relationship (perhaps a scorned lover?[13]). In any case, Rayne certainly appears to want revenge against Giles when he transforms him into a demon ("A New Man" 4.12). Giles is unable to communicate with anyone except Spike, who demands money in exchange for his help. Buffy, believing that the demon has killed Giles, almost kills the demon before realizing what has happened. Rayne is imprisoned by the Initiative and Buffy promises to be more forthright with Giles in the future.

Other men who practice magick on *Buffy* are the Troika, or Trio, a group of misfit nerds with delusions of grandeur. The three are Andrew, Jonathan Levinson, and Warren Mears. They have graduated from being ignored or bullied at school to being angry and ready for revenge against the world. Warren is particularly violent, especially against women (see Chapter

3). Jonathan and Andrew simply want some respect and are easily bullied by Warren. These three are extremely bright, possessing some very good technological skills. After all, it was Warren who built both the robot April and the Buffybot ("I Was Made to Love You" 5.15; "Intervention" 5.18). The three also create various rays that have effects designed to increase their power over Buffy or other women. For instance, they create an invisibility ray ("Gone" 6.11) that accidently makes Buffy disappear from sight. Later they create a compulsion ray ("Dead Things" 6.13) which is designed to make women (want to) have sex with them. Their intelligence is not to be underestimated; they are very bright and it seems incredible that they have not been recruited by the Initiative or another government agency. Nonetheless, they can also be very stupid, setting their sights only on battling the Slayer and "ruling" Sunnydale. As stated, the Troika also use magick in this quest for power, at various times resorting to spells or other incantations to access dark magick. They use these spells for a variety of reasons: to rob banks ("Flooded" 6.4); to masquerade as demons and discover Buffy's weaknesses ("Life Serial" 6.5); to steal demonic power ("Seeing Red" 6.19); and, in order to misdirect attempts to foil their capers or keep from being caught by either Buffy or the law. It is Warren's increasing anger at Buffy for thwarting their attempts to become "crime lords" (Kaveney 296) that results in the horrendous events culminating in Tara's death ("Seeing Red" 6.19). Willow's grief at Tara's death almost destroys the world (see below); her revenge against Warren is horrific, although not fatal, as we learn in the Season Eight comics (Whedon et al.).[14]

Objects in the Buffyverse also assume magical power and influence events, objects such as amulets and masks. The latter, an African mask that Joyce brings home from her gallery, figures prominently in "Dead Man's Party" (3.2), when the Scoobies are forced to forgive Buffy for her desertion after killing Angel ("Becoming" (Part 2 of 2) 2.22). The quiet dinner party Joyce plans to welcome Buffy home turns into the social event of the year, as word of the party spreads throughout the high school. The mask has the power to reanimate the dead and as the dead around Sunnydale rise and converge on Buffy's house, the Scoobies band together to stop the zombies from killing everyone.

An amulet figures prominently in the episode "Once More, with Feeling" (6.7). Buffy is depressed after her return from the dead. She felt that she was at peace, she tells Spike, and believes that she was in Heaven. Dawn has stolen an amulet and wears it on a chain, not knowing that the charm will call the demon "Sweet." This demon challenges the Scoobies to reveal the secrets they have been keeping from each other, in song. Sweet comes to Sunnydale to claim Dawn as his prize, and all is revealed. It turns out that Xander first took the charm so that he could see if all would end well, but then Dawn stole the charm. Sweet does not wish to claim Xander and leaves the Scoobies to face the truths that they have been hiding from one another.

Communication is a major problem on *Buffy*, with various characters not speaking of what they really feel for one another, or what they mean by their actions. For instance, Buffy is unable to tell Riley how she feels (or does not feel) about him, and so he leaves her. Dawn does not believe that Buffy loves her, because she is not "real," and she thinks that the others probably feel the same way, hence her constant need for attention and approval (Rambo). Oz is unable to tell Willow about the terror he feels about not being able to control his animal self; rather than ask for her help, he leaves. Xander uses a magick spell on Cordelia, trying to force her to admit that she likes him. Later, Xander is unable to share his fear of the future with Anya and, thus, jilts her on their wedding day. The list could go on and on. Even after Sweet forces the issue with his spell, the Scoobies go their separate ways and are still unable to share their innermost feelings with each other. Willow is horrified to think that she tore Buffy out of Heaven, but instead of talking to Buffy, she casts a spell, hoping to erase Buffy's memories of Heaven (and Tara's memories of their arguments over magick) ("Tabula Rasa" 6.8). This spell goes horribly wrong, as Tara realizes what Willow has done, and it is safe to say that this is the beginning of the end for the two lovers. Willow's actions are too much for Tara and she leaves. The quirky young woman we met in Season One is gone, having been replaced by one seduced by power and unable and unwilling to control it.

Willow Rosenberg began the series as a timid and shy young woman. As discussed in Chapter 1, Willow was often overlooked by her peers. Her most important asset (as far as her schoolmates were concerned) was her intelligence, and then only if she would use those assets to help them. We can almost see Willow being bullied into writing someone's paper for them or being forced to allow someone to cheat off of her test. Her best friend, prior to meeting Buffy, is Xander Harris, another powerless misfit at Sunnydale High School. It is only when she meets Buffy and becomes one of the Scoobies that Willow begins to develop a sense of purpose and a sense of power. As she learns more and more about the world of Slayers, vampires, demons, and witches, Willow begins to be attracted to that world. Jong (3) notes that

> adolescence is a time when witchcraft exercises a great fascination. Disempowered by society and overwhelmed with physical changes, teenage girls fall in love with

the idea of forming covens. Whatever bric-a-brac of magic[k] is around, they will pick up and shape to their own uses.[15]

This is quite true of Willow, who learns just enough in the beginning to be a little dangerous, but who becomes even more dangerous as time passes. Her initial interest in magick seems innocent; an attempt by an inquisitive young woman to increase her knowledge, especially when she knows that it can be helpful to Buffy (Riess). However, as her skill with the magick increases, her power likewise increases, and this, notes Jong (69), is nothing new:

> We intuitively understand that during the long centuries when women were the semislaves of society, they were naturally drawn to witchcraft as a cure for their powerlessness, a means of manipulating a world that otherwise painfully manipulated *them*.

Willow has been overlooked throughout her life, not only by her peers but by her parents as well (see Chapter 1), thus the power afforded to her by magick becomes increasingly seductive, just as the power Buffy wields as the Slayer is also seductive.

It must be noted that Willow's use of magick does not always have negative consequences; sometimes positive effects result from her actions. One early example was Willow's use of the curse originally employed by the gypsies to give Angelus a soul. After Jenny Calendar's death at the hands of Angelus ("Passion" 2.17), Willow takes over her job as computer teacher at the high school.[16] Finding a disk that contains fragments of the curse, Willow attempts to recreate it. She is successful and manages to restore Angel's soul; unfortunately, it happens when Buffy stakes him and he is sucked into Hell ("Becoming" [Part 2 of 2] 2.22). Another example occurs in Season Four when Willow casts a spell that allows the Scoobies to merge their "power" into a super–Buffy, which gives her enough strength to vanquish the human-demon-cybernetic hybrid Adam ("Primeval" 4.21). In Season Five, Willow uses various spells in various episodes to keep Glory from finding Dawn and manages to recapture Tara's sanity from Glory ("The Gift" 5.22). Finally, we cannot forget that Willow was powerful enough to bring Buffy back from the dead ("Bargaining" [Part 1 of 2] 6.1).

Although Willow's journey on the slippery slope of magick addiction has already begun prior to events occurring at the beginning of Season Six, it is the ritual that Willow performs in order to recall Buffy that accelerates her descent. Willow violates the first rule of Wicca, "Harm None," when she kills the fawn for its blood for the spell:

Witches have a very strict belief in the Law of Three which states that whatever [is sent] out into [the] world shall return ... three fold either good or bane. With this in mind, a "True Witch" would hesitate in doing magick to harm or manipulate another because that boomerang ... will eventually come back ... much larger and harder then [sic] when [thrown].[4]

Such prophetic words will be evident throughout Season Six as Willow's use of magick escalates and finally culminates in the murder of Warren Mears. There is no greater sin in the Buffyverse than the murder of a human being, and Willow commits that act (although as noted, Warren apparently still lives in Season Eight, albeit without his skin). After Xander manages to pull Willow back into this world and away from her alter-ego as Dark Willow ("Grave" 6.22), she becomes frightened of her power. Willow gradually begins to regain her confidence, but is almost undermined by Amy's attempts at revenge ("The Killer Inside Me" 7.13). Willow manages to fight against Amy's machinations with the help of the Potential Kennedy, who provides her with much-needed succor and a kiss, which breaks Amy's spell. In the end it is Willow who casts the spell that empowers the Potentials and allows Buffy, the Potentials, and Spike to stop the First ("Chosen" 7.22).

As noted, Willow's use of magick begins in Season One and continues throughout the early years of Buffy, and she becomes even more adept in its usage after she starts college. She joins a Wicca group on campus but is disappointed when they do not appear to be interested in casting spells and engaging in other types of magick. The only good that really comes from the group is meeting Tara Maclay, with whom Willow falls in love (see Chapter 2). We observe Willow's use of magick becoming increasingly problematic as her relationship with Tara continues (see Chapter 3). Tara loves Willow and worries about Willow's use of magick. Willow uses magick for silly reasons that have no purpose other than the ability to actually do it, like conjuring party decorations rather than buying and preparing them by hand. Willow and Tara begin to fight over the fact that Tara believes Willow is using magick too often, and that she does not know when to quit. Willow pouts, then replies that she knows what she is doing, that she can control herself, and that she can stop using the magick any time she wants to. Each of these phrases is indicative of addiction, and Willow displays many of the signs of an addict.

A complete discussion of the issue of Willow's addiction to magick is beyond the scope of this chapter. However, it is my opinion that Willow's use of magick was an addiction, just as harmful as any addiction. Indeed we could argue that Willow's addiction is more dangerous because of the potential for harm, considering what happened to Tara, but that would be like arguing over who is more evil, Spike or Angel (see Chapters 2 and 3). Willow's use of magick accelerated over the course of time: she began to hide what she was doing and she lied about what she was doing. In addition, she harmed people she professed to love. All of these can be taken as signs of addiction. For an addict there is nothing more important than the thrill of the next rush and the release that comes from alleviating the withdrawal symptoms which have accumulated since the last "fix." After Dark Willow's "birth" following Tara's death and its attendant results, we see a Willow afraid to use her magick until her Season Seven transformation into Willow the White, when she has learned to control her abilities.[17] Jacqueline Lichtenberg[18] argues that, for Willow, magick

> was so alluring ... [because] it was a renewed hope that here at last was the tool she could use to become self-confident, to find her self-esteem, to define her identity, to cause the world to accept her — or at least stop forcing her to appease [129].

In addition, magick allows Willow to find a place in which to belong (South). This is especially true when she enters college, thereby giving her access to the information she needs to help her in her quest to learn more about magick. It is also at college that she meets Tara.

As this short discussion shows, magick and witchcraft are used with varying degrees of success in the Buffyverse. However, the use of both exacts its toll on the practitioners of these supernatural tools. Those who have not been schooled in the ways of either can be left with an inability to control the forces unleashed by their actions. Buffy is a Slayer, but we must remember that Buffy was called because another Slayer, whom we have never met, died. As such, she must still be trained in the ways of actually being a Slayer: the super-strength, agility, ability to heal, et cetera, may be hers because she was born a Potential, but the timing makes all of the difference. Unlike Kendra, Buffy did not know that she would be called upon one day ("What's My Line" [Parts 1 and 2] 2.9 and 2.10) and, thus, she did not begin her training until adolescence.[19] Hence Buffy's need for the education that Giles has to offer.

However, Giles is so busy helping Buffy and taking Willow's science and computer skills for granted that he does not notice what is happening right under his nose. That is, he notices that Willow is learning about magick and practicing seemingly insignificant spells. Nevertheless, he does not seem to be aware of the depth of Willow's obsession nor the degree of her involvement with magick. It is only later, when Willow begins using magick in trivial ways, and especially when she uses it to manipulate her friends, that Giles begins to notice and chastise her for the usage. His lessons with Buffy notwithstanding, it is unclear why he has left Willow to probe the secrets of the magical world without providing a guiding hand, especially as Giles' knowledge is not just intellectual, but rather practical (Jowett). One could argue that she is doing it behind his back, and that is probably partly true; however, it seems as if he is perfectly willing to let Willow "play with" magick as long as it is helpful to Buffy and Buffy's mission. When Willow begins to seriously use and abuse magick, into Seasons Four through Six, Giles becomes increasingly irritated with her and she becomes increasingly irritated with him as well. Luckily for the planet he has the wisdom of his years, the help of a coven in England, his knowledge of the psychology of this gifted young woman, and her very best friend to keep her from destroying the world.

Magick and Witchcraft in the Angelverse

Magick and witchcraft also figure prominently in *Angel* by virtue of its relationship with the magical world of *Buffy*. As a vampire with a soul, Angel is a supernatural creature who walks a fine line between the forces of light and the forces of darkness. Although Stacey Abbott (*Reading* 3) states that Angel is a "curious hybrid" of Angel and Angelus, Angel can actually be conceived of as a multiple personality, with his psyche containing three parts: the pre-vampire human Liam, the vampire Angelus, and the vampire with a soul named Angel. Angel wages a constant battle against the man he was, a thorough reprobate, and the vicious vampire who slaughtered his way across several continents. Indeed, Whedon has stated that Angel is similar to a recovering alcoholic, who is one step from taking his next drink (Commentary *Angel* Season One DVD). Already a preternatural being, Angel is aware that there are others of his kind as well as demons of different types.[20] Unable and unwilling to remain in a platonic relationship with Buffy, Angel relocates to Los Angeles ("City Of" 1.1), where he once lived ("Are You Now or Have You Ever Been?" 2.2). It is in L.A. that he encounters the half-demon, half-human hybrid Doyle, who informs Angel that the Powers That Be have declared that Angel has a mission: to help those who are in need of help, including himself, in order to atone for his past sins.

Doyle will aid Angel in this quest for atonement until Doyle atones for his own sins in the episode "Hero" (1.9). Doyle's last act before dying is to kiss Cordelia and transfer the ability to receive visions to her. The visions are the Powers' way of communicating about those who need help and they are, thus, supernatural in origin. These visions, however, were never meant to be received by a non-demonoid creature and Cordelia becomes increasingly ill over the course of time, almost dying (see Chapter 5). However, Cordelia has changed a great deal since her early days as a member of the Scooby gang. She realizes that she actually wants to help the less fortunate and is thus unwilling to surrender the visions to the person intended to next receive them, the Groosalugg ("Through the Looking Glass" 2.21). Instead, Cordy will agree to become part-demon in order to keep the visions ("Birthday" 3.11). She believes the sacrifice to be worth the price, although her happiness will be short-lived. The fact that she is now part-demon may help in her growing attraction to, and love for, Angel. But as with all of the relationships on the various Whedon series, true love does not run smoothly or well (see Chapter 2). Indeed, Cordelia is frequently tormented and tortured during four seasons of *Angel* (see especially Chapter 3). Even becoming a Higher-Being and ascending to a Heavenly dimension ("Tomorrow" 3.22) does not keep Cordelia from being used as a pawn in a game by a deity known as Jasmine, who is intent upon obtaining a corporeal body in our dimension and then ruling it (e.g., "Shiny Happy" 4.16; "Peace Out" 4.21).

Angel made much more use of the concept of alternative dimensions than did *Buffy*. One such dimension is Pylea, which figures prominently in a story arc during Season Two. Pylea is the home dimension of the demon Lorne, who escaped by accident, but never wants to return because they do not have music. Cordelia is accidently transported to Pylea and enslaved, until it is discovered that she has visions. She is then proclaimed Princess. The Priests plan to steal the visions from her, by mating her with the Groosalugg, a very handsome (but slightly dumb) warrior. While in Pylea, the gang discovers a woman named Fred who has been living a very hard existence as an escaped slave. It turns out that Fred is a highly gifted physicist who was transported to Pylea by a professor jealous of her work ("Belonging" 2.19; "Supersymmetry" 4.5). The gang rescues Fred and she becomes a valued member of the team, but this is complicated by the fact that both Gunn and Wesley fall for her.

Another dimension that figures prominently in *Angel* is the Hell dimension Quor-toth. After Wesley kidnaps Angel's son, Connor, the boy is almost killed by a demon named Sahjahn, who has vowed vengeance on Angel (we do not learn why as Angel cannot remember Sahjahn; "Sleep Tight" 3.16). Rather than have the boy die, Holtz grabs Connor and jumps into Quor-toth. Time does not work the same in these dimensions as it does in our own. Several weeks later, Connor, now a teenage boy, returns ("The Price" 3.19). During his years in Quor-toth Holtz has taught the boy to hate Angel and to vow revenge. Holtz is the only father that Connor has ever known, but Holtz understands that Angel loves his son. Holtz only wants revenge for the death of his family at the hands of Angelus, and he does not care if Connor kills Angel or if Angel kills Connor, although he will be most happy if the latter happens. Unfortunately for Holtz, Angel is able to make a deal with Wolfram and Hart that removes Connor from "play." Connor's memories are erased and he is able to live the remainder of his life as a normal human being ("Home" 4.22).

Other examples of the supernatural on *Angel* are directly related to magick and witchcraft, but I will only mention a select few given the sheer number of such examples. A number of magical events occur in the episode "To Shanshu in LA" (1.22). A scroll stolen in the previous episode ("Blind Date" 1.21) contains a prophecy stating that Angel will die. Wesley determines that the scroll actually foretells that the demon Angelus will "die," and, thus, Angel will become human again. Also in this episode, Holland Manners of Wolfram and Hart sends for the demon priest Vocah, who kills the Oracles and summons Darla back from Hell. Learning that he may be able to become human again has profound effects on Angel, almost making him forget his true mission from the Powers. He remembers the hard way, when he accidently kills the demonic protector of a young, pregnant woman ("Judgement" 2.1). Angel seeks Lorne's help by singing "Mandy," which allows Lorne to "read" Angel and then help him find the woman. Angel serves as her champion before a mysterious Tribunal, convened on the streets of LA and apparently invisible to "normal" Angelenos. Angel manages to kill his opponent, thus granting the woman safety for the daughter she carries. Meanwhile, Darla is slowly recovering from her return from Hell and begins to link psychically with Angel. The events that occur during Season Two with Darla will cause a rift between the members of Angel Investigations, eventually culminating in a complete break between Wesley and the others. As on *Buffy*, the failure to communicate will drive a wedge between Wesley and Gunn over their feelings for Fred, between Angel and Cordelia over their feelings for each other, between Wesley and Angel over the prophecy that Angel will kill Connor, between Connor and Angel over what really happened with Holtz in the past and in the present, between Fred and Gunn over his murder of Professor Seidel, et cetera.

The fact that Angel and Cordelia will not talk about their growing feelings for each other, as well as the fact that true love never runs smoothly in the Angelverse, partially explains events that occur in Season Three with respect to the Groosalugg. Groo, as Cordy affectionately calls him, fell so hard for his Princess in Pylea that he travels through a portal to find her again ("Waiting in the Wings" 3.13). Given that Groo is a very handsome young man, Cordy wants to have sex with him, but is afraid that doing so will deprive her of her visions. Remember that the visions help Angel Investigations in their mission to help the helpless, but the visions also confer power upon Cordelia, beyond the power she has as a beautiful, intelligent, and witty young woman.[21] Cordy charges Angel with finding a potion that will allow her to have sex with Groo but retain the visions ("Couplet" 3.14). He does so reluctantly, but then sends the two off on holiday, probably so he will not be reminded constantly of the fact that they are having sex (and he is not). Also in this episode, Fred and Gunn investigate the strange behavior of an engaged man; his fiancée believes that he is being seduced by a witch. The two find that he has been lured out by a tree-flesh demon that attracts its victims via the internet and then sucks the life out of them.[22] Angel and Groo rush to help Fred and Gunn, who have been attacked by the demon. Groo is also captured by the tree, but Angel is able to save them all when he goads the tree into trying to suck the life out of him. It is at the end of this episode where Wesley deciphers the prophecy stating that "the father will kill the son."[23] Another incident involving memory (see Chapter 6) occurs in the Season Four episode "Spin the Bottle" (4.6). After returning from her state as a Higher Being, Cordy experiences memory loss. Lorne attempts to recover her memories but the spell backfires, leading everyone to believe they are 17 years old again, despite the physical evidence to the contrary. Everyone panics believing they are trapped inside the Hyperion with a vampire and a demon. Connor arrives to once more do battle with Angel and to rescue Cordy as well since she is his first love. Lorne eventually completes the spell and Cordy's memories are returned, including the one in which she and Angel were in love. However, from this point onward in Season Four Cordelia is doomed by the machinations of the deity who will be known as Jasmine.

Earlier in this book (see Chapter 1) I pointed out how the characters in the various Whedonverses are powerless, and it is easy to see just how powerless the characters in *Angel* are when the magick controlling their lives is factored into the equation. Neither Doyle nor Cordelia asked to receive the visions bestowed upon them. For Cordelia those visions are dangerous (see Chapter 5). Not only that, but Cordelia becomes a pawn to be used by

Jasmine in her bid to restore goodness and order to our dimension. Such a ploy would rob the people who inhabit this planet of the freedom to make their own choices about how to act, in other words, it would render them powerless (Richardson and Rabb).

Fred was definitely powerless throughout most of the series. First, she was sent to Pylea by a professor jealous of her intellectual abilities. In Pylea she was enslaved. When rescued by Angel and company, she had to confront that same professor and was robbed of the power to harm him (or not) by Gunn. Finally, she was possessed by Illyria, completely losing herself, body and soul, to the demon. Gunn has been powerless in stopping the vampires that infested the streets of L.A. Over the years he lost numerous friends and, finally, a sister to the vampires. Joining Angel Investigations gave him colleagues in the fight and knowledge to use in that fight as well as a new love, named Fred. Unfortunately for Gunn, his choice to kill Professor Seidel, rather than letting Fred do the deed, had serious repercussions for their relationship and his conscience. Gunn was unable to stop what happened to Fred, yet another illustration of the powerlessness that affected the Angel gang.

Wesley was also unable to help Fred; he developed a relationship, of sorts, with Illyria but he gradually sank deeper and deeper into the bottle as his depression over events deepened. Finally, there is Angel. He managed to stave off the cravings for blood that consumed (almost) his every waking moment. His actions over the years helped many humans and demons, but he was unable to help his nearest and dearest: Connor, Cordy, Fred, Gunn, and Wesley. He has his soul, but at what cost? Using magick, making deals with demons, traveling to Hell dimensions and beyond, nothing has worked. The machinations of other beings, generally supernatural, have controlled Angel's actions throughout the course of the series. Such was not the case on *Firefly* and *Serenity*.

One Incident on Firefly

Because *Firefly* takes place in a 'verse that mirrors our own, supernatural entities did not exist. Any monsters or demons found in the 'verse were completely human, and Whedon's purpose in creating *Firefly* was to demonstrate how people form communities and families in an attempt to be a part of something with meaning. Each episode of the short-lived series can then be "read" as a microcosm of society and how each of the worlds that the Serenity visits attempts to create such a place.

In the episode "Safe" (1.5) the crew visits the colony of Jiangyin in order to off-load the cattle they are transporting for Sir Warwick Harrow ("Shindig" 1.4). After arriving at Jiangyin and attempting to negotiate for the sale of the cattle, local law-enforcement personnel arrive and Shepherd Book is seriously wounded. It is only at this point that Mal realizes that Simon is missing. Simon has been kidnapped by a group of people who live outside of the established colony of Jiangyin. They are in need of a doctor and kidnap Simon after they overhear Mal call Simon "Doc." Simon tries to help as many people as possible during the short time he is there. Unfortunately for her, River is taken captive as well. River is given into the care of a woman named Doralee, whom we learn was also kidnapped by the hillpeople when they needed a teacher. Apparently Doralee has accepted her fate and now considers herself to be one of this group. Whilst in the care of Doralee, River is able to communicate telepathically with a young girl named Ruby. She has been mute ever since her mother killed her sister and tried to kill her (perhaps Ruby's mother was also kidnapped and could not accept that fate, unlike Doralee). Doralee immediately denounces River as a witch and calls the other people in the community as witnesses. When questioned by the Patron, the leader of the hill-people, River reads his mind and discovers that he gained his title by killing his predecessor. The Patron declares that River is a witch and must suffer the fate of all witches, death by burning. Luckily for River and Simon, Mal, Jayne and Zoe arrive in time to rescue them both.

River has been the subject of much experimentation by Alliance scientists. This meddling enhanced River's natural psychic tendencies as well as her physical ones (see Chapters 5 and 7). Although this meddling makes her a very powerful weapon, it does so using science and not magick or other supernatural means. Nevertheless, River is almost immolated because superstitions about witches manage to survive into the 26th century.[24]

Conclusions

People in both the Buffyverse and the Angelverse used a variety of supernatural means to exert power and gain control over others, friend as well as foe. This was especially true on *Buffy* when characters as diverse as Amy, Anya, Dawn, Jonathan, Xander, and Willow cast spells to help or harm others. Even Buffy uses magick to determine if it is a spell that is causing her mother's illness ("No Place Like Home" 5.5). In Buffy's world the supernatural is real, and thus magick is as well. Just like we "fight fire with fire," Buffy uses all of the tools at her disposal to fight the forces of darkness. Sometimes she uses magical tools, such as spells, potions, amulets and other objects, along with vampires and demons, which fight on her side. Sometimes she uses normal tools, such as guns and rocket launchers. For Buffy it's the goal that is important, and almost any method will be used as long as it does not harm humans. Magick controls Buffy's life in the sense that she is the Slayer and her actions must be predicated upon how they influence her mission. As the Slayer she has some modicum of control over demons, vampires and other things that go bump-in-the-night. At various times other people and things have attempted to control Buffy's actions and fate via the use of magick, and they generally do not succeed. Buffy has her own arsenal of magick tricks along with some pretty formidable friends to help her in her mission. And, in the end, it is magick that allows her to share her power, defeat the First, and hope for some semblance of a normal life in the future (but see Note 14 again).

The picture is much darker in the Angelverse. Angel, by virtue of his age and vampire status, has a great deal of knowledge about the world of darkness, although his quest for redemption forces him to use that knowledge and not always for good purposes. Temptations are constantly around him — the power the magick affords as well as the relief he would feel if he would but succumb to the temptation to take a drink (of blood). In the early days of his most recent sojourn in L.A., he is joined by people whom he counts as good friends, perhaps family, even if they do betray him at one point or another (Lorrah[25]). In many respects, however, Angel and his allies are the pawns of various demons who use them for their own nefarious purposes,[26] usually having to do with grabbing some power and then keeping it all for themselves.

Magick was a tool used by Buffy, Angel, and their compatriots in the fight against the forces of darkness. Sometimes this tool was useful and its usage brought about beneficial results, such as saving the world. Sometimes this tool was dangerous and its usage brought about horrific results, such as losing the girl. But magick is not a weapon that can be used to exert control over people in the "real" world, given that the magick itself is not real. Thus, more mundane methods must be used, and these will be explored in the next three chapters.

Chapter 5

Manipulating the Brain as a Method of Control[1]

Also, I can kill you with my brain.— River Tam, "Trash" (*Firefly* 1.11)

Joss Whedon is fascinated by the brain. In the DVD commentary to Season One's *Dollhouse* episode "Man on the Street," he notes that people want to be the best that they can be. According to Whedon, people want perfection and they are willing to do whatever it takes to achieve that perfection, without thinking of what they might be doing to other people or even to themselves in that pursuit. In *Dollhouse*, he says, you can cut out the part of yourself that "causes pain, have Topher slice it out, and Poof! It's gone." Whedon also explored the idea of perfection in his short-lived, much-missed, series *Firefly*, and its sequel film, *Serenity*. Both of these endeavors reflect the theme of what could be done to make a perfect person, a perfect world, a perfect weapon. In this chapter I explore the ways in which Whedon envisioned the disastrous effects of neurological manipulations in the quest to achieve that ideal existence. I discuss *Firefly*'s River Tam, saving a discussion of *Dollhouse*'s memory manipulations for Chapter 6, and various pharmacological manipulations for Chapter 7. In addition to the discussion of River Tam, I also focus on three primary examples of neuroscience and neurology as they apply to *Buffy*: the creation of Adam, Joyce's tumor, and Spike's chip. Finally, I will discuss the effects of Cordelia's visions on her brain.

A Short Lesson on the Nervous System

The basic building block of the nervous system is the neuron. Neurons are composed of three parts. The cell body or soma controls the vital functions of the cell (i.e., nutrition, metabolic activities, elimination of waste products, manufacture of proteins and other necessary chemicals). The dendrite is considered the receiving end of the neuron, accepting information from adjacent neurons. Dendrites may also serve as receptors. Dendrites consist of fine, treelike branches (the better to receive information) with knobby protrusions called dendritic spines. If you think of what a tree looks like in spring, with no leaves but lots of buds, then you have a good image of the dendritic arborization of a neuron. The third basic part of the neuron is the axon, the transmitting end of the neuron. It sends information from a receptor into the Central Nervous System (CNS), from the CNS to a muscle or gland, or it transmits information in a neural link. Axons can be quite long or quite short. Information flows in a neuron in the following direction (always): dendrite to axon. In the nervous system itself, information flows in the following direction: sensory or afferent into the CNS, where a decision about the information is made; and, motor or efferent from the CNS to the effector where a response is made. Thus, as I drive home from work the receptors in my eyes capture sensory information and relay it into the CNS. My brain analyzes the input in order to determine what I am seeing: the other cars on the road, exit signs, et cetera. I am able to drive safely because my brain is constantly processing information about where I am and what is happening around me. My brain relays information to my muscles and glands, allowing me to react to the input it is receiving, such as brake lights (slow down to assess the threat), indicator lights (someone's car is moving — into my lane?), exit signs (is this my exit?). And, much of this occurs without my being conscious of the activity.

The nervous system can be divided into two major parts: the Peripheral Nervous System (PNS) and the Central Nervous System. The PNS can also be divided into two parts: the somatic nervous system which controls striate muscles, those involved in voluntary movement; and, the autonomic nervous system which controls smooth muscles and glands. The autonomic nervous system can be subdivided into the parasympathetic nervous system, which controls the so-called "vegetative" functions such as resting heart rate and blood pressure, and the sympathetic nervous system, which prepares the body for "fight or flight" in response to a stressor. The CNS consists of the brain and the spinal cord.

The spinal cord serves the body below the shoulders and provides sensory and motor functions via peripheral nerves. It is surrounded by a column of bones called the spine. The spinal cord constitutes only 2 percent of the total volume of the CNS, but it serves four very important functions. First, it is the conduit through which sensory information from the body reaches the brain. Second, the pathways for voluntary control of skeletal muscles are located in the spinal cord. Third, neural systems of the spinal cord provide the physiological basis for integrated and coordinated movement of limbs through spinal reflexes. Finally, neural systems that regulate much of the functioning of the internal organs are located here. The spinal cord is, thus, our link between the environment and the brain. The spinal cord enters the skull through an opening called the foramen magnum to form the brain stem.

The brain is also composed of neurons and fiber tracts. Some of these are covered with a fatty substance called myelin. Unmyelinated neurons in the brain are located on the outside, hence the name "gray matter" for the cerebral cortex. Separating the brain from the skull is cerebrospinal fluid. Depending upon who you read, the brain can be divided in several ways. One way is to separate the brain into three major parts: the cerebrum (the largest part of the brain occupying the upper cranium), the cerebellum, and the brain stem, both of which lie inferior to the cerebrum. Other authors separate the brain into two parts, brainstem and cerebrum.

The brain stem is a direct continuation of the spinal cord and, as such, shares many features in common with it. It serves three major functions: (1) it connects the cerebrum, the spinal cord, and the cerebellum; (2) it provides the face and neck with sensory and motor functions via the cranial nerves; and, (3) it is a center for integration both for the cranial nerves and several visceral functions (such as control of respiration). The brainstem can be subdivided into different parts, so separated because of function.

The medulla is direct continuation of the spinal cord. All nerves coming from the body into the brain travel through the medulla; the majority of nerves entering the brain cross over to the opposite side of the brain at the level of the medulla. This structure controls respiration via CO_2 receptors and the cardiovascular system via several groups of cells that control heart rate and peripheral blood flow. The medulla also contains the centers for swallowing, nausea, and vomiting.

Sensory nerves continue their journey from the periphery through the pons, a relay center for visual and auditory information. The bulge of the pons is due to the fibers descending from the cerebrum which synapse there and then course to the cerebellum, the only link between the cerebellum and the rest of the brain. Neurons here appear to regulate rapid eye movement (REM, or dream) sleep. In addition, the pons contains numerous groups of cells that regulate the functioning of the nervous system as a whole.

83

Located superior to, or above, the pons is the midbrain, with structures that coordinate eye movements, regulate the size of the pupil in response to light, mediate pain, and aid in the coordination of visual and auditory reflexes.

The cerebellum, or "little brain," controls posture and balance as you move about in space. It also maintains muscle tone and coordinates the movement of the head and body with sights and sounds in the environment. It is concerned with the accuracy (the force and range) of movement (that is, the correct amount of force, when to start and stop, et cetera.). It apparently is also involved with certain language and learned motor skills.

The most rostral, or forward, portion of the brainstem is called the diencephalon, which is composed of two structures. The most superior is called the thalamus. It serves as a relay station for all sensory fibers (except those from the nose) entering the cerebrum. The thalamus communicates with cortical areas in a reciprocal fashion. It also receives input from various motor systems, such as those located in the midbrain as well as those in the cerebellum.

Lying inferior to the thalamus is the hypothalamus, a group of nuclei lying at the base of the brain just above the pituitary gland and the optic chiasm. It contains the primary centers for control of body temperature, appetite, and water excretion. It is also believed to mediate primitive emotions. The hypothalamus provides the link between the nervous system and the endocrine system.[2]

The forebrain is the largest part of the human brain and contains several groups of structures related by function. One of these groups is called the basal ganglia. Research evidence indicates that the basal ganglia are important for simple, routine movements and providing movement appropriate to context. People with Parkinson's disease and Huntington's disease have damage in this part of the brain. The limbic system is a group of structures whose functions are believed to be involved in learning and memory as well as primitive emotional responses.

Most of the functions with which people are familiar are controlled by the cerebrum, where the final integrative or conscious actions occur. We can consider the cerebrum to be the thinking center of the brain. It is also the largest part of the brain: 80 percent of the brain's total mass is cortex. The cerebrum is covered by a very thin layer of cells called the cerebral cortex (cortex means bark) approximately one-eighth-inch thick, about the size of the tip of pen. These cells are arranged in layers (lamina) of which there are six, although not all areas have all six. Underlying the cortex is the cerebral white matter.

The cerebrum is composed of two hemispheres, connected to each other by a broad band of myelinated fibers called the corpus callosum. Each hemisphere is believed to serve different functions; however, that is not totally clear. We do know that in 95 percent of right-handed and 65 percent of left-handed people, the left hemisphere is dominant, referring to language capability. The remaining people are right dominant or non-dominant. The left hemisphere contains the structures which control the production and comprehension of language. The right hemisphere analyzes and processes information about visual and spatial tasks, as well as recognition of nonverbal sounds (such as music and environmental noise) and faces. Although each hemisphere is specialized for different functions, it is not appropriate to say that one hemisphere is artistic or spatial and the other is not. That is much too simplistic. Each hemisphere is dependent upon the other to carry out the tasks of everyday life. You cannot do without one or the other (and it is absolutely not true that we only use 10 percent of our brains!).

The cortex is quite distinctive in appearance because of its convolutions. The bumps or ridges on the surface of the brain are referred to as gyri (singular, gyrus) whereas the valleys are referred to as sulci (singular, sulcus). Very deep sulci are also referred to as fissures. It has never been done, but if the cortex were "smoothed" it is believed that it could be anywhere from two to six square feet in area. The reason your brain is so wrinkled is to increase its surface area. Imagine that you wanted to increase the intellectual ability of an organism, making it capable of tasks like speaking and planning for future events. You could increase the size of the brain, but that would be problematic since the size of the head would also have to increase. Babies are already born with incredibly large heads for their small bodies, so imagine trying to increase it even more. It might become difficult for women to give birth to such babies. Nature's way of solving this problem appears to be to simply fold the brain tissue over onto itself; in effect taking a larger brain and making it look smaller. (You can demonstrate this to yourself easily enough by taking a piece of paper and crumpling it into a ball. It is still the same amount of paper.)

Each hemisphere can be divided into four lobes named for the skull bones that overlie the tissue in that area; they are not quite mirror images. The occipital lobe lies at the back of the brain. Why is it referred to as the visual area of the brain, when about 50 percent of the total area of the cortex analyzes visual information? Let me explain. When the optic nerves leave the eyes, they travel to the brain. These nerves enter the brain at the base of the skull at an area near the hypothalamus. The optic tracts then travel to specific nuclei in the thalamus where the fibers synapse. From this point, the fibers travel to the occipital lobe where they synapse again. This pathway is considered the direct connection between the eye and the brain; we refer to the area where these fibers synapse as V1, or primary visual cortex. Cells in this area "see" the world as a collection of lines of various orientations, lengths, and colors. The remainder of the occipital lobe is involved with organizing and interpreting visual sensations. Analysis of visual input related to language takes place only in the dominant hemisphere.

Using this fact and nomenclature then, we know that primary auditory cortex (A1), the direct connection from the ear to the brain, lies in the temporal lobe. A1 receives auditory input from each ear. It cannot actually be observed on the surface of the brain; rather, it lies within the inner slope of the lateral fissure. Conscious patients report hearing tones or noise when this area is electrically stimulated. Also located in the temporal lobe in the dominant hemisphere is Wernicke's Area, the part of the brain involved in speech comprehension (interpreting sound as words). There is some evidence that the same region in the nondominant hemisphere is involved in musical discrimination. There are several areas in the temporal lobe that are involved in visual processing (e.g., shape constancy). Evidence also exists for temporal lobe involvement in memory. Patients with temporal lobe damage frequently report various types of memory deficits (see Chapter 6).

Primary somatosensory cortex (S1) is located in the parietal lobe. The somatosenses, or skin senses, are touch (pressure), temperature on the skin, and nociception (pain). Each area of the S1 receives impulses from the sensory receptors in the skin. Without S1 we would be unable to locate a sensation. That is, we can "feel" pain, touch, and pressure, using brain stem structures; however, we cannot determine where the sensation is coming from if S1 is damaged. The remaining portions of the parietal lobe are involved in higher order sensory discrimination (e.g., recognizing a number drawn on the back of the hand or being aware of the contralateral body).

Primary motor cortex (M1), the direct connection *from* the brain to the muscles of the body, lies in the frontal lobe. The corticospinal tract arises in M1 and descends through the brainstem to the spinal cord to the muscles of the body. The left frontal lobe (but not the right) contains Broca's Area, which is the center for speech production in humans. Anterior to M1 is the premotor cortex (or supplemental motor area), which is concerned with more complex motor movements such as speaking and throwing a ball. The most anterior portion of the frontal lobe, as well as the inferior portions, are referred to as the prefrontal area and are involved in the control of emotional behavior. Speculation based on patients who have suffered damage to this area (accidentally or through prefrontal lobotomy), such as Phineas Gage, suggests that this area exerts inhibitory control over primitive and socially undesirable behavior (Mashour, Walker, and Martuza). Gage was a railroad worker in Vermont in the mid–1800s who had a tamping iron driven through his skull following an accidental explosion. Gage survived the accident, but his personality was never the same (Macmillan). With this summary understanding of the nervous system, let's now look at some of the ways that the brain is "portrayed" in the Whedonverses.

Neurology and Neurosurgery in the 'Verse

The physically and psychologically fragile River Tam has been subjected to various types of neurological tampering at the hands of government scientists, although the type of tampering is never made clear. Simon says that River is a paranoid schizophrenic ("Safe" 1.5), although she displays several characteristics of someone who is hebephrenic.[3] In addition, he states that Alliance scientists treated her mind like a "rutting playground" ("Safe"). Later, he will tell Jayne that those scientists "stripped" her amygdala ("Ariel" 1.9), probably meaning that Alliance scientists destroyed these structures. Simon continues to talk to Jayne, saying, "You know how you get scared. Or worried or nervous. And you don't want to be scared or worried or nervous, so you push it to the back of your mind. You try not to think about it. The amygdala is what lets you do that — it's like a filter in your brain that keeps your feelings in check. They took the filter out of River. She feels everything. She can't not." But Simon is wrong. This is not what the amygdala does.

It is true that the amygdalae[4] are involved in emotions by virtue of their location and involvement in the limbic system, a set of subcortical structures comprising an emotional circuit responsive to primitive emotions, such as fear (Kandel, Schwartz, and Jessell). The limbic system lies in a "ring" or border around the brainstem, inferior to the cerebral cortex. Amygdalae connect to the hypothalami, which monitor the internal environment of the body, and also to the peripheral nervous system, the endocrine system, and the autonomic nervous system to affect reactions to the presence of both physical and psychological stressors. Another component of the limbic system is the hippocampus, the gateway to memory. The amygdalae actually sit on the most anterior aspect of the hippocampi. The hippocampi serve as the bridge between short-term, working memory and long term memory, apparently transferring those short-term memories into the long-term stores. It is this part of the brain that is damaged in patients with anterograde amnesia, Alzheimer's disease, and other disorders of memory. It is probably the case that the amygdalae, by virtue of their connections with the hippocampi, contribute the emotional tone to the memories transferred to the long-term memory (LaBar; LeDoux). Patients with temporal lobe damage also frequently experience uncontrollable anger and even rages, presumably because their amygdalae are also damaged, or the connections between the amygdalae and cortical areas mediating rational thought are damaged (LeDoux).

As Daniels noted, River shows no signs of amygdalar damage (136). Damage to the amygdala results in a condition known as Klüver-Bucy Syndrome.[5] Typical symptoms of Klüver-Bucy are hyperorality, visual agnosia, memory and emotional impairments (including loss of fear of usually feared objects), and hypersexuality. We definitely know that River does not display these symptoms, with the exception of the memory and emotional problems, and it is my hypothesis that the primary reason is that the scientists *did not finish* with her; Simon rescued her before they could do what they meant to do.

Daniels suggests that River suffers from Post Traumatic Stress Disorder (PTSD). She has many of the classic symptoms, such as heightened arousal, hypervigilance, and disturbed sleep patterns (DSM-IV-TR). Research data suggest a link between the amygdalae and PTSD, with increased activity in the amygdalae being observed in people with PTSD (Shin, Rauch, and Pitman). Daniels notes that if the Alliance had stripped River's amygdalae, it would make it more difficult for her to develop PTSD symptoms as the "most integral brain region associated with the experience of fear (central to the development of PTSD) would be destroyed" (138). Further, he suggests that if the Alliance wanted to create symptoms similar to the behavior symptoms of PTSD the Alliance scientists would want to stimulate her amygdalae, not destroy them. But I do not think that was the point. The Alliance scientists *wanted* to destroy her amygdalae so she would not feel fear prior to a mission. The amygdalae are apparently important for reactions to other people's emotions, especially fear. Damage to the amygdalae causes "psychic blindness," or the inability to recognize fear in other people's facial expressions or voices. This ability would be very important to someone who has to kill people on a mission. In addition, amygdalar damage means that River would not feel any remorse afterwards, especially if the links between her amygdalae and her frontal lobes were damaged, and it appears that they were. As Connor states: "River is a frail young girl, but neural manipulation had made her into a homicidal monster" (187–188). In actuality, the Alliance was trying to create a super-soldier, a weaponized woman (Marano 46), in other words, an "Operative."

However, manipulating River's amygdalae would not make her psychic, and we know that she is. River displays precognition as well as telepathy, empathy, and she is most certainly telekinetic, as evidenced by her statement to Jayne that she can kill him with her brain[6] ("Trash" 1.11). Certain conversations in the episode "Objects in Space" (1.14) let us know that the crew increasingly understand and fear River's powers. Mal says that she is "a reader.... She understands, but she doesn't comprehend." The comment that River "knows things she shouldn't or couldn't" foreshadows the plot of *Serenity*.

Connor states that perhaps River's psychic ability is innate (188). The extended sequences of sessions that culminate in Session 416 (*Serenity* Collector's Edition) provide support for this hypothesis. As River talks about her life at school in Session One, the interviewer suggests that she is highly intuitive, that she knows things. River replies, "People tell you things all the time without talking ... the way they move, the way they aren't talking.... Simon says I was born with a third eye." I believe that River was chosen to enter the Institute because of this ability. Much as Psi Corps in the series *Babylon 5* (Keyes) constantly monitor the general population in an attempt to discover latent telepaths, the Alliance would also be monitoring schools and other institutions looking for "a few good kids" for their programs. A close examination of the River sequences and sessions, along with her own comment, leads me to believe that the true purpose of their experimentation on River was to activate and then exploit that third eye.

The third eye is another name for a small, pine-coned shaped endocrine gland called the pineal gland located at the center of the brain, just inferior to the thalami and posterior to the hypothalami. The fact that this gland is located deep within the brain and that it was the last of the endocrine glands whose specific function was discovered led to much speculation about its function. Today some associate it with

> the sixth chakra[7] whose awakening is linked to prophecy and increased psychic awareness as consciousness ascends.... Mystical traditions and esoteric schools have long known this area ... to be the connecting link between the physical and spiritual worlds. Considered the most powerful and highest source of ethereal energy available to humans, the pineal gland has always been important in initiating supernatural powers. Development of psychic talents has been closely associated with this organ of higher vision.[8]

The ancient Greeks were aware of the pineal gland and claimed it was the gateway to "realms of thought." The great philosopher Descartes wrote extensively on his belief of the duality of man, who was part machine, but who also possessed a soul. The interface of the body and the soul was the pineal gland, at the ideal location for an interconnection between body (brain) and soul (mind). Descartes wrote:

> My view is that this gland is the principal seat of the soul, and the place in which all our thoughts are formed. The reason I believe this is that I cannot find any part of the brain, except this, which is not double. Since we see only one thing with two eyes, and hear only one voice with two ears, and in short have never more than one thought at a time, it must necessarily be the case that the impressions which enter by the two eyes or by the two ears, and so on, unite with each other in some part of the body before being considered by the soul. Now it is impossible to find any such place in the whole head except this gland; moreover it is situated in the most suitable possible place for this purpose, in the middle of all the concavities; and it is supported and surrounded by the little branches of the carotid arteries which bring the spirits into the brain [Adam and Tannery 19–20; Grayling 277–78].

Using the pineal gland as an intersection between the real and the mystic is not a new theme is literature or film. H. P. Lovecraft used Descartes' hypothesis about the pineal gland's function in his short story "From Beyond," citing Descartes' premise that the pineal gland, as a sensory organ, sends visual images to the brain, and its activation could allow us to reach the unseen world of the mind.[9] The belief in the pineal gland as the seat of mysterious powers was also used in Shaun Cassidy's short-lived series *American Gothic* (1995–1996), in which Satan, in the guise of Sheriff Lucas Buck, reigned supreme in Trinity, SC. In an attempt to destroy Buck, an ice pick was jabbed into his head, damaging his pineal gland and thereby depriving Buck of his supernatural powers.

It is my contention that the Alliance "recruited" River Tam and others like her for their innate intuitive powers. Alliance scientists then began experimental surgery, which was sometimes successful and sometimes not (Session 416), in an attempt to create something no one had ever seen before. As mentioned earlier, part of River's problem is that the scientists had not finished with her before Simon rescued her. Of course, I do not suggest that Simon should not have rescued her, but it is probably safe to say that she would have ended up as a formidable weapon, a cross between the Operative and Jubal Early, with a little of Adelai Niska thrown in for good measure. That is, the surgical, biochemical, and psychological manipulations would have led to a woman with no ability to feel either psychic or physical pain, no emotions, no memories of happier times, with a highly conditioned body able to kill with the simplest of weapons, like a pen ("Session 416"), or without weapons, using only her raw physical or mental power ("War Stories" 1.10; *Serenity*). River was correct when saying to Kaylee, "No power in the 'verse can stop me" ("War Stories").

Neurology and Neurosurgery on Buffy *and* Angel

No discussion of the Whedonverses would be complete without discussing the three primary instances of neurology and neurosurgery in *Buffy*. These three are Adam's creation, Spike's chip, and Joyce's brain tumor. I also briefly mention Cordelia's problems in *Angel* Season Three.

Buffy Season Four brought us the year of the Initiative and Buffy's love affair with Riley Finn. The Initiative, a military organization designed to capture and contain supernatural beings such as vampires and demons, is secretly operating in Sunnydale, with an elaborate complex located beneath the campus of UC-Sunnydale. Unbeknownst to Buffy, her new beau (who happens to be her psychology teacher's assistant) is involved with the Initiative. One of their first actions is to capture Spike, Hostile 17 ("The Initiative" 4. 7). If the Initiative's intent is to render Hostiles harmless, then they are entirely successful with Spike. Initiative scientists implant a chip in Spike's brain that inhibits his ability to feed on humans; he is also unable to harm them in any other way. However, Spike should not feel pain following his attempts to harm people,[10] although I speculate that Spike might feel pain because his chip is connected to a pain processing center. However, that fact would not explain why he grabs his head and cries out as if he is in pain. He also should not be grabbing the right side of his head when the chip appears to be located in his left hemisphere.

The Scoobies have great fun at Spike's expense over his inability to "do anything" anymore, making jokes about his impotence and his neutering (e.g., "Something Blue" 4. 9). Even Spike makes such comments, for example, when he says, "Spike had a little trip to the vet, and now he doesn't chase the other puppies anymore" ("Pangs" 4.8). But more than rendering Spike unable to harm a human being, they have also rendered him capable of change. Spike goes to Buffy for help against the Initiative ("Pangs"). As he falls in love with her, he wishes to do anything to please her and help her in her mission. When he discovers that he can harm demons and other vampires ("Doomed" 4.11), he quickly becomes one of the Scoobies, at least as far as he and she are concerned. Buffy relies on Spike more and more throughout Seasons Four through Seven.

However, before that occurs, Spike attempts to have the chip removed, leading to a rather silly scene in the fifth season episode "Out of my Mind" (5.4). Spike kidnaps the doctor who is supposed to repair Riley's heart. Harmony holds the doctor at gunpoint (well, crossbow point) as the doctor works on Spike. Harmony is her usual dimwitted self, asking the doctor questions and annoying Spike, who wants the doctor to concentrate completely on the task at hand. She is entranced by the surgery because Spike is awake, not realizing that neurosurgery frequently occurs with the patient awake and able to talk with the surgeon.[10] Yes, Spike is awake, threatening both Harmony and the doctor with harm. What Spike is not, is restrained. Patients would have their heads stabilized by a specialized piece of equipment that keeps the head from moving while the surgery is taking place. Imagine if the surgeon accidently touched the head and it slipped — *oops*! Brain surgery is quite delicate; one slip of the knife and some crucial part of the brain could be destroyed. In addition, the visual images of Spike's surgery indicate that the doctor was attempting to remove the chip from Spike's left parietal lobe, not a part of the brain one would normally consider to be important for emotional (e.g., hating humans) and behavioral (e.g., eating them) expression. We can only speculate about the placement of Spike's chip. If poor Spike had been captured by the Initiative 60 or 70 years ago, he might have been lobotomized. That would certainly have made him manageable. Of course, it would have also destroyed his personality, but some might think that was worth the "price." Today Spike would be a candidate for Deep Brain Stimulation (DBS), a procedure used primarily for the treatment of patients with Parkinson's disease who do not respond to medication. In this type of surgery a neurostimulator is implanted into the affected area of the brain. The device, which is similar to a pacemaker, stimulates the brain in order to control the tremors and abnormal movements indicative of the disease. Clinical trials are also being conducted to determine the viability of using DBS for the treatment of Obsessive-Compulsive Disorder (Greenberg et al.) and Major Depressive Disorder (Mayberg et al.).

Season Four also finds the Scoobies fighting against Dr. Maggie Walsh's creation, Adam. Formed of the body parts of humans and demons with much electronic enhancement, Adam is Frankenstein's monster rendered whole. This monster knows who his parent is; he calls her "Mommy" even as he kills her ("The I in Team" 4.13). Also, he is born fully sentient, unlike the poor creature in Mary Shelley's famous novel (1818, 1831). Unlike the original, however, Adam is bent upon starting a war against humanity. He has no compunctions about using any means necessary to win the war, promising

Spike that he will remove his chip if Spike will serve as a double-agent against Buffy and the Scoobies. Adam's plan is to create a race of "demonoids" just like himself, part demon and part human. Of course, he will be the master of them all. Like his creator, Maggie Walsh, he, too, plans to create a race of beings who will call him God (Whale).[11]

Joyce's illness occurs in Season Five and culminates in her death. The episode "Out of Mind" (5.4) introduces us to Joyce's illness. As Joyce prepares Dawn's breakfast, she becomes momentarily distracted, pausing in her banter with Dawn, to ask, "Who are you?" before falling to the floor in a faint. Joyce is taken to the hospital where a battery of tests is conducted to determine the cause of these symptoms. As the next few episodes progress, Joyce begins experiencing headaches, which become increasingly severe. Although her doctor has prescribed medication, it does not appear to be helping, and he finally sends her to the hospital for observation and more tests ("Fool for Love" 5.7). The episode "Shadow" (5.8) opens with Joyce entering the CT scanner,[12] while Buffy and Dawn wait anxiously for the test to be over. Dawn asks Buffy to tell her about the "Cat" scan, wondering if it has anything to do with cats, but Buffy replies that she thinks it is a kind of X-Ray (she's right). Because the CT scan only reveals a shadow, Joyce is immediately prepped for a biopsy. Although not mentioned in this episode, Joyce almost certainly undergoes an MRI as well.[13] The test results show that Joyce has a low-grade glioma, in actuality an oligodendroglioma, a type of tumor that affects the myelin coating of neurons. These types of tumors are most likely to be found in the cerebral hemispheres and Joyce's tumor is considered to be a Grade II tumor. This type of tumor has a good prognosis, with a median survival rate of 4 to 10 years.

Joyce's doctor tells her that the tumor is located in the left hemisphere; however, he does not indicate whether the tumor is located in the frontal or temporal lobes. The doctor tells Joyce and the girls of the symptoms she can expect to experience, and that the symptoms will progress very quickly (although he does not say why, we can guess it is for dramatic effect). The symptoms include those one would expect of someone with a tumor in the frontal lobe (e.g., lack of muscle control and mood swings). You would expect someone with a tumor in the frontal lobe to also have disturbances in language, specifically aphasia. Based upon the location of Joyce's bandage, her tumor is quite anterior and looks to be temporal; hence, she should not have had problems with movement or muscle control. She also should not have had mood swings; rather her mood should have been flattened.

Although Joyce's surgery is successful, the aftermath is not. The doctor tells her that she will need some follow-up treatments and tests, but he glosses over the details. In fact, given the severity of Joyce's symptoms and the rapidity with which they displayed, she would have likely needed quite aggressive treatment, including radiotherapy, despite the doctor's assurances that he "got it all" ("Into the Woods" 5.10).

Almost all of the information presented with respect to Joyce's illness is incorrect.[14] Dr. Moshe Feinsod of the Technion Institute of Technology (Israel) states, "An intrinsic brain tumor in a middle-aged woman is much more likely to be a glioblastoma or a metastatic brain tumor than a low-grade glioma. The CT appearance of such tumors is very distinctive and cannot be described as a 'shadow.' In a left hemispheric glioblastoma neurologic deterioration is quite rapid. Mental symptoms will appear quite soon." Dr. Samuel Greenblatt of Brown University (U.S.A.) adds that a Grade II oligodendroglioma actually has "tentacles" that extend out into the brain. There is no way any surgeon could guarantee that he or she got it all. Indeed it would be impossible to take it all because of the extensive damage that would result from such a procedure. Most of these tumors would actually be associated with epilepsy, according to Dr. Peter Koehler of the Atrium Medical Center (The Netherlands), and would, in all likelihood, deteriorate into a high-grade tumor with time.

Given that this is only fiction, one can perhaps forgive the writers for not getting the details correct, but they certainly should not have made the mistakes found in "The Body" (5.16). The paramedics who respond to Buffy's call upon discovering Joyce's body guess that she died of an aneurysm, which is an abnormal widening in an artery due to weakness in the wall of the blood vessel.[15] Such weakness can be caused by trauma, and it is presumed (in the episode) that Joyce's surgery led to the aneurysm. Because of the sudden death, Joyce must be autopsied to verify and/or establish cause of death. The doctor performing the autopsy (who just happens to be Joyce's doctor) states that the on-site report was accurate; however, this is a blatant ethical violation, not to mention downright stupid. *No* hospital would ever allow a physician to perform an autopsy on his or her own patient; the physicians who perform autopsies are specialists. You wouldn't want a pathologist to perform neurosurgery, so why would you want a neurosurgeon to perform pathology? As I said, no hospital would allow this, especially in today's litigious society. All three of my aforementioned colleagues agree that a patient with such a tumor would not die of an aneurysm. Based upon his extensive experience, Dr. Feinsod speculates that such a death would result from a hemorrhage into the tumor. The odds that a patient would have both a tumor and an aneurysm in the same part of the brain are astronomically high.

The last example of neuroscience and neurology involves Cordelia in *Angel.* Following the death of Doyle, Cordelia begins to have visions that inform Angel and the gang that someone is in trouble. Cordy's visions become increasingly painful, and we begin to see the toll they take on her. By Season Three she is taking large quantities of powerful drugs in order to stop the pain. In addition she has had several CT and MRI scans which show that her brain is gradually shutting down. However, in the episode "Birthday" (3.11), we learn that Cordy has apparently also had a functional MRI, which allows neurologists to examine neural activity in the brain. Blood oxygen levels can be detected with the MRI scanner. The computer can create an image showing activity levels in various parts of the brain. For ease of interpretation, levels of activity can be color-coded, generally with red indicating high activity. In Cordy's case, her brain scans were mostly green, indicating very little activity. The speculation is that the intense visions are altering her brain chemistry as well as her anatomy, apparently killing her brain cells. Continued visions will result in her death, hence her decision to become part demon.[16] The visual images used in "Birthday" are striking and look as a genuine scan would. The presumption is that abnormal activity in the brain will have cumulative, devastating consequences for the individual, and this is true. Physical disorders, such as Alzheimer's disease and epilepsy, and mental disorders, such as schizophrenia, can result in significant neurological damage over the course of time.

Conclusions

Joss Whedon's fascination with the brain led him to explore various ways in which that organ can be manipulated. Brains can be enhanced, leading to increased abilities, and this was the goal of the Alliance scientists who experimented on River Tam. Not only did the Alliance want to create a better world (see Chapter 7), they also wanted to create a better weapon to help them create that world (*Serenity*). Maggie Walsh's goal in creating Adam was to design a better being. Not only would her creation hail her as Mother, she would also be as God. However, manipulating the brain can also have detrimental effects, as with Cordelia, whose visions will increasingly damage her brain and might eventually kill her. In Spike's case, manipulating his brain allowed him to control his homicidal impulses and reclaim his soul.

Spike's chip as a means of controlling his behavior is, thus, analogous to the use of drugs or psychosurgery to control the behavior of mentally ill patients. And, finally, there is Joyce Summers, whose death from brain cancer illustrates how quickly something can go wrong with the brain and how devastating the consequences of that damage can be.

In conclusion, one way people can control other people is by interfering with them physically, altering their body or their body's ability to adapt to the changes that continually occur in their environment. It is our brains that allow us to detect the changes that occur around us. It is our brains that allow us to make the adaptations necessary for life. Whether we are conscious of those changes or not, our brains are constantly monitoring both our external and internal environments for information that will allow us to protect ourselves and continue to live. Joss Whedon has explored various ways to interfere with people physically, with neurological manipulations and neurosurgery specifically in *Buffy*, *Angel*, and *Firefly*. He has also explored mental manipulations, manipulations that are the subject of the next chapter.

CHAPTER 6

Manipulating Memory as a Method of Control[1]

It isn't mine. The memory, it isn't mine. And I shouldn't have to carry it. It isn't mine. Don't make me sleep again.— River Tam, *Serenity*

Memory is defined as the ability to recall events and experiences, knowledge and information, and skills (Memory). This definition indicates that three types of data are stored in our memory banks, and psychologists label these three types as episodic, semantic, and procedural memory, respectively. Each type of memory is different from the other two, but all three can and do hold the details of our memories. And, it is these memories that serve as the basis of our identity, yielding a conception of self that arises around the age of 18 months and lasts a lifetime. Memory manipulation, via deletion, implantation, and re-creation, lies at the core of Joss Whedon's *Dollhouse*, and the purpose of this chapter is to examine how Whedon and his writers envision that manipulation. I will first present a short overview of the psychological theory of the three aforementioned types of memory and then discuss how Whedon illustrates each in various episodes of *Dollhouse*, followed by his treatment of memory in his other three series.

Manipulating memory in order to alter reality is a fairly common theme in science fiction. Examples of such manipulation can be found in numerous feature films such as *Dark City* (1998), *The Island* (2005), and the *Matrix* (1999), as well as novels and short stories, such as Roger Zelazny's *Nine Princes in Amber* (1970) and Philip K. Dick's *Do Androids Dream of Electric Sheep?* (1968). This theme has also been explored in a number of television series. J. Michael Straczynski used the idea of erasing a person's episodic and autobiographical memories via a mind-wipe as a form of capital punishment in the *Babylon 5* episode "Passing through Gethsemane" (3.4). This "death of personality" erased the convicted person's memories of the criminal self and reprogrammed the person to serve humankind. The person's memory, the very identity, was erased, and memories of a new identity were created. Joss Whedon also explored this idea in several episodes of *Buffy the Vampire Slayer*, notably including "Tabula Rasa" (6.8). The entire Season Five story arc of *Buffy* involved manipulated memories. Dawn was placed into the Slayer's family for protection, and memories of Dawn were created for Buffy, her mother, and the Scoobies. Even after Buffy learned that Dawn was The Key (to tearing down the boundaries between Earth and Hell) and, thus, not real ("No Place like Home" 5.5), she continued to *remember* events of their lives together, even though she *knew* that the memories were false (more about this distinction later).

One could consider that this story arc foreshadows the theme underlying Whedon's series *Dollhouse*, that memory can be programmed, wiped, and reprogrammed without seeming to leave a trace of such manipulations behind. Such an idea is appealing to many: just consider the interviews conducted with the "Man on the Street" (1.6). During this episode a reporter randomly interviews men and women to determine if they believe in the mysterious Dollhouse, whether such a place really exists or whether it is merely an urban legend, and if such a place does exist, whether it would hold any attractions, why or why not? Many of those interviewed could conceive of a world in which such manipulation would be useful, and indeed, even necessary.

Each of the episodes of the two seasons screened presented both positive and negative examples of such manipulations. For example, a widowed man still in love with his wife could relive a dream day with her, a man whose daughter was kidnapped could receive help from the very best negotiator for her release, an obsessed collector could steal a priceless work of art, and a deranged hunter could stalk the ultimate prey, a human being. Nevertheless, the majority of [real] people do not want their memories erased and would consider that to be one of the worst fates to which they could succumb. Memories are what make us who we are; we remember information about ourselves and these memories serve as our selves. Losing their memories, losing their selves, is a very real fear for many people, and unfortunately a very real possibility, given the incidence of diseases which produce cognitive deficits, such as Alzheimer's and other dementing diseases.

A Short Lesson on Memory

Although memory loss is not inevitable with age, people fear that they will lose their memories as they grow older (see Halpern). Indeed, many people not only fear loss of memory, but fear the major pathological cause of memory loss: Alzheimer's disease (Alzheimer's Assoc.). Some people will develop a dementing illness such as Alzheimer's: 5–10 percent of the population over the age of 65 present with symptoms of the disease. Some scientists state that all people over the age of 85 exhibit pathological signs of the disease (Schneider et al.). However, these people do not necessarily exhibit the behavioral or cognitive symptoms of Alzheimer's. The fear that people feel over this issue is real, because at its heart Alzheimer's disease slowly erases all memories that make someone the person he or she is. Eventually, memories of family and self will disappear as will memories of motor programs that allow one to act upon the world and the general knowledge of all one has learned about the world over the course of a lifetime. Stated simply, Alzheimer's disease destroys the three major types of (long-term) memories that scientists have identified, and debated about, for several decades.

Before discussing these types of memories it is important to note that scientists divide memory into multiple storage depots. Although there is disagreement about some of the details, most agree that we can divide memory into a short-term, working memory and long-term memory. A very helpful analogy for understanding memory is to compare it to a computer. This analogy has been in use for several decades now because early cognitive scientists realized that the computer provided a good model for understanding the ways in which humans and other animals process information. First, information from the environment is captured by the body's sensory receptors, which are located in the eyes, ears, nasal passages, on the tongue, and in the skin. This information is held for a very brief moment of time; less than one second in the visual registers, for example. If the information captured is important[2] it is transferred to the short-term, working memory (STWM). Many people have heard of the short-term memory; however, most are mistaken as to its duration. STWM lasts for a very brief period of time, generally less than 30 seconds. One can extend the life of a STWM, but only by continually repeating the information, an activity termed maintenance rehearsal. If the information is important then it can be transferred to the long-term stores, where it can be held indefinitely. The STWM would be analogous to the monitor on a computer. It is visible and you can work with it, but if you do not save the information to your hard drive, then the information will be lost. The hard drive is analogous to your long-term memory (LTM), and like your LTM, this information is available to you whenever you need it.

However, as we all know, our memories are fallible, and access to particular memories may be difficult. There are a variety of reasons why we might fail to retrieve a memory that is needed, but two reasons for memory failures are interference and cue loss. Cue loss simply refers to the inability to find a memory because the cue used to locate it has been lost. For example, most of us have lost a file on our computer's hard drive because we simply cannot remember where we filed the darn thing. Apparently, our memories can be affected the same way, which is why when you walk into the kitchen and forget why you are there, you can retrace your steps and perhaps retrieve the memory. Or you can remember events from your youth when talking to someone who can provide the cues necessary for retrieval. Interference happens all of the time and can occur in two ways: old memories can interfere with the recall of new information, which is called proactive interference, and new memories can interfere with the recall of old information, which we term retroactive interference. I use the examples of "foreign" languages to illustrate this. On my recent trip to Paris, I continually mixed Italian phrases in with my French. My sentences would frequently consist of a blend of the two. Both of these languages have their roots in Latin and they are very similar to each other, hence the interference.

Long-term memory is our permanent storehouse of knowledge; most neuroscientists believe that memories are created and stored physically, although they have not determined exactly how this process occurs (and not for a lack of trying!). Nevertheless we believe that LTM contains (at least) three different types of memories.

These three major types of memories have been identified based upon analysis of case studies of patients presenting with various kinds of brain damage. Some of these patients experienced damage from illnesses such as encephalitis (e.g., Clive Wearing) and some of these patients experienced damage following surgical procedures (e.g., Henry M.). In the cases of Clive Wearing (Sacks) and Henry M. (Hilts), both of whom suffered massive damage to the temporal lobes, particularly the hippocampi, each experienced an almost total anterograde amnesia, or memory loss for events occurring subsequent to their trauma. Each did retain memory of events prior to the trauma, although such memories were not necessarily directly accessible (more about this later). These tragedies have given us much information on the processes that underlie the physiological basis as well as the cognitive and behavioral aspects of memory.

One of the simplest ways in which to distinguish memories is on the basis of the types of information held (for an introduction to the material in this paragraph, see Hunt & Ellis). Episodic memories, or memories of specific episodes, include all memories that take place in a person's presence. It also includes autobiographical memory or the memory of a person's life. Episodic memories are organized according to time, and their retrieval requires conscious effort. For example, what were you doing last weekend? Most people have to stop and think to find the answer in their memories. Cognitive psychologists state that episodic memories are those we remember, as in "I remember that was the weekend of the PCAS conference and we all went to the Firefly Cafe." Semantic memories on the other hand are our general knowledge stores, basically our dictionaries, encyclopedias, and hard drives (depending upon which metaphor you prefer to use). These memories are organized conceptually and are accessed automatically. For instance, you do not have to consciously access your memory for the meaning of the words you are reading; you do so automatically. Cognitive psychologists state that semantic memories are those that we know, as in "I know that many people get laryngitis when they get sick." Finally, procedural memories are our "how to" memories, that is, our memory of how to do something. These memories are stored as motor patterns and, with experience, their production becomes increasingly automatic. So when I talk about my first car, you can remember your first car as I discuss mine. We remember our first driving experiences and know how to drive those first and subsequent cars. We can carry on a conversation because we share a common language and many common experiences that the words access.

One further distinction that can be made with respect to memory is whether we intend to remember the information or not. If we intend to remember a prior event, or we are aware that we are experiencing an event that occurred previously, then such memories can be said to be *explicit*. On the other hand, if we do not intend to remember a prior event, or if we are unaware that we are experiencing an event that occurred previously, then such memories can be said to be *implicit*. Recall of procedural and semantic memories is thus implicit, whereas recall of episodic memories is explicit.

Memory Mayhem in Film and Television

Moviegoers have been entertained for many years by plots relating to memory loss and memory enhancements. Amnesia, the partial or total loss of memory, is a frequent plot device, although writers sometimes confuse the amnesia which results from organic causes, and the amnesia which results from psychological causes.[3] Psychogenic amnesia does not have a structural or organic cause; it results from a psychological trauma, such as a rape or sexual assault, or witnessing a traumatic event. Organic amnesia, on the other hand, occurs following damage to the brain, from illness or injury.

As mentioned earlier, numerous examples of memory loss can be found on both film and television, although a thorough discussion of this issue is beyond the scope of this chapter. One of the best cinematic portrayals of amnesia occurs in Christopher Nolan's *Memento* (2001). This film's protagonist, Leonard Shelby, suffered a severe head trauma attempting to save his wife from a murderer. As a result of this encounter Leonard experiences complete anterograde amnesia, that is, he is unable to create new memories, much as patient Henry M., mentioned earlier. Lenny's attempts to remember information relevant to the solution of his wife's murder by, for example, tattooing his body are quite compelling. One memorable scene in the movie shows the dozens of post-it notes that Lenny has stuck to the wall above his bed. In this visually stunning film that tells the story of the murder in both real-time and flashback, color-coded to distinguish the two timelines, one significant scene involves Leonard telling his story via telephone to an unknown caller. The scene provides a lesson in how memory works and is especially relevant to the case of patient Henry M.

The recent FOX television series *Fringe* (2008–) developed a plot line involving memory manipulation in Seasons Two and Three. Agent Olivia Dunham, through a series of inadvertent events, becomes stranded in a universe somewhat parallel to our own. Her twin has infiltrated our world in order to destroy it (for quite valid reasons). Our Olivia, held captive in the alternate universe ("Over There [Part 2 of 2]" 2.23), is subjected to repeated drug treatments designed to destroy her memories of her former self and implant the memories of the alternate universe's Olivia into her mind ("Olivia" 3.1; "The Plateau" 3.3). It is unclear if the alternate world scientists realize that Olivia was subjected to brain-enhancing experiments when young ("Jacksonville" 2.15); however, those treatments apparently allow her "real" memories to interfere with this programming, thereby saving Olivia from losing herself mentally much as she is physically lost in the alternate world.

Manipulating Memory in Dollhouse

With engaging plots that provided much food for thought, Whedon and his writers, nevertheless, made several errors with respect to the ways in which the brain works and the ways in which memory was depicted and manipulated in *Dollhouse*. For example, the Actives exhibit some basic memories, although their memories supposedly have been wiped. They answer to their names, albeit their "Active" names. They understand language as evidenced by their ability to talk and understand what is said to them. They also remember basic motor programs. That is, they can all walk and talk and engage in other activities designed to keep their bodies supple (e.g., yoga) and provide them some basic mental stimulation (e.g., painting). Victor's growing love for Sierra is manifested in a "man reaction"; that is, he experiences an erection whenever he sees her naked ("True Believer" 1.5), an example of procedural memory. A more chilling example is Sierra's reaction to Victor's touch in "Man on the Street." She screams when he places his hand on her shoulder, a reaction that leads to the discovery that she has been raped by her handler, Hearn. In the episode "Needs" (1.8), Echo notes that she can remember information such as the days of the week and the capital of Nebraska, but nothing about herself. In Season Two, when Victor's contract with Rossum expires and he is re-integrated into the "real" world, vestiges of his Dollhouse imprinting bleed into his life. For example, he cannot sleep in a bed. Instead, he takes his pillow and blanket off the bed in his room and sleeps in his bathtub, which physically resembles the sleeping pods in the Dollhouse ("Stop-Loss" 2.9). Examples such as these indicate that the Rossum Corporation is manipulating only the Actives' episodic memories, wiping any memories of the original personality. Although an intriguing idea, completely destroying one type of memory without affecting other types does not appear possible. Even brain-damaged patients continue to have memories of their lives prior to their trauma, even if they can no longer create new explicit memories.

However, in one respect, Whedon and the other writers depicted the reality of the neural basis of memory. As the series progressed through Season One it becomes increasingly clear that Echo is remembering information from her past imprints, a programming impossibility according to the Rossum Corporation. Theoretically, an Active's true personality is to be wiped "clean," downloaded onto a disk and stored until the Active's contract with Rossum is terminated. During the five-year contracting period an Active is designed to be imprinted multiple times, usually with a new personality. No "bleed through" is supposed to occur between imprints. Each Active is to be imprinted with the requested personality and then wiped clean after a time period specified by the client. However, Echo clearly shows awareness of those implanted personalities, as well as her original, primary personality.

In the episode "A Spy in the House of Love" (1.9), the suggestion is made that there is a mole in the Dollhouse and that this person has tampered with Echo's program. Episodes prior to this one show that Echo is already remembering bits and pieces of previous imprints; we do not learn the identity of the mole or the mole's true purpose until later in Season Two ("The Hollow Men" 2.12). A complete review of the theoretical basis of Echo's "awakening" is beyond the scope of this chapter; however, memories are constructed through association. Memories become associated with each other for a variety of reasons and are stored as vast networks of memories. Activating one memory in turn activates a host of other memories associated with that event through a spreading activation. For example, memories of my first car will activate memories of the day my mother drove it home because I could not drive a straight-drive, which will activate the memory of my mother, which will activate memories of a life-time spent with my mother, which will activate other memories of my lifetime, et cetera. Thus, as Echo remembers one piece of information, she will increasingly remember other pieces, despite the best efforts of Topher and his attempts to wipe and re-implant memories as requested by Echo's clientele.

This is especially evident in the Season Two episode "Vows" (2.1). Although Echo remembers Whiskey when encountering her early in the episode and even talks to her about Whiskey's past ("You were number 1."), it is the blow to the head Echo receives at the hands of her client "husband" Martin Klar that affects her memory. As he repeatedly hits her, Echo begins to see flashes of her previous imprints. Echo tries to reassure him that she is really his wife, but ends up saying, "I will always be Eleanor Penn." Of course, that is the wrong imprint, which Echo realizes as soon as she says it. Later on, when she is back in the Dollhouse, she speaks with her handler, former FBI agent Paul Ballard, about her memories of the imprints. She tells him that she is lost, that she does not know who or what is real. Echo is remembering information from the women she has been with her various clients. That is, episodic memories of these women have been created and stored in her brain. They have not been wiped clean, and the fact that she can access these memories of her "selves" leaves her with a sense of fragmentation. She has no clear memory of a specific self, but rather memories of multiple selves. Her semantic memory is intact as well; however, recall that semantic memory is generalized knowledge. Echo knows that she has been, and is being, programmed repeatedly, but these memories are not personal, i.e. episodic, memories of her self. Indeed, she has some problems with the reality of the memories as well. And that is another flaw in the way that memory is presented on *Dollhouse*.

This flaw is the very real inability that we possess of knowing whether our memories are actually accurate. Numerous research studies have demonstrated the fallibility of memory and the ease with which false memories can be created (Loftus). We know that memories are reconstructed with use, which means that any memory may not actually be "real." That is, are the memories that I have of any childhood event real, or have I recreated those memories to coincide with what I thought was true, or what I believed was true, or what I hoped was true? When Echo and the other Actives are imprinted with another person's memories, it is presumed that that person's memories are their actual, "real" memories. Once again, given the ease with which false memories can be created, this assumption may not be true. The episode "Ghost" (1.1) illustrates this fact quite clearly (more about this later).

"Ghost," the first episode of the series, introduces us to the imprinting procedures used in the Dollhouse. Whenever an Active is requested for an assignment, she or he receives a "treatment" in which the requested personality is imprinted upon her or his brain. It is apparently painful to wipe and insert memories, as witnessed by the facial expressions and vocalizations of the Actives. Given that the brain has no pain receptors there should be no pain in the process (see Chapter 5). Memory of the treatment itself is apparently forgotten also, as evidenced by the Actives' question, "Did I fall asleep?" after each wipe. We know that Echo is different from the other Actives when we see her walk up the stairs to watch Sierra's programming. Her facial expressions let us know that she is aware that something is happening, even if, at this point, she is unsure of what it is. Wiping an Active's memory is compared to cleaning a slate, as if one were erasing all the information on that slate. As Echo's original personality Caroline notes, however, you cannot clean a slate ("Ghost"); you can always see what has been written prior to the erasure. The escaped Active Alpha reinforces this metaphor later. In the Season Two episode "A Love Supreme" (2.8) he notes that you can never delete a program, as "once it's created, it's alive."

Dollhouse's Actives are programmable people; they are "made to order." Topher, their programmer, considers himself to be "the man behind the gray matter curtain" ("The Target" 1.2), referring to the outer covering of the brain (the cerebral cortex, which consists of neuronal cell bodies that appears "gray" to the naked eye). As noted earlier, Joss Whedon is fascinated by the brain (Season One DVD Commentary) and *Dollhouse* allowed him to speculate about the neurological basis of behavior and its potential for manipulation. The graphics used to illustrate the brain in "Man on the Street" (1.6) are quite real. Still, much of the neuroscience and neurology discussed in the program is not only impossible at this time but unlikely to be developed, given our current state of knowledge. However, one aspect of the series' programming is within the realm of possibility, and that concerns the pharmacological manipulation of behavior. Drugs that have effects on memory have been featured on a couple of episodes of *Dollhouse*.

Echo begins remembering events from her past in the episode "The Target" after her client, Richard Connell, drugs her. His plan is to make her more malleable and more easily hunted, and he almost succeeds. The episode "Echoes" (1.7) centers on a drug N7316, created by the Rossum Corporation. N7316 is a memory drug that works by breaking down natural inhibitions in the hippocampus to awaken the "sleeping" parts of the brain. According to Rossum, the drug is still in its experimental stage. Phase I intake produces giddiness and light hallucinations, making it euphorigenic. Phase II intake results in a complete loss of impulse control. According to Topher, the drug supposedly acts by "attacking the inhibitory centers in the hippocampus, breaking down repressed memory blocks." This causes the user to experience a memory glitch, which is especially troubling when the Actives, particularly Echo, begin recovering their memories of lives before the Dollhouse. The fact that the Actives begin remembering those lives speaks to my earlier comment about the spreading activation of memory. As a memory is accessed, it will lead to other memories, which will lead to still more memories, et cetera. A useful metaphor might be to think of this spreading activation as a snowball rolling down a hill. It may start small, but as it rolls, it will get larger and larger, and as it gets larger, it may become dangerous. This is certainly the case with Echo; she has already begun remembering her life as Caroline, and the N7316 enables Echo to access even more of Caroline's memories. This episode ends with the suggestion that the drug's effects have dissipated; but it seems that this is not the case, at least with respect to Echo.

Whedon's commentary on "Man on the Street" notes that we are a society in love with drugs. We use these drugs "to help us focus, be less depressed, and help us in every way, and more and more drugs [that] can target areas of memory. People's response to this is to give me those drugs." He is correct. We do indeed have drugs to help us focus (e.g., Ritalin, nicotine), be less depressed (e.g., SSRI's), and help us in every way (e.g., anti-anxiety drugs, anti-hypertensives, anti-cholesterols, anti-fat, alcohol, opiates, etc). And, yes, we do have drugs that affect memory, such as Aricept, the function of which is to delay the inevitable memory loss accompanying advanced Alzheimer's disease. Presumably, Rossum's intention with respect to N7316 is to make it easier to program their Actives. However, a major advantage would be to mass-produce the drugs and make them available to the general population. It is clear that Rossum Corporation is making large amounts of money from their clients who use the Actives from the various Dollhouses. Nevertheless, the costs associated with maintaining the various Dollhouses must be astronomical. The initial costs associated with creating a drug with the capability of controlling memory would also be astronomical; however, the ultimate profits would be staggering as people bought and used the drug in their attempts to, as Whedon states, cut "out the part of us that causes pain ... to be the best version of themselves that they can be." It does not take much stretch of the imagination to realize that a drug that can break down memory blocks (i.e., allow access to every memory stored in one's brain), could have powerful repercussions, not only for the person who wants access to those memories, but to the person who can gain that access as well. There would be no secrets, and potentially catastrophic events, as explored in "Ghost," would not happen. *Dollhouse* programmers, such as Topher Brink and Bennett Halverson, would have easier jobs in the sense that the Actives could perhaps be imprinted more easily and less painfully.[4]

One reason for *Dollhouse* programmers' ease in imprinting the Actives may have to do with neural plasticity. Plasticity refers to the brain's ability to mold itself over the course of development. Increasingly, research indicates that even "older" brains, that is, brains beyond the age of maturity (which is roughly 25 years) are capable of rewiring and perhaps healing themselves after damage. The fact that the human brain itself is capable of being re-programmed may also underlie the assumptions of *Dollhouse*. Topher states that he is in "neuroplastic heaven" ("A Spy in the House of Love"), and several episodes feature Topher's manipulations of Echo's basic neural processing. For example, in "Ghost," Echo is imprinted with a nearsighted hostage negotiator named Eleanor Penn. For this mission, Echo wears glasses and truly cannot see without them. Topher states that he can mess up the neural connections to her eyesight and change the way that her brain processes information. Indeed, he states that he can make her whatever *he* wants her to be. Later, in "True Believer," Topher operates on Echo, inserting a camera into her visual system. Visual information perceived by her eyes bypasses her cortex — she is in effect rendered blind — but the signals are in actuality being recorded and broadcast back to the Bureau of Alcohol, Tobacco, Firearms, and Explosives (ATF).

In Season Two's "Belle Chose" (2.3) Topher tries a remote wipe of Victor, much as Alpha had done to Echo in the Season One episode "Gray Hour" (1.4). The nephew of one of the Dollhouse's patrons, a man named Terry, has been seriously injured. Terry is in a coma and, as Topher maps Terry's brain, he discovers that Terry is a psychopath who has abducted several women. Victor is imprinted with Terry's memories in an attempt to rescue these women. Terry escapes from the Dollhouse with the aid of his uncle, whom he subsequently injures. Terry's escape leads Topher to try a remote mind wipe which only succeeds in having Echo and Victor exchange imprints. Echo attempts to complete Terry's murderous urges, and she almost succeeds. This episode's end lets us know that Echo has retained Terry's memories of violence. The emotions that accompany those memories—the rage against his mother, the sexual excitement he feels when engaging in violence—are intense and emotional memories that are very easily accessed.

Echo's recovered memories are extremely strong and emotional. These types of memories are apparently not as easily wiped as Topher thinks. In "Ghost," Miss Penn is confronted with the man who sexually assaulted her when she was a child. Miss Penn's fear of this man almost overpowers Echo's programming. The fact that Miss Penn had been sexually assaulted as a child was not part of her file and, thus, could not be downloaded into an imprint. Even if the Dollhouse programmers create artificial memories that serve to augment an Active's imprint, traumatic memories that have perhaps been repressed by the primary might bleed through those artificial imprints. If someone's memories are not accurately "recorded," then the inaccurate memories would be downloaded and imprinted on an Active rather than the actual memories or the memories that imprinters create.

As Season One continues we observe other instances of Caroline or Echo's memories bleeding into Echo's current program. All of these memories are extremely strong and intensely personal. At various times Echo remembers Alpha's massacre ("The Target"), Dominic's attempt to kill her ("True Believer"), and the death of her lover ("Echoes"). Even Boyd is aware of the correlation between strong emotions and imprint disruption ("A Love Supreme"). Each of these examples provides evidence of the difficulty of programming or reprogramming memories, especially those that involve strong emotions, such as love, anger, or fear.

Emotional memories are mediated by a subcortical area of the brain known as the amygdala (LaBar; LeDoux). The amygdalae are located at the anterior ends of the hippocampi, in the temporal lobes. It is the hippocampus that apparently transfers short-term memory into the long-term stores, and it is this part of the brain that is damaged in patients with anterograde amnesia. Patients with temporal lobe damage also frequently experience uncontrollable anger and even rages, presumably because their amygdalae are also damaged, or the connections between the amygdalae and cortical areas mediating rational thought are damaged.[5] The amygdala and the hippocampus are part of the limbic system, a set of subcortical structures comprising an emotional circuit responsive to primitive emotions, such as fear (Kandel, Schwartz, and Jessell). When Echo awakens in "The Target" and realizes that Richard is hunting her, she experiences the typical fight-or-flight endocrine response. The sheer amount of stress hormones flooding her body initially interferes with her ability to respond rationally to the threat. These naturally occurring chemicals, in conjunction with the drugs given to Echo by Richard, begin to interfere with the neural imprints created by Topher. Research increasingly indicates that the chemicals released by the body during stress interfere with memory (for a very brief discussion of this see Lemonick). What this episode also demonstrates is that memories are stored physically, that the memory trace of any event, piece of information, or program is stored as a physical locus that cannot be erased as easily as one would wish. Perhaps what Topher is actually doing is not so much wiping the Active's memories as rendering those Active's memories inaccessible. In other words, the memories are not wiped prior to, and following, an imprint. Instead, they are simply blocked from conscious access. Echo may not remember her life as Miss Penn or Kiki, but she can occasionally use the information learned from those imprints to help her solve problems. Data from patients with brain damage support this hypothesis. Although patients such as Clive Wearing and Henry M. cannot create new explicit memories, continued observation and study of these patients indicate that their memories prior to their trauma are intact and, in some instances, they can create new implicit memories. Henry M. cannot tell someone how to find the restroom in his nursing home, for example, but he can show them where it is.

As Season Two progresses, Echo is increasingly revealed as someone and something new. Whereas the Rossum Corporation is increasingly vying for power and control of an unsuspecting population, their manipulations are having consequences of which they are unaware. Echo, while special, is something new and something unanticipated. Echo increasingly remembers her previous imprints and can make use of the information imprinted upon her. In the episode "Meet Jane Doe" (2.7) Echo uses memories from her Active past to allow her to escape from the prison and free Galena. As Echo and Paul talk, she mentions that she has 36 personalities, and she tells Paul about some of them (e.g., seven of the imprints were gay). But although Echo has some flashes of memories of Caroline, she does not have them all. Echo is determined to obtain these missing memories even though she is leery of what she will find. Her torture by Bennett ("The Left Hand" 2.6), as well as her flashes of Caroline, increasingly indicate that Caroline was not a nice person. For instance, Caroline befriended Bennett primarily to obtain her security clearance for the Rossum Corporation's laboratory and then left her to suffer after the bomb they planted exploded ("Getting Closer" 2.11).[6] Knowledge such as this worries Echo: she wonders about recovering Caroline's memories. She is especially concerned about what will happen to this new entity named Echo when Caroline returns.

Topher is quite taken with Bennett, his counterpart in the DC office. She is beautiful and nearly as intelligent as he is, or so he thinks. As they discuss various details of the imprinting process, Topher notes that Senator Daniel Perrin is in actuality a hybrid. He has had a replacement imprint superimposed upon his existing mind: in effect, his imprint has been "married to an existing consciousness" ("The Left Hand"). Topher wonders whether such a procedure would make the person schizophrenic, and Bennett states her belief that the human mind is capable of containing multiple consciousnesses. When Topher asks whether she means a composite person, Bennett replies no, stating that the result would be "something new, something better." In this episode it is unclear if Bennett is speaking from experience, as her behavior is decidedly odd. It does seem as if she is unaware that Echo might be one of those "new, composite beings," who are capable of holding multiple consciousnesses in their minds.

One thread in this episode and others involving Echo and her awareness of those multiple episodic memories has to do with the concept of schizophrenia. Although the word "schizophrenia" means split personality, the condition is not understood by the average person and is frequently referenced incorrectly. People with schizophrenia experience a split, a disconnection, between their thoughts and their emotions (American Psychiatric Association [*DSM-IV-TR*]). Their thoughts are frequently disorganized and delusional. Their emotions are flattened and inappropriate for the situation. Schizophrenics do not have separate, dual, or multiple personalities. That condition is now referred to as Dissociative Identity Disorder (DID); it was once called Multiple Personality Disorder (MPD). There is controversy about this condition; many doctors doubt its existence. Often, patients with DID are not aware of the condition. Hence, Topher's use of the term "schizophrenia" in reference to Actives with the awareness of multiple consciousnesses is incorrect. We know that Alpha and Echo are both aware of these multiple personas. We also know that Whiskey is becoming increasingly aware; she remembers that she was once the most-requested Active and that

Alpha hurt her so that Echo could be "Number 1" ("Vows"). But all three know that they are different somehow, something new. Whiskey/Claire Saunders says, "I am in someone else's body and I'm afraid to give it up" ("Vows"). Her angst concerns whether she will continue to exist and she flees the Dollhouse for some time rather than relinquish this new self. Alpha is so determined not to lose his new self that he destroyed his "primary" (i.e., original) personality ("Omega" 1.12). Echo, although much more stable psychologically than Alpha or Whiskey, says that she is "not real. I'm not who I think I am" ("The Public Eye" 2.5) and later "I'm afraid of Caroline. If she comes back, where will I go?" ("The Left Hand"). Echo and Caroline are able to resolve this conundrum and coexist ("Epitaph Two: The Return" 2.13), although one could argue that it is their desire to destroy the Rossum Corporation's stranglehold on the world that allows for Echo's acceptance of the Caroline persona, and vice versa. Both of them are needed to restore humanity to its pre-imprinting reality.

The premise underlying Joss Whedon's *Dollhouse* concerned whether human memory could be manipulated in such a way as to delete previously stored memories, implant new memories, or create artificial memories. Those people who entered the Dollhouses wishing to escape from the pain and suffering in their lives, such as Whiskey and November, could have those painful memories excised and new, less painful memories created. Other Actives, such as Sierra, who was forced into servitude by a rejected lover ("Belonging" 2.4), would have the memory of her abuse at this man's hands erased, but would have memories of her life prior to her entry into the Dollhouse erased also. Echo, devastated by the death of her lover, volunteered to have the memory of her loss erased; however, given that she was facing imprisonment, she could not actually be said to "volunteer." Although a premise that some might envision as helpful in certain circumstances ("Man on the Street"), many people cannot conceive of the reality of losing their memories, nor would they want to. Patients presenting with traumatic brain injuries or diseases such as Alzheimer's, with the concomitant amnesia, serve to illustrate the devastation such memory loss brings to its victims.

Manipulating Memory in Whedon's Other Worlds

As mentioned earlier, the Season Five story arc in *Buffy* concerned the nature of memory and the definition of family. In order to protect the gates between the dimensions, the Key is sent to the Slayer in the form of a sister. Should the Key open the gates between these dimensions, the universe would be destroyed as the dimensions begin to bleed together. The monks who transformed the Key into human form created memories of Dawn so that Buffy and Joyce would accept her as part of the family. Reality was altered in such a way that, even after Buffy and Joyce learned the truth about Dawn, they continued to have memories of their life together. And, the love they felt for a sister and a daughter continued to be felt. Even though they *know* Dawn is not really a member of the family, their memories include her — they remember her.

Memories were also manipulated in *Buffy* by Willow when she feared her addiction to magick was creating too many problems in her relationship with Tara. The episode "All the Way" (6.6) is a perfect example. Willow uses magick to decorate the house at Halloween rather than doing it the old-fashioned way (by hand), upsetting both Tara and Giles. Later, when Buffy discovers that Dawn is not really sleeping over at Janice's, the gang looks for her. Tara and Willow arrive at the Bronze to find it very crowded, but Willow simply uses magick to clear out the crowd. Tara continues to be upset with Willow, until Willow puts a spell on her, causing Tara to lose her memory of what happened that night. However, Tara discovers what Willow did to her and threatens to leave unless Willow renounces magick. Willow promises that she will stop for one week, but she is unable to go 24 hours without using magick. The morning after her promise, she casts a spell on both Buffy and Tara, but it backfires and wipes all of the Scoobies' memories clean ("Tabula Rasa" 6.8). Once the spell is broken, Tara leaves; she is simply unable to live with Willow any longer, knowing that Willow would abuse her in such a fashion (see Chapter 3).

As mentioned in Chapter 5, River Tam was subjected to both psychological and neurological torture at the hands of Alliance scientists. One result of that trauma was a fragmented memory. In various episodes in *Firefly*, River does not recognize her brother or her location (e.g., "The Train Job" 1.3), thinking that she is home rather than aboard Serenity. One could argue that her incoherent ramblings are the result of precognitive visions interfering with her conscious awareness ("The Train Job" 1.3). Thus, it might be that her ability to create accurate memories is disrupted by the visions she sees. Nevertheless, her memories of her torture are intact, as evidenced by her nightmares, flashforwards, and flashbacks (e.g., *Serenity*).

The manipulation of memory figures prominently in Season Four of *Angel*. Cordelia returns from the realm of Higher Beings at the end of "The House Always Wins" (4.3) in which her first remark to the gang is, "Who are you people?" Unfortunately for Angel and Company, their attempts to protect Cordy arouse her suspicions, and when one of Lorne's clients attacks her, she is rescued by Connor, with whom she leaves ("Slouching toward Bethlehem" 4.4). Cordy's remarks about her memory are a reflection of Echo's remarks that she can remember factual information (i.e., semantic memory), but she cannot remember personal information about herself (i.e., episodic memory) ("Spin the Bottle" 4.6). Cordy will recover her memories as events unfold in Season Four; however, Connor, Angel's son, will lose his memories of his entire life in an attempt to stop him from becoming a mass murderer ("Home" 4.22). Just as the Powers That Be created the Key and built memories of her for Buffy, Joyce, and the rest of the Scoobies, the Powers That Be removed the memories of Connor from everyone associated with Angel, except Angel.

Conclusion

Dollhouse in particular and, to a lesser extent, the other Whedon series can be viewed as intellectual exercises in how memories might be manipulated for both nefarious (e.g., stealing artworks) and altruistic (e.g., rescuing kidnapped women and children) purposes, and how such manipulations might affect those involved (e.g., saving a young man from his own depression and despair). Although Whedon and the other writers on these series made several errors with respect to the ways in which memory was depicted, they also presented several instances of the reality of human memory. Because there are multiple types of memory, apparently mediated by different neurological structures and pathways, disrupting one type of memory will leave other types intact. Thus, it is possible to remove someone's memories of self without affecting their ability to walk or talk or perform other skilled operations. It is unclear, however, whether it is possible to dissociate certain aspects of semantic memory from personal memory. Is it possible to forget moral lessons that one has learned? For example, is it possible for Echo to forget the basic values that Caroline possessed? Values such as the sanctity of human life might be difficult to erase. The writers certainly reinforced cultural stereotypes when they had Echo's "maternal instinct" activated in the *Dollhouse* episode "Instinct" (2.2),[7] the assumption being that motherly love can be imprinted and will override not only all other emotions but logic as well. However, even a complete loss of identity did not keep Buffy from realizing that she was a "superhero" ("Tabula Rasa").

Memory is what makes us who we are. It allows us to situate ourselves in the world and establish connections between our pasts, our presents, and our futures. People without memory are cast adrift in a world that they do not understand, a world that is foreign and alien, one that makes little sense. Could there be a worse fate?

CHAPTER 7

Exerting Control
with Pharmaceutical Agents[1]

I was actually at Woodstock. That was a weird gig. Fed off a flower person and spent six hours watching my hand move.— Spike, "School Hard" [*Buffy* 2.3]

As noted in Chapters 5 and 6, people can control others by manipulating the ways in which their brains work or the ways in which they remember information. They can also exert control over others using chemicals such as drugs. At various points in the four series in question, Whedon's characters are exposed to drugs, generally in order to control some aspect of their behavior. The characters also use some drugs willingly, such as alcohol, and others for their therapeutic benefits. It is important to note that drugs can affect memory, as mentioned in Chapter 6. Drugs also exert their effects via the brain (see Chapter 5). In this chapter I will discuss the ways in which drugs were used to control behavior as depicted by Whedon, expanding on information presented in the previous chapters.

A Short Lesson on Neurons

Neurons signal information electrically. This is accomplished by changing the polarity of the neuron from negative to positive by alternating the passage of ions through the cell membrane. As one section of the axon depolarizes, the signal is attracted to the next section of the axon because this section's polarity is opposite in sign to the signal. This transmission occurs repeatedly down the length of the axon, but it is a relatively slow process:

information travels at a speed of about 10 m/sec. Some axons are so long that they must have help in transmitting the traveling signal. In these types of axons, the neuron has evolved two mechanisms that allow for fast conduction of information. These mechanisms are myelin and the node of Ranvier. Myelin is a protein coating composed of a certain type of glial cell and gives the axon a whitish appearance, hence the term "white matter." Myelin serves as an insulator for the neuron. Located throughout the myelin sheath are openings called nodes of Ranvier, in effect, bare spots on the axon. It is at these nodes that depolarization occurs, aiding in the propagation of the signal, the action potential. In effect, the nodes act as boosters of the action potential and, in myelinated axons, information can travel at a speed of about 100 m/sec, or 275 mph (electricity travels about 300 million m/sec).

Neurons are separated from one another by a very small space (approximately one ten-millionth of a millimeter wide) called the synaptic gap. The action potential cannot jump the gap; therefore, the neuron must transfer information through a different means. This involves chemicals called neurotransmitters. When the action potential reaches the terminal buttons of the axon, calcium channels are opened along with the sodium channels. The calcium causes a change in the vesicles located throughout the terminal buttons, causing them to migrate to the end of the button and fuse with the cell membrane of the button. The neurotransmitter is then released into the synaptic gap. It diffuses across to the receiving neuron where it causes sodium channels to open, depolarizing the adjacent neuron. However, the neurotransmitter will only affect the adjacent neuron if that neuron has a receptor for that particular transmitter. Think of the receptor as being a lock and the transmitter as being a key. Several poisons (e.g., botulinum toxin and curare) work by blocking receptors; that is, they attach themselves to the receptor and do not allow the transmitter to do its job. Some drugs work by interfering with synaptic activity. For example, cocaine causes the excess release of dopamine. This neurotransmitter appears to mediate the reinforcing properties of those things that humans find pleasurable, and even addicting, such as sexual activity, gambling, and drugs.

Psychoactive Drugs

A drug is an exogenous chemical that affects physiological processes (Cooper, Bloom, and Roth). The effects of psychoactive drugs include alterations in psychological states or processes, such as attention, memory, judgment, time-sense, self-control, emotion or perception. These drugs can be placed on a continuum, ranging from stimulant to depressant, and those terms refer to the actions of the drug within the Central Nervous System, not to their behavioral effects. Physical dependence upon a drug occurs when the user must compulsively use the drug to maintain bodily comfort; in psychological terms we say that the person is addicted. Dependence is usually accompanied by tolerance, in which the user must take larger and larger doses of the drug to produce the desired effect. In addition, a person who is dependent upon a drug experiences withdrawal symptoms when the drug is no longer available. Because these withdrawal symptoms are very unpleasant, and for some drugs downright dangerous, the user is compelled to use the drug again. The elimination of their withdrawal symptoms is negatively reinforcing, which is much more powerful than positive reinforcement.[2] Negatively reinforced behaviors are highly resistant to extinction, and this type of reinforcement guarantees that the individual will continue to use their drug of choice to avoid any future withdrawal symptoms. Users may also experience psychological dependence, which occurs when the user feels that the drug is necessary to maintain emotional or psychological well-being.

Most psychoactive drugs act directly on the Central Nervous System, which consists of the brain and spinal cord (see Chapter 5). The majority of drugs work by affecting activity at the synapse. Drugs may affect synaptic activity in a variety of ways; for example, by mimicking naturally occurring neurotransmitters or interacting with their receptors; by blocking receptors for naturally occurring neurotransmitters or altering their sensitivity; by altering neurotransmitter synthesis or storage; by altering neurotransmitter release from presynaptic terminals; by altering neurotransmitter breakdown or re-uptake; by destroying neuronal cell bodies or terminals; by mimicking naturally occurring hormones; or, by altering electrical activity of neurons at the membrane level (Julien, Advokat, and Comaty).

There are seven pharmacological classes of psychoactive drugs (Cooper, Bloom, and Roth). These are psychomotor stimulants, sedative-hypnotics, opiates, hallucinogens, major tranquilizers or antipsychotics, antidepressants, and anxiolytics (Bloom, Iversen, Roth, and Iversen). The latter three— major tranquilizers, antidepressants, and anxiolytics— are therapeutic for certain mental disorders: schizophrenia, depression, and anxiety disorders, respectively. Of the seven classes, four produce dependence in human beings: psychomotor stimulants, sedative-hypnotics, opiates, and anxiolytics. Psychomotor stimulants include drugs such as cocaine, methamphetamine, ecstasy, caffeine, and nicotine. Sedative-hypnotics include drugs such as alcohol and barbiturates. Opiates include drugs such as heroin and morphine, and anxiolytics are anti-anxiety drugs, such as Valium and Xanax.

These addictive drugs work by activating the brain's reward circuitry. Certain areas of the brain are specialized for responding to rewarding consequences; these areas are active when we engage in activity that is related to survival, such as eating when we are hungry or drinking liquids when we are thirsty. This part of the brain is also active when we engage in sexual activity. The neurotransmitter dopamine is associated with this reward circuit — actions that increase activity in the reward circuit increase the release of dopamine from the neurons in the circuit. This release of dopamine is pleasurable; that is, it creates a pleasurable sensation. Because drugs of abuse also increase the release of dopamine in the reward circuit, people are likely to re-use a particular drug in order to obtain that pleasurable sensation. In addition, the reward circuit is connected to those parts of the brain that mediate memory, so the user remembers the pleasurable sensations elicited by the drug. Thus, they will seek out the drug in the future when they remember that the drug produced pleasure (Abadinsky 78). With repeated use, however, the user's response to the drug is diminished.[3]

Drugs in Science Fiction and Fantasy

The use of drugs and other biological treatments, such as hypnosis and psychosurgery, has a long history within the fields of medicine and psychiatry. They are also common plot devices in science fiction and fantasy (SFF). Authors ranging from Mary Wollstonecraft Shelley in the early 19th century to Joss Whedon in the early 21st have explored the myriad ways in which psychoactive drugs are used as methods of control. The noted science fiction author Robert Silverberg proposed that drug themes within SFF belong to one of the following categories: drugs as euphorics, mind-expanders, panaceas, mind-controllers, intelligence-enhancers, sensation-enhancers, reality-testers, mind-injurers, and means of communication. Silverberg's analysis of these themes was based on his reflection upon the times: the majority of the stories and novels he examined dated from the post–1965 period, when "the use of drugs first pervaded the national life to its present extent" (vi).

Silverberg proposed that the drugs depicted in SFF could be categorized as mind-controllers. However, one could argue that all drugs, at least the psychoactive ones, are mind-controllers. That is, they all work in the brain leading to multiple effects on behavior. It must be noted that Silverberg's classification does not exactly match the seven classes of psychoactive drugs. Nevertheless, his classification scheme is still timely, even if 25 years old. Drugs in several pharmacological classes can be deemed euphorigenic: opiates, sedative-hypnotics, hallucinogens, stimulants, and even anxiolytics in sufficient quantities. Hallucinogens can be considered mind-expanders and sensation-enhancers as well as reality-testers and even mind-injurers, if one considers the reality of "bad trips." And, some psychomotor stimulants, by virtue of their ability to focus attention, may even be deemed as intelligence-enhancers. The sheer numbers of prescriptions written for anxiolytic drugs would seem to suggest that they be considered panaceas, universal remedies for what ails an anxiety-riddled society or to calm and sedate a population into happiness and bliss.

Just such a world was imagined by Aldous Huxley's *Brave New World*, one of the first science fiction novels to explore the use of drugs as a means of controlling the population. Huxley's book is a marvelous satire of a consumer-driven, technology-hungry society, much like our own 21st century, carried to extreme limits. The novel is filled with characters who do everything they can to avoid facing the truth about their situations. Nearly everyone uses the drug soma as a means of self-delusion. Soma clouds the realities of the present and replaces those realities with happy hallucinations. In doing so, it promotes social stability. According to Mustapha Mond, the Resident World Controller of Western Europe, the World State prioritizes happiness at the expense of truth by design: he believes that people are better off with happiness than with truth (Huxley; see also the Sparks Notes on the novel). Using Silverberg's categories, soma would be classified as a euphoric, a mind-controller, and a sensation-enhancer. In addition, soma is a panacea, a universal remedy for a contented population, one that does not question the authority of its leaders and knows itself to be happy. Certainly Huxley conceived of soma as such. In his essay *Brave New World Revisited*, Huxley wrote: "Soma was not only a vision-producer and a tranquilizer; it was also (and no doubt impossibly) a stimulant of mind and body; a creator of active euphoria as well as of the negative happiness that follows the release from anxiety and tension" (300).[4] The citizens of his *Brave New World* were happy because they had been told so since childhood, and they had a drug to ensure that they never encountered any information to the contrary. Soma was the epitome of mind control, and it had rendered Earth's citizens powerless.

Although the use of drugs as agents of population control can be found in many SFF novels, they have also been used repeatedly in SFF television programs. Examples include all versions of *Star Trek*, *Odyssey 5*, *Babylon 5*, *Farscape*, *Stargate SG-1*, *Stargate Atlantis*, *Sanctuary*, *Fringe*, *Buffy the Vampire Slayer*, *Dollhouse*, and *Firefly*, to name only a few. These series provide examples of ways in which drugs are used to control populations, individuals, or both. Drugs as depicted on these series can be classified using Silverberg's taxonomy as well as the psychopharmacological taxonomy, and their effects are both reinforcing and addictive.

Drug Use in the Buffyverse

Although there are various episodes on *Buffy* in which drugs figure prominently, I will first speak about Spike's drinking problem. Vampires in the Buffyverse are apparently capable of ingesting and digesting human food.[5] Spike certainly loves his blooming onion, even going so far as learning how to make one ("Empty Places" 7.19). He likes chicken wings also. But what Spike really loves is his booze. He is not too picky, appearing to drink Scotch whisky, gin, vodka, wine, bourbon, beer, you name it. Spike's drinking is out of control in several episodes. The first occurs when he returns to Sunnydale after Drusilla leaves him for a chaos demon ("Lovers Walk" 3.8). Spike's arrival is heralded by a wreck; the interior of his car is strewn with bottles and he is so drunk that he passes out. Later he kidnaps Willow to force her to create a spell that will make Dru return to him. Drunk but still deadly, Willow is terrified of Spike and attempts to do his will. Spike will return to Sunnydale in Season Four, during which he will be captured by the Initiative ("The Initiative" 4.7). Although he escapes, he learns that Initiative scientists have implanted a chip in his brain (see Chapter 5) which renders him unable to harm a human being. Spike's depression returns as does his tendency to alcohol abuse. It is only when Spike realizes that he can hurt demons that his depression begins to clear, and he does not drink quite as much ("Doomed" 4.11).

Played for comic relief, Spike's alcohol abuse occurs following periods of what psychologists would diagnose as depression. As a matter of fact, the three most commonly diagnosed mental disorders in the United States and Canada are anxiety, depression, and substance abuse (NIMH). Women are more likely than men to receive a diagnosis of depression, and men are more likely than women to receive a diagnosis of substance abuse (NIMH). Nevertheless some clinicians believe that men who abuse alcohol and other drugs are actually experiencing depression and anxiety (NIMH). Rather than admit the latter problems, men are likely to "treat" their depression in ways that are socially sanctioned, like working too much or abusing drugs (NIMH). Giles, for example, abuses alcohol throughout Season Four. He loses his sense of identity and sense of purpose, beginning with his dismissal from the Watchers' Council ("Helpless" 3.12), which is followed by the destruction of high school (and, hence, his library) ("Graduation Day" [Part 2 of 2] 3.22), and culminates with Buffy's "crush" on Professor Walsh in Season Four. Giles' use of alcohol dulls his senses and renders him less able to discern what is happening around him. For example, he gets so drunk when out with Ethan Rayne one night, that he is unaware of the fact that Rayne casts a spell on him, turning him into a demon that is almost killed by Buffy ("A New Man" 4.12). In addition, we can argue that Spike is attempting to medicate himself through his use of alcohol. The alcohol would dull the pain of losing Dru and then Buffy. It would also dull the pain of losing the only identity that he has had over a hundred years or so— that of a stone-cold killer, one who knows just how far one has to go to hear the girls cry before you kill them.

Unlike Spike, Buffy cannot handle her alcohol. Visiting him in his crypt one night, the two get drunk, or at least Buffy does ("Life Serial" 6.5). She is thoroughly depressed by her life, having been summoned from heaven by her well-meaning, but selfish, friends. Only Spike knows how badly Buffy feels about her life, and she is actually horrified to find that she is becoming increasingly attracted to him. Although the two do begin a sexual relationship that eventually develops into friendship (see Chapter 2), Buffy does not continue to drink alcohol.

Other examples of the negative consequences of drug use in *Buffy* occur in the episodes "Go Fish," "Band Candy," "Beer Bad," and various Season Four and Five episodes involving Riley Finn and the other Initiative commandos. Both "Band Candy" (3.6) and "Beer Bad" (4.5) also involve the use of magick. "Go Fish" features one of the fans' favorite *Buffy* scenes: Xander in a very small swimsuit. Apparently the only sports team at Sunnydale High School that is consistently good is the swim team. Unfortunately, something is not quite right with these young men, and Xander joins the team in order to learn what it is.[6] He discovers that the team's coach has developed a drug that enhances the team members' ability to swim. Unfortunately, it does so by altering their DNA, eventually turning them into fish.

The plot of "Band Candy" centers on yet another demonic tribute, in this case the sacrifice of four newborn babies to the demon Lurconis. The candy causes any adults who eat it to revert to their adolescent selves. Thus preoccupied, the adults do not notice that anything strange is happening in town (although, arguably, very few adults seem to notice the high death rate in Sunnydale). Whether something has been added to the chocolate bars or whether Ethan Rayne has put a spell on the candy is not quite clear; however, Sunnydale's adults clearly lose their inhibitions and act irresponsibly. Giles reverts to his "Ripper" persona, smoking cigarettes, stealing a coat for Joyce, and beating up a police officer. Joyce drinks liquor and flirts outrageously with Giles. They eventually have sex, not once but twice, and apparently on top of a police car! Just as the episode "Reptile Boy" (2.5) warned of the dangers inherent in college fraternities, the episode "Beer Bad" warned of the consequences of alcohol overindulgence. Buffy, still smarting from her one-night stand with Parker, gets drunk with four college men while Xander looks on helplessly. Reeling from the hangover following the first night of drinking, Buffy goes back to the bar and drinks more. Xander realizes that someone has been tampering with the beer: it makes those who drink it revert to a Neanderthal state (which just might be an insult to Neanderthals). The young men who have been drinking the beer become increasingly barbaric, chasing women, and getting into fights. The twin morals — that drinking beer and having casual sex are bad — are not metaphorical at all in this episode. In Buffy's case she has now had sex with two men in her young life. The first guy turned into a monster literally after having sex with her. The second guy was just a cad, looking to score with the new girls on campus. It is a terrible fact that first-year college girls are referred to as "fresh meat,"[7] and Parker is just the type who would do so.

Drugs also figure rather prominently in episodes from Seasons Four and Five when Riley and his fellow soldiers learn that they have been fed drugs by Dr. Walsh ("Goodbye Iowa" 4.15). These drugs, probably comparable to anabolic steroids, are designed to make the soldiers stronger and tougher than the average human, in order to better prepare the soldiers for the work they must do in the fight against the forces of darkness. However, much like anabolic steroids, these drugs have negative consequences for Riley, the most notable being cardiac arrhythmia. As a matter of fact, Riley's arrhythmia becomes so dangerous he must undergo emergency surgery ("Out of My Mind" 5.4). It is in this episode that we begin to learn that Riley is not actually happy that his girlfriend is stronger than he is, and more capable of fighting. Although attracted to Buffy because of her strength and determination, when it comes down to it, Riley cannot handle that strength and determination and betrays her trust and love (see Chapter 2).

Two other examples of drug use in the Buffyverse should be mentioned. The first involves using a drug to control someone else, in this case, Buffy. On her 18th birthday Buffy must face a test called the "Cruciamentum" which will determine if she really has what it takes to be a Slayer ("Helpless" 3.12). Unbeknownst to Buffy, Giles injects her with drugs that will eliminate her Slayer powers; these drugs include muscle relaxants and epinephrine (i.e., adrenaline) antagonists. The adrenal hormone epinephrine aids the body in its reaction to stressors in the environment, increasing heart rate and blood pressure among other things, which prepare the body for "fight or flight." Obviously, muscles cannot be relaxed when their power is needed, like when one needs to stake a murderous vampire.

A final example of drug use in the Buffyverse occurs in the third season episode "Beauty and the Beasts" (3.4). A young man named Pete, who doubts his ability to control his girlfriend Debbie, develops a potion/drug that turns him into a more masculine but brutish man à la Robert Louis Stevenson's Mr. Hyde. The potion increases his violent tendencies and Pete hits Debbie, after which he begs for forgiveness (see Chapter 3). Like an idiot she forgives him, and his violence escalates to the point where he need only get angry and the transformation will occur. Pete eventually kills Debbie and tries to kill Buffy, but Angel kills him instead.

Drug Use in the Angelverse

Joss Whedon has stated that Angel has alcoholic roots; he is one step away from slipping back and becoming a "drunk" again (*Angel* DVD Special Features). Thus, one could argue that whereas the magick is the addiction for Willow, the vampirism is the addiction for Angel. He is able to handle the cravings because that is what he has learned to do. Once Angel regains his soul and develops a conscience as well (see Chapter 1), he slowly learns how to control the craving for blood and violence.

As with many drugs of abuse, the street trade can be dangerous. Angel learns just how dangerous when he discovers that Kate Lockley's father is working with a gang of demons who sell drugs to other demons, the Kwaini, who are generally peaceful ("The Prodigal" 1.15). The drug is similar to phencyclidine (PCP), which was developed as a surgical anesthetic and generally produces a feeling of being "out-of-body." Effects at low doses are similar to alcohol intoxication. This drug is highly addictive and produces multiple effects, from poor muscle coordination to suicidal and homicidal behavior. In the Kwaini the drug apparently causes their adrenal glands to grow, increasing their need for the drug as well. The gland, in turn, apparently becomes quite desirable, with Kwaini adrenal glands fetching a high price on the black market.

Later in Season One, Angel is approached by a Hollywood starlet named

Rebecca Lowell who wants to hire Angel Investigations to protect her from a stalker. In actuality the starlet knows perfectly well what Angel is and wishes to become a vampire as well, so that she will never grow old ("Eternity" 1.17). In order to facilitate Angel's agreement to turn her, she drugs him, placing a bliss-inducing tranquilizer named Doximal into his champagne. Lowell's plan is that Angel will experience a moment of pure happiness and transform into Angelus, which he does, although Cordelia and Wesley are on hand to ensure that he does not remain that way or vamp Rebecca. Too bad the writer of this episode did not read up on Doximal; she might have learned that it is not available for sale in the U.S. and it is not a tranquilizer at all. Rather, this drug is a broad-spectrum antibiotic, used for the treatment of bacterial infections. It is unlikely to make anyone euphoric unless they are happy to have gotten rid of an infection.

The last instance of drug abuse in the Angelverse I will discuss concerns Kate Lockley's self-induced overdose ("Reprise" 2.15) and subsequent rescue ("Epiphany" 2.16). Kate is devastated following her father's death. All she has ever wanted was his approval, which is one of the reasons that she joined the police force, to be just like him. However, Trevor Lockley is not an easy man to know and he finds it difficult to discuss his feelings with his daughter. This inability to share feelings with another person is characteristic of most of the relationships on *Angel* (see Chapter 2). Following her dismissal from the force, Lockley returns to her apartment in despair. She removes a pill bottle from her medicine cabinet and washes the pills down with alcohol. One of her last acts is to phone Angel, who arrives the next day, but still in time to save Lockley. It is apparent that Angel is meant to save Lockley, as he is able to enter her apartment even though she has never invited him in. Given that Lockley pretty much disappears from the series after this indicates that the Powers That Be meant for Angel's rescue of Kate to awaken him from the blackness in which he has been enveloped throughout Season Two. It apparently works, as Angel returns to his former office and asks Wesley, Cordelia, and Gunn to let him come to work *with* them.

Drug Use in the 'Verse

Drug use figured prominently in both *Firefly* and *Serenity*. As mentioned in Chapter 5, Simon thinks that River is suffering from paranoid schizophrenia, which is characterized by auditory hallucinations, such as hearing voices, and delusions, such as believing a co-worker wants to poison you, along with anger and violence (DSM-IV-TR).[8] In my opinion she actually exhibits the symptoms of hebephrenic schizophrenia (see Note 3, Chapter 5). Until Simon is able to take River to the planet Ariel ("Ariel" 1.9) for a neural scan he treats her as if she is schizophrenic, and apparently in the 26th century (as in our own), the standard treatment is medication. If River were schizophrenic then she would be treated with an antipsychotic drug, of the class major tranquilizer. These drugs work by blocking the action of dopamine at their receptor sites in the brain. The astute observer would note that Simon keeps trying different drugs on River; the side-effects she experiences, such as nausea and vomiting, are typical of antipsychotic medications. Also, these medications take several weeks before blood concentrations of the drug reach therapeutic efficacy. Finding the correct drug for any given patient is a time-consuming process, and it should not be surprising to learn that many patients give up in the attempt to find a drug that will manage their symptoms without producing unpleasant side effects.

Simon learns the truth about the Alliance's experimentation on River when he is able to scan her on Ariel. After this scan, Simon continues to try various pharmaceutical treatments on River. At this point, I would speculate that he is attempting to control the fear and anxiety that she is experiencing, using antidepressant drugs or antianxiety drugs of the class minor tranquilizer. Antidepressants work by enhancing the action of the neurotransmitters serotonin or norepinephrine or both. Antianxiety drugs work by enhancing the action of the neurotransmitter gamma-amino-butyric acid (GABA), which is the major inhibitory neurotransmitter in the brain. Antianxiety drugs have the disadvantage of producing tolerance and dependence in humans; that is, they are addictive. They may also have dangerous side effects. Antidepressant drugs are not addictive, but their therapeutic effects may take four to six weeks to develop.

The evidence of River's psychic ability was visible as early as "The Train Job," although the crew did not understand that most of what she said referred to future events. They understood that she was afraid, but they did not realize that her fear was real. River was not suffering from post-traumatic stress for what she experienced at the hands of Alliance scientists. She was experiencing the very real fear of the fact that the Alliance wanted her back and was willing to do whatever it took to get her. She was also experiencing the fear of what had happened on Miranda, her fear of falling asleep being a very real manifestation of the millions of people on that planet who just "laid down and died" (*Serenity*).

Another instance of possible drug use on *Firefly* concerned the mysterious contents of Inara's syringe ("Serenity" 1.1). Many have speculated over this and Whedon has refused to answer questions about it (*Firefly*, Vol. Two). Some speculate that Inara has a mysterious illness and the syringe's contents are medicine. Some speculate that the contents confer some type of youthfulness to her.[9] Both of these are perfectly reasonable explanations and pique our interest about Inara's past and the mystery behind why she left her former post to take up residence aboard Serenity.[10] Nevertheless, another very reasonable explanation for the syringe is that Inara is living on the fringe of the 'verse and flirting closely with Reaver space. Just as some might carry a weapon with them as insurance "just in case," Inara may carry a syringe filled with poison to prevent a fate worse than death — what could be worse than being raped, eaten, and killed, in whichever order such events might occur?

Introduced in his short-lived series *Firefly*, the Reavers were the bogeymen of the 'verse. Discussions of their actions (raping, killing, and eating people) terrify even battle-hardened soldiers (*Serenity*). Their origins were mysterious; some claimed that they were once men who had seen the edge of space and gone mad. It was not until *Firefly*'s sequel motion picture that Whedon gave us an explanation of the Reavers' "birth." Reavers were born from the Alliance's desire to create a perfect human and a perfect world. On a world named Miranda, located on the edge of space, colonists were exposed to an air-borne drug called Pax (Latin for peace, ironically), G-32 Paxilon Hydroclorate [sic], which

> was supposed to calm the population. Make a peaceful ... it worked. The people here stopped fighting. And then they stopped everything else. They stopped going to work, stopped breeding, talking ... eating ... [T]hey all just let themselves die ... [A]bout a tenth of a percent of the population had the opposite reaction to the Pax. Their aggressor response increased ... beyond madness. They've become ... they've killed most of us ... not just killed, they've done ... things [Whedon 128–129].

Once Mal Reynolds learns that it was the Alliance at the root of the Reavers' madness, he is determined to broadcast the news to the other worlds of the 'verse. Mal believes that the Alliance will try again, one day, and he is of the opinion that people should have control of their own minds and their own destinies. The Reavers show the extreme to which "meddling" can go and serve as another statement on the horror than can ensue when technology runs amuck (Rabb and Richardson).

Both Rabb and Richardson and Bussolini note the similarity between the Pax used on the population of Miranda and the antidepressant Paxil which is used in large quantities in contemporary American society. As mentioned earlier, use of antidepressants is not a panacea. Not all clinically depressed patients will respond to these drugs, and some of their side effects can be life threatening. The side effects of Paxil and other antidepressants can be suicidal ideation, hyperactivity, sleep disturbances, loss of libido, anger, aggression, and impulsivity. On a more cautionary note, pharmaceutical companies rely more and more on out-sourcing the clinical trials that must be conducted on the safety and efficacy of their drugs prior to FDA approval. Some scientists and physicians question the reliability of the data obtained from such out-sourcing.[11] One final note about this issue. While I am not suggesting that we blame people for their problems, we must note that people are sometimes complicit in their victimization. People want a quick fix for their problems and often look to drugs to provide that quick fix. Need to lose weight? Take a drug. Need to feel better about yourself? Take a drug. The similarities between Paxil and other antidepressant drugs and Huxley's soma are striking.

Drug Use on Dollhouse

Whedon's newest series, *Dollhouse*, also explored drugs, but in this case, their effects upon individual members of the titular collective rather than the group as a whole. The episode "The Target" (1.2) concerned using a drug to render the Active Echo defenseless. She is engaged by an apparently wealthy young man named Richard. After a day of outdoor adventures coupled with sexual pleasure, Richard evicts Echo from their campsite and tells her that she is his prey. We are led to believe that Richard plans to hunt and then kill Echo from the remarks he makes about how "she" will be a worthy target because a nameless "he" told Richard so. To facilitate his hunt, Richard—in a very unsportsmanlike fashion—drugs the water that Echo finds in a Ranger's cabin. Whatever the drug is, her actions indicate that it is some type of hallucinogen. As the drug enters her system she gradually begins to remember previous imprints and those memories help her escape from, and eventually kill, Richard. The results of the drug's actions are to break down the bonds that have apparently kept her primary memories from interfering with her imprints (see Chapter 6). Hallucinogens are believed to result in a "mind expansion," which is one reason that they were so popular during the 1960s, a decade dedicated to "turning on, tuning in, and dropping out."[12] This belief is also the reason why some indigenous peoples in various countries around the world use psychoactive drugs in their religious practices

(Fuller). Although never discussed with respect to *Dollhouse*, it is possible that Whedon chose to have Echo drugged with a hallucinogen because these drugs would seem to be the logical ones to release inhibitions and serve as mind-enhancers/expanders. He explored this idea further in a later episode.

"Echoes" (1.7) centers on a drug designated N7316 created by the Rossum Corporation, which they say is still in its experimental stages. N7316 is a memory drug that works by breaking down natural inhibitions in the hippocampus in order to "awaken" the so-called sleeping parts of the brain.[13] Phase I intake produces giddiness and light hallucinations, making it euphorigenic. Phase II intake results in a complete loss of impulse control. The drug supposedly acts by attacking the inhibitory centers in the hippocampus, breaking down repressed memory blocks. This causes the user to experience a memory glitch, which is especially troubling when the Actives, particularly Echo, begin recovering their memories of life before the Dollhouse. Luckily for the Actives' keepers the drug wears off, or does it? By producing a tranquilizing effect in its users, the N7316 could have many possible advantages, mind control being the most obvious one. Blocking memories would be an effective method of mind control, a theme explored in many SFF novels and films, including *The Island*, *The Matrix*, and *Dark City*.

The last example[14] of drug use in *Dollhouse* that I will mention involves Priya/Sierra. As discussed in Chapter 3, Priya was placed in servitude to the Rossum Corporation by a violent suitor named Nolan. When she rejected his advances, Nolan imprisoned Priya in a mental hospital and began giving her drugs to make her delusional. When Topher Brink, the Dollhouse's programmer, went to the hospital to recruit Priya, he believed that her comments about Nolan drugging her were simply a manifestation of the paranoid schizophrenia with which she had been diagnosed. Topher maps Priya's brain upon her entry into the Dollhouse, and he believes the scans that indicate she is schizophrenic are real. It is only later, in the episode "Belonging" (2.4) that Topher realizes he was wrong, and that the scans were actually produced by the variety of drugs with which Nolan was injecting Priya. As discussed earlier, drugs have a variety of effects depending upon the drug in question and their site of action in the brain. It is certainly possible for someone to display the symptoms of certain psychological disorders after receiving a drug injection. For example, people who abuse amphetamines will eventually develop "amphetamine psychosis," exhibiting symptoms very similar to paranoid schizophrenia. Because of their effects on the brain physiologically it is possible that these effects will be permanent.

Conclusion

Whedon's use of drugs in *Buffy*, *Angel*, *Firefly* and *Serenity*, and *Dollhouse* serve to illustrate the myriad ways in which these agents can serve as methods of mind control. The programs and drugs presented herein ranged from those used to control individual beings to those used to control entire populations of unsuspecting beings. Given the ways in which drugs are used and abused in contemporary U.S. society, it is no wonder that the drugs have found their way into popular culture. Silverberg said that "science fiction is more often a reflection of existing [social] trends than a prediction of trends to come" (vi). The upsurge in drug use that he described in 1974 was "precisely mirrored by the upsurge in use of such themes in science fiction" (vi). Silverberg believed that "science fiction is as much a guide to where we are as it is a vision of where we are going" (vi), which is why so many SFF programs can be examined for their ability to reflect issues that currently affect our lives, including drug use and abuse.

Silverberg proposed that drugs used in SFF could be divided into several categories based upon their actions on the user. Drugs used in the four Whedon series in question fit into these categories as well as the seven pharmacological classes currently used to classify psychoactive drugs. Therapeutic drugs such as anxiolytics, antidepressants, and antipsychotics apparently played a role in controlling the behavior of several characters, most notably River Tam in *Firefly* and *Serenity*. Drugs with hallucinogenic properties were administered to characters as diverse as Jayne Cobb (*Firefly*) and Echo (*Dollhouse*). Psychomotor stimulants, which include the most widely used drug in the world (caffeine), also figured in each series, as did sedative-hypnotics such as alcohol. Although all of the psychoactive drugs have therapeutic uses,[15] several of them can be abused, and we did observe characters that appeared to have problems with their use, such as Spike and Giles and their abuse of alcohol.

In conclusion, psychoactive drugs have many uses, in medicine, psychiatry, and psychology. They are not just for inducing pleasure or reducing pain. No one can deny that these drugs have alleviated the sufferings of countless people diagnosed with various mental disorders. Indeed psychoactive drugs revolutionized the care of patients confined to mental institutions in the middle of the 20th century. Nevertheless these drugs are powerful chemicals; their use may result in both tolerance and dependence, and their side effects can be dangerous. Because of the potential for abuse, many of these drugs are sold on the black market. Unfortunately, some are also sold in our schools. A quite lucrative, but illegal and illicit, industry has grown from the sale of both legal and illegal psychoactive substances. As Whedon's and others' work illustrate, those who control access to drugs needed by other beings can be said to have control over that being, and that control can be dangerous not only to the individual, but to society as well.

CHAPTER 8

Other Methods of Control[1]

Couldn't be Reavers. Wasn't Reavers. Reavers don't leave no sur-
vivors.— Jayne, "Bushwhacked" [*Firefly* 1.3]

If they take the ship, they'll rape us to death, eat our flesh, and sew our
skins into their clothing. And, if we're very, very lucky, they'll do it in
that order.— Zoe, "Serenity" [*Firefly* 1.1]

People may exert control over each other using a variety of techniques.
Some of these include material means, such as administering drugs or sub-
jecting someone to surgical or mental manipulations. Other methods can be
more psychological, like giving or withholding love, or threatening or inducing violence. Given the nature of the Whedonverses some of these methods
are more supernatural in agency, such as using magick to effect control over
others' actions, beliefs, memories, et cetera. The preceding chapters explored
a number of ways in which characters in four Whedon series exerted control
over each other and the other beings, human and otherwise, with which
they came into contact. This last chapter will provide a sampling of other
ways in which power can be wielded in order to exert control not only over
others, but upon one's self as well. Examples of these types of power are the
use of symbols, the induction of fear, the expression and repression of knowledge, and the creation of family.

Using Symbols to Exert Control

A symbol is "something that represents something else by association,
resemblance, or convention, especially a material object used to represent
something invisible."[2] Jewelry and clothing are symbolic in the Whedon-

verses, as are religious symbols in both *Buffy* and *Angel*. The most obvious of the religious symbols is the cross. Buffy wears a cross in a number of episodes, and that she does so is interesting considering the fact that she is not presented as very religious. This would serve to indicate that the symbol has the power rather than the individual possessing the symbol. One could then argue that the demon possessing the vampire is repelled by what the cross stands for. For example, the cross is symbolic of Protestantism and indicates that a man, Jesus of Nazareth,[3] was crucified, buried, and rose from the dead. That is, the cross is empty because Jesus rose from the dead and ascended into Heaven. According to Protestants, Jesus' death fulfilled Biblical prophecy that a Messiah would return to Earth and intercede with God, expunging the sins of mankind. The crucifix, the cross with the figure of Jesus imposed, is symbolic of Catholicism and reminds the faithful that Jesus of Nazareth was crucified, that he died for their sins. Other symbols of Christianity, such as holy water, are also displayed and used in *Buffy* and *Angel*.

The fact that symbols of other religions do not serve to repel vampires is never explained. For example, the Star of David, the symbol of Judaism, does not repel vampires, even though Jesus of Nazareth was a Jew. The most interesting explanation I have ever seen with respect to this issue was presented in Patrick Lussier's film *Dracula 2000*. We learn in this film that Dracula's sin was treachery. Dracula, in actuality, is Judas Iscariot, whose actions resulted in Jesus' death at the hands of the Romans. Judas is doomed to eternal life and torment for his sin, hence his fear of Christian symbols. These symbols serve to remind Dracula/Judas that it was his actions that condemned Jesus.

Apparently, Whedon only chose certain aspects of Stoker's *Dracula* to include in the Buffy and Angelverses rather than all of them. For example, Whedon's vampires can engage in sexual intercourse. They can eat solid food and drink liquids other than blood. They do not sleep and can be up and about in daylight, although direct sunlight does harm them. Of course Whedon's writers did frequently forget previous plot lines and "canon" and make mistakes with respect to vampire lore. The most obvious example had to do with how to make a vampire. In some episodes it appears that a vampire only needed to kill a human and the human would come back as a vampire. This would be the most obvious explanation for the sheer number of vampires in Sunnydale. In other episodes the plot indicates that there was more involved, with a vampire having to decide whether or not he or she would sire another vampire. According to Buffy, "To make you a vampire they have to suck your blood. And then you have to suck their blood. It's like a whole big sucking thing" ("Welcome to the Hellmouth" 1.1).

Another major symbol on *Buffy* is the claddagh ring.[4] This ring, legend has it, was crafted by a young man named Richard Joyce from County Galway Ireland (which just so happens to be where Liam [Angel's pre-vampire persona] is from). Joyce was sold into slavery and learned metalwork while enslaved. Eventually freed, he returned to Ireland to find his sweetheart awaiting his return. They married and lived happily ever after. The ring itself contains three parts: two hands holding a centrally located heart with a crown resting atop the heart. The two hands symbolize friendship, the heart stands for eternal love, and the crown symbolizes fidelity and loyalty; some say it also honors King William III who had negotiated with the Moors for the return of the slaves. Angel gives Buffy a claddagh to symbolize their love for each other.

Obviously, the most potent symbol on *Buffy* and *Angel* is the stake. Unlike the vampires depicted in the Universal and Hammer Studios films, vampires in the Buffy and Angelverses can be killed easily enough. All it takes is a stake through the heart and the vampire turns to dust. Buffy never leaves home without a stake, apparently. She always seems to have one secreted somewhere on her person.[5] Traditional vampire lore stated that vampires could only be destroyed if they were staked and decapitated. Other traditions stated that the vampire had to have its heart removed as well. Driving a stake through a vampire's heart would, thus, combine two of the methods by which a vampire can be destroyed. The stake through the heart also serves a double purpose: not only does the vampire die, but the soul or the demon inhabiting the vampire can escape from the body as well (Mascetti 223) presumably to find its eternal rest. Vampires on *Buffy* and *Angel* immediately turn to dust whenever they are staked, although technically we should state that the *body* turns to dust and the demon inhabiting the body returns to the Hell dimension from whence it came, otherwise how could we explain Darla's return from the "dead" ("To Shanshu in L.A." *Angel* 1.22)? When Darla is summoned by the demon priest, Vocah, how is it that she returns in her original body?[6]

Items of clothing are symbolic in the Whedonverses, such as Spike's leather duster, but I will only discuss a few examples from *Firefly*. The brown coats that Mal and Zoe wear are very potent symbols, indicating their service in the War for Independence. Although the war has been over for a number of years, the fact that they continue to wear the coats reminds those with whom they come into contact about their history. Pride in one's uniform or other items of clothing would be much like in our own time when men and women wear symbols of their military service, such as camouflage gear, hats, boots, et cetera, even after said service is over. Of course, not everyone will appreciate the statement that Mal and Zoe make with respect to their brown coats, as in "The Train Job" (1.2) when they get into a fight because they were wearing their brown coats on Unification Day.

Another item that may be symbolic is Zoe's necklace. Some have speculated that it could be a shoelace from the boots that she wore in the war (*Firefly* Vol. One).[7] Others have speculated that the string is symbolic of her marriage to Wash (Commentary to "Shindig" 1.4). Zoe is not the type to wear a wedding band. Indeed in their century husbands and wives may no longer wear such jewelry. It is possible that gold is far too expensive to display on one's appendages—you might have your finger chopped off or be killed for such sentimentality. However, Zoe is wearing the necklace in the episode "Out of Gas" (1.8), before she meets Wash, suggesting that the former explanation is closer to the truth. Although one could argue that clothing, such as brown coats and necklaces, do not control one's actions, these objects do have power over their wearers: the power of sentiment and nostalgia, for lost youth, lost ideals, and a simpler time of life.

Another example of clothing as symbolic would be Inara's elaborate and richly colored costumes which indicate her position as a Companion. Inara's costumes are generally red or gold as are the furnishings of her shuttle and her boudoir in *Serenity*. Although never explained, it is possible that these are Companion Guild colors and would be understood as such by the population in general, instantly notifying anyone in her presence that she is a Companion. Much as in contemporary American society, red and gold symbolize richness and sensuality,[8] characteristics one would expect to find in a Companion. As Whedon indicates in *Serenity: the Official Visual Companion*, Inara represents the Alliance's positive features, including "enlightenment, education, self-possession, [and] feminism" (11), which explains some of the tension between Inara and Mal.

Symbols, by their very definition, serve to remind us of something else, something not present or visible, yet their power over us cannot be denied, else why would we use them? In the Whedonverses various symbols exert power over the characters because these symbols have meaning for the character beyond the actual meaning of the object. For instance, a cross is simply two pieces of wood or metal placed at right angles to each other, forming the letter "t." However, to Christians it has the meaning conferred upon it by what it represents, the death of the man considered to be the source of their faith. A piece of jewelry is simply some item of adornment made of metal usually and sometimes containing precious stones. However, jewelry has no meaning other than what it signifies to its owner: friendship, love, marriage, anniversaries, birthdays, et cetera. Likewise with clothing which has the practical purpose of keeping the wearer warm and covering his or her nakedness. These symbols have power over us because of their significance; we allow this power because of what the symbols represent to us and how we feel about them. We can love and cherish the symbol, as in "I love my spouse and my wedding ring symbolizes that love." We can also hate or fear the symbol, as in "That swastika is symbolic of the Nazis and reminds me of the millions of people killed in its name."

Using Fear to Exert Control

Fear is an emotion, a "feeling of agitation and anxiety caused by the presence or imminence of danger."[9] Paul Ekman considers it to be one of the six basic emotions that can be recognized reliably from facial expressions. These six are anger, surprise, disgust, happiness, fear, and sadness. Research data indicate that people living in 37 different countries on five continents recognize the six basic emotions when presented with photographs of faces expressing each emotion.

Although one would expect that the characters on *Buffy* and *Angel* experience fear by virtue of their fight against the forces of darkness, these characters experience fear for other reasons as well. Buffy fears the loss of her friends and family, as does Angel. For instance, Buffy worries about Dawn's growing crush on Spike and whether Spike can be trusted with her. She fears that Social Services will take Dawn away following their mother's death. Xander is afraid that he will become abusive, just like his father, and subject a wife and potential children to the same kind of life he has led. Willow fears that she will not be able to control herself following the events that occur after Tara's death.

Fear was easy to observe in the 'verse. Living on the fringes of society would produce fear. People would fear for their families: would there be enough to eat, could you provide them with the resources necessary to sustain a reasonable life, could you keep them safe from villains? We learn very early that the Reavers are the bogeymen of the 'verse. Everyone is afraid of them; apparently they rape, eat, and kill their victims— in that order ("Serenity" 1.1). Of course, if the Reavers kill their victims, then how does anyone know what they do? Reavers figure prominently in *Serenity* (see Chapter 7), but are introduced in *Firefly*. In "Bushwhacked" (1.3) the crew actually finds a survivor of a Reaver attack. Mal knows, before the others, that the young survivor will not be able to live with the memories of the attack, and, in a gross parody of the old saying "If you can't beat 'em, join 'em," the boy will mutilate his body in an attempt to become a Reaver. The possibility of encountering Reavers is real enough that most spaceships are either armed against the possibility or steer well clear of Reaver space. A number of fans have speculated upon Inara's syringe.[10] She reaches for it in the pilot episode "Serenity" (1.1) after the ship encounters Reavers while trying to elude the Alliance. Mal realizes that Serenity is unlikely to outrun the Reavers should they be attacked. It makes perfect sense to me, and Occam is generally correct about the simplest explanation being the best, that, if one lived with the possibility of a Reaver attack, one might keep poison close at hand for an easier death than the one predicted by the scary stories about these bogeymen.

Dollhouse characters also feel fear. Most everyone in the Los Angeles Dollhouse fears Alpha, the Active who downloads his Dollhouse imprints to create a composite personality. Following that event, Alpha escapes from the Dollhouse but not before slashing Whiskey's face and killing several of the employees, including the original Dr. Saunders (see Chapter 3). Alpha gradually learns to integrate the various personalities into one; however, DeWitt, Topher, and Whiskey, among others, fear that Alpha will return and finish what he started. Several of the Actives are fearful of discovering who they were prior to their entrance into the Dollhouse. Whiskey wonders what will happen to her if her original personality returns; Echo wonders the same thing about Caroline. And, Echo is frightened of what the Rossum Corporation's true intentions are with respect to the imprinting technology, a fear that is all too real given the events that happen at the end of Season Two when the entire population is subjected to enslavement at the hands of a wealthy few. The knowledge that Echo gains from her imprints helps her in the fight to reclaim the world.

Events that occurred in the Whedonverses awakened fear in its inhabitants. In both the Buffy and Angelverses fear could be inspired by natural sources, such as the fear of whether a loved one was seriously ill; where the money would come from to pay the bills; whether people really liked you; whether you turn out like your parents; would the "dark side" claim your soul again. Fear could also come from supernatural sources, such as whether a vampire could enter your home uninvited; would the visions have deleterious effects on your health; would you ever be able to forgive yourself for your past transgressions. The fear occurring on *Firefly* and *Dollhouse* came from natural sources only, such as unscrupulous businesspeople, bandits and thieves, the government, and powerful corporations with secret agendas. Regardless of source, the fear felt by the various characters was real and that motivated each to plan and execute a strategy to control their fear, as best they could. They were not always successful, of course, but it was not generally from a lack of trying. One successful strategy was forming bonds with others who felt similarly. Another was collecting as much information about the source as possible.

Controlling Knowledge and Information

Controlling the amount and type of information others receive is one way of achieving and maintaining power. It is not surprising, then, that most revolutions begin by limiting access to information. Whedon explored this issue in all four of the series discussed herein, with each series illustrating the issue in different ways.

Knowledge was power in the Buffy and Angelverses. It was the key to vanquishing the powers of darkness. Although various people have laughed over the misuse of Sunnydale High School's library,[11] Rupert Giles amassed a vast collection of esoteric tomes with the express purpose of helping Buffy in her quest to "fight the forces." Although Buffy patrols the streets of Sunnydale after dark, she needs help to fight demons intent upon mischief, hence the Scooby gang. Buffy and the gang frequently encounter unknown demons, in which case they have to do research to determine the type of demon they have encountered, its strengths and weaknesses, and most important of all, how to kill it and return it to Hell.

To situate Buffy and the other Scoobies in the modern day, the internet was also used as a source of information, with Willow being the science nerd ("Prophecy Girl" 1.12) and computer geek able to understand all things in the chemistry and biology labs as well as in cyberspace.[12] Willow was quite adept at hacking into places where the typical high school student does not tread: police records, Sunnydale city plans, the morgue, et cetera. As a matter of fact, Willow even notes that she is "probably the only girl in school who has the Coroner's Office bookmarked as a 'favorite place'" ("Some Assembly Required" 2.2). The fact that research is important to Buffy's mission certainly reinforces the saying that "knowledge is power."[13]

Although interested in ridding the world of evil, Angel's mission is somewhat different than Buffy's. In Angel's world, demons are not always evil, just as in Buffy's not all vampires are bad.[14] Sometimes they are in need of help and Angel Investigations is perfectly willing to help all who are helpless ("City Of" 1.1). Nevertheless, Angel and his team need information, and they look to Wesley to provide them with that information. Trained as a Watcher, just like Rupert Giles (but with much less experience in the field when we meet him in Buffy[15]), Wesley's knowledge of demonology is especially helpful in their mission. I think it is rather interesting that Cordelia becomes increasingly adept at using the computer as *Angel* progresses. Thus, on *Buffy* and *Angel*, Whedon has two female characters serve as the computer nerds (Willow and Cordy, respectively), a reversal of the gender stereotype of the male computer geek.[16]

Unlike Buffy, Angel has sources of information other than ancient tomes and dubious internet sites. During Seasons One and Two, Angel relies on a police detective named Kate Lockley for information about his various cases. Theirs is an uneasy relationship because, despite the sexual attraction,[17] she knows that there is something not quite right with Angel. She eventually discovers his secret and is horrified ("Somnambulist" 1.11), especially when she believes that he killed her father ("The Prodigal" 1.15). She is completely confused when Angel is able to rescue her from a suicide attempt. She has never invited him into her apartment and yet he is able to enter it in order to save her life ("Reprise" [Part 1 of 2] 2.15), apparently at the behest of the Powers That Be.

Angel also gets information from Brother and Sister Oracles who are able to commune with the Powers That Be. The Oracles are willing to help Angel occasionally in exchange for some money or other trinkets ("I Will Remember You" 1.8). Unfortunately, like all Oracles, their information is often cryptic and, by the time it is deciphered, it is usually too late. It would also be too easy to get information that way, so the Oracles are killed to prevent Angel's reliance on them and the conduit they provide to the Powers That Be ("To Shanshu in L.A." 1.22).

Probably Angel's best source of information is Doyle's visions, which are transferred to Cordelia following Doyle's death ("Hero" 1.9). The visions provide Angel Investigations with enough information to help someone in need, although, much like the Oracles' often cryptic prophecies, the visions sometimes get mixed up in "translation." One such example occurred in the episode "I've Got You Under My Skin" (1.14). Angel and team convince a mother and father to let them exorcize their son Ryan, believing the child to be possessed by an Ethros demon. In actuality, the demon longed to escape from the psychopathic child. Although Angel mortally wounds the demon before learning the truth, he is able to save the boy's family from Ryan's attempt to kill them.

Angel relied upon a variety of sources of information to aid him in his work. Some of these sources were more reliable than others; some were downright unreliable, even false. Planting false information is a time-honored way of confusing one's enemies and misdirecting them away from the truth. An even more effective way of hiding the truth is to erase the information from the records, to render the information unavailable and inaccessible. This is the tactic used by the Alliance on *Firefly/Serenity*.

As discussed in chapters 5 and 6 the Alliance experimented upon the population residing on a planet named Miranda. In an attempt to create a better human being, one which would be less violent, Alliance scientists created a drug designed to tranquilize the population, with disastrous effects. The Alliance has hidden knowledge about this event. We learn in *Serenity* what happened: they were too successful. The population on Miranda was so tranquilized that they stopped all activity, including eating, and starved to death. Unfortunately, the drug, called Pax, had the opposite effect on some of the population, increasing their anger and rage. These people, eventually named Reavers, become exceedingly violent, killing those members of the population who have not already died. In addition, the Reavers practice particularly barbaric acts upon their victims and upon themselves. Apparently their rage is so great that they must violate their own flesh.

A young girl named River Tam has been subjected to various types of surgical and pharmaceutical manipulations at the hands of Alliance scientists. One of the effects of this experimentation is the creation, or unleashing of, psychic ability (see Chapter 5). One of her doctors is so intent upon reaping the glory of his work (and probably continuing to receive funding for the project) that he allows Alliance politicians to watch River in action. He may or may not be aware that River is psychic, but she learns the secret of Miranda when he allows "key Members of Parliament" to observe her. River vacillates between being a fragile and frail, mentally unstable, young woman unable to understand the knowledge she holds in her head, and being an incredibly strong and gifted fighter. As time passes after River's rescue from her prison, Serenity's crew becomes aware that River knows something damaging about the Alliance, and that is why the Alliance wants her so desperately. River is finally able to piece together enough information and stay coherent long enough to impart the knowledge to Captain Mal Reynolds. Once Mal learns the secret, he and the rest of Serenity's crew are determined to disseminate the information to the people inhabiting the worlds of the 'verse. Mal states quite clearly that he does not believe that the Alliance has the right to withhold information from the people, and he will broadcast the information about what happened on Miranda so that everyone will know. He is of the opinion that, although Alliance scientists failed in this attempt to create a better world, they will try again in the future. Mal fought a war so that he could have the freedom to make his own decisions. He does not believe that the Alliance has the right to control the information they present to the citizens of the 'verse. Such a view is mirrored in our time as people argue as to whether the government has the right to keep information from the public "for its own good."

One way to gain control over something is to learn what you can about it. To fight vampires you must consult the knowledge accumulated over the years about them by those who have been in contact with them. To fight a demon, you must learn what type of demon it is. To fight a government that is intent upon creating super weapons or mass tranquility, you first have to know about it. To keep people from stealing other people's memories, you must first learn how to regain your own. The various members of the Whedonverses were often hampered in their actions by their lack of knowledge about the events that were transpiring around them. This need meant that they were at the mercy of events with only one way to re-establish control: get the knowledge necessary to fight back. The knowledge needed came from a variety of sources and these sources were not always to be found in some esoteric tome or computer program. Sometimes the source needed was a person, someone who possessed knowledge, or strength, or kindness; someone to befriend, someone to love, someone to call family.

The Creation of Family

The traditional definition of a family would be a "fundamental social group in society typically consisting of one or two parents and their children." However, such a definition does not reflect the type of families created by Joss Whedon on the four series in question. Rather, family in the Whedonverses is more accurately defined as "two or more people who share goals and values, have long-term commitments to one another, and reside usually in the same dwelling place."[18] A number of people have analyzed the various Whedon series in terms of family (see for example Abbott; Battis; Koontz; Stafford; Stoy), so I will not go into great deal here. Suffice it to say that Whedon is aware of the changing demographics of the American population and understands that families in contemporary American society have become whatever works for the people involved. Parents in the Whedonverses are not as critically important as traditionally considered in today's society.[19] Indeed, parents in the Whedonverses are often disengaged from their children, or missing altogether. As such, a birth family may be "difficult and cruel ... [but] you have the power to create your own family. Your new family can be more important, more real, than the family you were born into" (Havens 74). And, this is what the various characters in the Whedonverses do: they construct their own families, which are much more important than the ones into which they were born.

I have already mentioned Willow's mother (see Chapter 2) and Xander's parents (see Chapter 3). The only other parent we encounter in the Buffy-verse is, of course, Buffy's mother. Joyce Summers appears to be a loving mother, but one who is distracted by the problem inherent in being a single mother — how to pay the bills. Women typically suffer financially following a divorce, although Joyce does not seem to. Nevertheless, her finances are not in good order considering what happens following her death, when there is not enough money left for Dawn and Buffy's expenses.

Joyce is also pretty clueless about her daughter's life. Buffy has had problems in the past, as recorded in the film *BtVS*. She has now relocated to Sunnydale in order to start over. Joyce does not seem to notice that her daughter is out every night (patrolling the streets of Sunnydale) and coming home with bloody clothes.[20] Buffy does not tell Joyce that she is the Slayer until the end of Season Two ("Becoming" [Part 2 of 2] 2.22). Joyce is unable to cope with that knowledge and tells Buffy not to come back home. Of course the two reconcile, but Joyce never quite understands Buffy's role as Slayer. She is also jealous of Giles.

Giles does understand Buffy's role and is able to provide her with the support necessary for the job. Giles grows to love Buffy over the course of the series and tries his best to be both Watcher and parent to the young woman whose own father no longer has time for her. Giles' feelings for Buffy eventually lead to his dismissal as her Watcher, although she refuses to abide by the Watchers' Council's decree. Buffy is instrumental in having Giles reinstated with the Council. Nevertheless, Giles becomes increasingly aware that Buffy relies upon him too much, especially after Joyce's death. His decision to leave Sunnydale and return to England will have tragic consequences for the Scoobies, but he will return to help set things right, just as a good daddy should.

If Giles serves as the father figure for Buffy's family, the other core members are Willow and Xander. Other people are occasionally allowed to join the family through their association with the core family members. Just as any family gains members when one of its sons or daughters marries, or become entangled with another (or loses them when the child divorces or disentangles); Buffy's family gains and loses members in the same fashion. Thus, at various times over the course of the Seven Seasons, the love interests of the core members are taken in and treated as family or lost. Indeed, in the episode "Family" (5.6), when Tara's father demands that she return home, Buffy tells Mr. Maclay that Tara will be staying with them, that Tara is now part of the Slayer's family. Even Spike becomes part of the Slayer's family after he falls in love with her and reclaims his soul. Thus, family in the Buffy-verse is constructed, with those who feel the bonds of love and friendship for one another building a relationship than can stand against, in their case, the forces of darkness.

Family in the Angelverse is also constructed, although the relationships that Angel and his gang build are not strong enough to stand against the darkness.[21] There are certain times when Wesley speaks of his parents, but the way in which he speaks informs us that theirs is not a good relationship. We learn nothing about Gunn's family other than that he has a sister who is vamped — he stakes her ("War Zone" 1.20). We do meet Fred's family a few times, and they appear to be very nice ("Fredless" 3.5), probably the only set of parents in all of the Whedonverses who are nice, with the possible exceptions of Jayne and Mal's mothers, and Joyce Summers. Angel's father was very disappointed in his wastrel son, Liam. Angelus kills his father and this, as Darla points out to him, affirms the father's low opinion of the son ("The Prodigal" 1.15). One could argue that Angel is not only trying to atone for the sins he committed as Liam and Angelus, of which matricide, patricide and fratricide are only a few, but he is also trying to prove his father wrong, which he can never do given that his father is long dead. Cordy's family, as we learned in *Buffy*, was quite wealthy, until her father was caught by the IRS and sent to prison for tax evasion ("The Prom," Buffy 3.20). Apparently, Cordy only thought of her father as a cash machine. She is more upset by the loss of her status than the fact that her father is in jail. Nevertheless, Cordy begins to change after joining Angel Investigations, especially once she begins receiving the visions that will allow her to help Angel in his mission of redemption. Cordy, although still her up-front and forthright self, also attempts to atone for her previous misdeeds, one of which was being a bully.

Firefly certainly illustrates the way in which a disparate group of people can come together and create a family. Dale Koontz provides a particularly lovely description of the crew as they sit around the table in the common space on Serenity. The various members of Mal's crew might, at first glance, seem too disparate to mesh into a family unit, but each member's strengths and weaknesses are complemented by others on the crew (and this is true in the Buffy and Angelverses as well). Mal certainly fits a parenting role as he is the one who provides for the members of his crew.[22] We do not learn anything about the families of the various crew members other than the Tams, whom Simon thinks are terrible parents because they refuse to believe that their daughter is in trouble (*Serenity*). Simon is the one who must rescue River and he is then the one who must keep her safe, until they meet Mal, that is, who takes them under his wing and makes them part of his crew. There is nothing that Mal will not do for his crew, his family.

Finally, there is *Dollhouse*. By no stretch of the imagination can we consider the characters of the Dollhouse a family, unless as a highly dysfunctional one. Rather I would state that the family created in *Dollhouse* only occurs after the Rossum Corporation loses the imprinting technology used in the various Dollhouses.[23] The imprinting tech is now being used upon the world's population, with those who have been imprinted programmed to kill those who have not ("Epitaph One" 1.13). The resistance that forms following this event can be considered a family, with Echo/Caroline and Paul serving as the heads of the family ("Epitaph Two" 2.13). Other members of this family include those who are attempting to maintain some semblance of normal life in the face of overwhelming odds, such as Priya and her young son, T, as well as the formerly rogue Active Alpha. Tony, Priya's lover and the father of her son, leads another resistance group, those who use technology to fight technology. It is only when the two groups pool their members and their resources that the resistance is able to begin reclaiming the world. Such an ending to the *Dollhouse* saga reinforces Whedon's message in all of his series: any group of people can be a family, and a family can do anything when it must.

Families control our actions in many respects. Certainly parents have great control over their children when the children are young. Parents control access to information as well as other people. They provide reinforcement for correct behavior and mete out punishment for incorrect behavior. Their function is to socialize their children, raising them to be responsible, and in our society, independent adults. Unfortunately, for some children their parents abdicate responsibility for their upbringing. Nevertheless, these children can grow to adulthood and create a family to provide them with the one they never had. Some people have perfectly adequate families, of which they are very fond. This does not stop them from creating other families to provide them with companionship and support when the family of origin is not available.

We have learned at some point that there is "strength in numbers." Clearly, the creation of a family can provide that strength, allowing one to wrestle control over the things of which one is afraid and over which one must gain power. This was beautifully illustrated in *Buffy*, when the Potentials, the Scoobies, Spike, and Buffy stood against the First. And again, when Angel, Spike, Gunn, and Illyria walk to meet the Circle of the Black Thorn. Yet again, when the six remaining crew members of Serenity fight together in order to give Mal time to upload the truth about Miranda to the people of the 'verse. And, finally, when Echo gathers together the disparate members of the Dollhouse to retake the world.

Conclusions

This chapter has discussed several ways of exerting control and establishing power over others. One such method, the use of symbols, binds together those who value the symbol. In the Buffy and Angelverses, crosses are one symbol that binds the living from the undead. The correct response to that symbol means the difference between life and a stake through the heart. Another way to gain control over others is through the use of fear. Being afraid of something gives that something power over you, whether it is being afraid of the bogeyman that might lurk just outside the light in the darkness or the darkness itself. Fear can be overcome, however, if one has the right tools, the right friends, or the right knowledge. It is no surprise that dictators try to control the flow of information in their attempts to establish and maintain power. We say that "knowledge is power," and that is apparently true. Knowing the truth about any situation, regardless of how frightening the information may be, can only help in the long run because now you know what you are up against and what the correct action to be taken is. And, having someone with whom to share the good times and the bad times can make those times easier to bear. Families "have our backs," or so we like to think. Whedon believes that our families will have our backs, if the families are those that we make.

Epilogue: Final Remarks

I hope we find me alive — Caroline/Echo, "Epitaph One" (*Dollhouse* 1.13)

The scholarship on the Whedonverses is vast, with more than 30 books published to date. *Slayage, The (Online) Journal of the Whedon Studies Association* began publishing peer-reviewed essays about all things Whedon over a decade ago. The Whedon Studies Association was founded in 2008, achieved tax-exempt status in 2010 and currently has over 200 members. It even has its own Facebook page. The fifth biennial Slayage Conference on the Whedonverses is planned for July 2012 at the University of British Columbia in Vancouver, Canada. That this book was written and published continues to attest to the popularity of Joss Whedon and his oeuvre.

My purpose in writing this book was to examine the various ways in which one could exert power over and thus control the thoughts and behavior of others. To that end I have explored issues as diverse as love and sex, violence and aggression, magick and witchcraft, drugs, and the manipulation of memory and the mind. This exploration was predicated upon the fact that I am a behavioral neuroscientist and thus "read" visual and verbal texts through the lenses of neuroscience and psychology. Joss Whedon has said that one must bring one's own subtext to his series. That is exactly what I have done within the covers of this book. Do realize that in 294 episodes of text there are many more analyses to be done. To all of those who wonder why people are still writing books about *Buffy* and the other Whedon series, all I can say is watch and you will see why. Other than that, well, you know it has been 400 years since William Shakespeare's time (1564–1616). Today we revere Shakespeare as a genius of English literature. In his day he simply wrote popular culture, designed to entertain his audience and make a few bucks. It looks to me like Joss Whedon has the same calling.

Whedonverses Character List[1]

Buffy the Vampire Slayer

Angel—Buffy's (apparent) true love. He is a vampire. He is a good vampire—he has a soul. As a human his name was Liam. He was worthless. As a vampire his name was Angelus. He was the epitome of evil. (It is very confusing.)

Anya—A former vengeance demon. She dates and becomes engaged to Xander, who jilts her on their wedding day.

Buffy Summers—the Slayer.

Cordelia Chase—One of the popular students at Sunnydale High, she eventually dates Xander and becomes one of the Scooby gang. She leaves Sunnydale after graduation, moving to Los Angeles. She eventually goes to work for Angel. Her nickname is Cordy.

Darla—A four-hundred-year-old vampire, she sired Angelus. She rejected him when his soul was returned. As Angel, he kills her. It doesn't "take." She is resurrected on *Angel* and bears Angel's child, Connor.

Dawn Summers—Buffy's little sister. She is the "Key."

Drusilla—A vampire. Angelus drove her insane before vamping her. Her insanity was not cured when she became a vampire. Her nickname is Dru.

Faith—Another Slayer. She joins forces with the powers of evil, in the form of the mayor of Sunnydale. He is killed on Graduation Day. Faith is eventually redeemed with Angel's help. She returns to Sunnydale to help Buffy train the Potentials and fight against the First (Evil).

Harmony Kendall—One of Cordelia's high school chums, she will be vamped on Graduation Day. Later she will "date" Spike and attempt to kill Buffy. She is very stupid.

Joyce Summers— Buffy's somewhat detached mother.

Oz— Willow's boyfriend. He plays guitar in the band, Dingoes Ate My Baby. He is also a werewolf.

Riley Finn— Buffy's boyfriend, for a short time. He is a member of the Initiative. He finds it difficult to date a Slayer. He loves her, but she does not love him.

Rupert Giles— Buffy's Watcher, charged with helping her train and providing other support for her in her mission to destroy vampires. He loves her and is her father figure.

Spike— A vampire, sired by Drusilla. He eventually falls in love with Buffy and reclaims his soul.

Tara Maclay— Willow's girlfriend. She is a witch.

Wesley Wyndam-Pryce— Another Watcher who is given the job of Buffy's Watcher after Giles is dismissed for being too emotionally involved with Buffy. Wesley is fired from the Watchers' Council and goes "rogue," eventually turning up in Los Angeles. He goes to work for Angel Investigations, but is tricked into kidnapping Angel's son, Connor.

Willow Rosenberg— Buffy's best friend, one of the Scooby gang. She is very intelligent and is a witch. Buffy frequently calls her Will.

Xander Harris— Willow's best friend since childhood, one of the Scooby gang. He is the class clown in high school. After high school he gets a job as a carpenter and is very good at it.

Angel

Characters from *Buffy* that "cross-over" to *Angel* include Angel (of course), Cordelia, Wesley, Faith, Drusilla, Darla, and Spike. Other *Buffy* characters occasionally visit, including Oz, Harmony, and Buffy herself.

Charles Gunn— A street-hardened young man battling the vampires in his neighborhood. His sister is vamped and he stakes her.

Fred Burkle— A brilliant physicist, exiled to the demon world Pylea and eventually rescued by the Angel gang. Both Charles and Wesley fall for her. She chooses Charles, but the relationship does not end well.

Kate Lockley— A police detective.

Lilah Morgan— An attorney who works for the evil law firm, Wolfram and Hart. She has an affair with Wesley. It ends badly.

Lindsey McDonald—An attorney who works for the evil law firm, Wolfram and Hart. He falls in love with Darla. She does not fall in love with him.

The Host—A demon who relocates to our dimension from Pylea and then stays because we have music. He is psychic and can read their "hearts" when people sing. Also known as Lorne.

Firefly and Serenity

Hoban "Wash" Washburne—Zoe's husband and the pilot of Serenity.

Inara Serra—A Companion. Inara rents Mal's spare shuttle. She and Mal are in love with each other, but neither will admit it to the other.

Jayne Cobb—A hired mercenary.

Kaylee Frye—Serenity's mechanic.

Captain Malcolm Reynolds—The captain of the firefly class transport ship, Serenity. He was a Browncoat during the War for Independence against the Alliance. His side lost. Call him Mal.

River Tam—Simon's little sister, who is wanted by the Alliance. They experimented on her and now they want her back. She is psychic and knows things she shouldn't.

Shepherd Book—A preacher with a mysterious past.

Simon Tam—A doctor who is on the run from the law.

Zoe Alleyne Washburne—Mal's second-in-command, his first mate. Zoe served with Mal during the war; he was her sergeant.

Dollhouse

Adelle DeWitt—The Director of the Los Angeles Dollhouse (LAD).

Alpha—A former Active, Alpha has downloaded all his Dollhouse imprints into one. He has gone rogue, but not before killing a number of people at the LAD and slashing Whiskey/Dr. Saunders' face.

Boyd Langton—Echo's handler and later head of security at the LAD.

Dr. Claire Saunders—The physician charged with keeping the Actives healthy. She was injured by the rogue active Alpha. In actuality she is an Active named Whiskey.

Echo—The number-one Active. Her "real" name is Caroline. She "joins" the LAD in order to escape prosecution for her crimes.

Laurence Dominic—The head of security at the LAD, he is eventually sent to the attic when his treachery is discovered.

Mellie—Her Active name is November. Mellie is a sleeper Active and is assigned to keep tabs on Paul Ballard, to feed him false information about the Dollhouse. She joined the LAD after the death of her child.

Paul Ballard—An FBI agent who falls in love with Caroline's picture. He believes that the tales of the Dollhouse are real and he is determined to find it. He eventually joins the LAD as Echo's handler.

Sierra—Her "real" name is Priya. A spurned lover had her incarcerated in the LAD.

Topher Brink—The LAD's programmer.

Victor—His "real" name is Tony. He joined the LAD after returning from service overseas. He falls in love with Sierra.

Series Episode List[1,2]

Buffy the Vampire Slayer
(Number / Title / Writer / Director)

Season One

1.1 / Welcome to the Hellmouth / Joss Whedon / Charles Martin Smith
1.2 / The Harvest / Joss Whedon / John T. Kretchmer
1.3 / The Witch / Dana Reston / Stephen Cragg
1.4 / Teacher's Pet / David Greenwalt / Bruce Seth Green
1.5 / Never Kill a Boy on the First Date / Rob Des Hotel and Dean Batali / David Semel
1.6 / The Pack / Matt Kiene and Joe Reinkemeyer / Bruce Seth Green
1.7 / Angel / David Greenwalt / Scott Brazil
1.8 / I Robot, You Jane / Ashley Gable and Thomas A. Swyden / Stephen Posey
1.9 / The Puppet Show / Dean Batali and Rob Des Hotel / Ellen S. Pressman
1.10 / Nightmares / Joss Whedon and David Greenwalt / Bruce Seth Green
1.11 / Out of Mind, Out of Sight / Joss Whedon, Ashley Gable, and Thomas A. Swyden / Reza Badiyi
1.12 / Prophecy Girl / Joss Whedon / Joss Whedon

Season Two

2.1 / When She Was Bad / Joss Whedon / Joss Whedon
2.2 / Some Assembly Required / Ty King / Bruce Seth Green
2.3 / School Hard / David Greenwalt and Joss Whedon / John T. Kretchmer
2.4 / Inca Mummy Girl / Matt Kiene and Joe Reinkemeyer / Ellen S. Pressman
2.5 / Reptile Boy / David Greenwalt / David Greenwalt
2.6 / Halloween / Carl Ellsworth / Bruce Seth Green

2.7 / Lie to Me / Joss Whedon / Joss Whedon

2.8 / The Dark Age / Dean Batali and Rob Des Hotel / Bruce Seth Green

2.9 / What's My Line? (Part 1) / Howard Gordon and Marti Noxon / David Solomon

2.10 / What's My Line? (Part 2) / Marti Noxon / David Semel

2.11 / Ted / David Greenwalt and Joss Whedon / Bruce Seth Green

2.12 / Bad Eggs / Marti Noxon / David Greenwalt

2.13 / Surprise (Part 1 of 2) / Marti Noxon / Michael Lange

2.14 / Innocence (Part 2 of 2) / Joss Whedon / Joss Whedon

2.15 / Phases / Rob Des Hotel and Dean Batali / Bruce Seth Green

2.16 / Bewitched, Bothered, and Bewildered / Marti Noxon / James A. Contner

2.17 / Passion / Ty King / Michael E. Gershman

2.18 / Killed by Death / Rob Des Hotel and Dean Batali / Deran Serafian

2.19 / I Only Have Eyes for You / Marti Noxon / James Whitmore, Jr.

2.20 / Go Fish / David Fury and Elin Hampton / David Semel

2.21 / Becoming (Part 1) / Joss Whedon / Joss Whedon

2.22 / Becoming (Part 2) / Joss Whedon /Joss Whedon

Season Three

3.1 / Anne / Joss Whedon / Joss Whedon

3.2 / Dead Man's Party / Marti Noxon / James Whitmore, Jr.

3.3 / Faith, Hope, and Trick / David Greenwalt / James A. Contner

3.4 / Beauty and the Beasts / Marti Noxon / James Whitmore, Jr.

3.5 / Homecoming / David Greenwalt / David Greenwalt

3.6 / Band Candy / Jane Espenson / Michael Lange

3.7 / Revelations / Douglas Petrie / James A. Contner

3.8 / Lovers Walk / Dan Vebber / David Semel

3.9 / The Wish / Marti Noxon / David Greenwalt

3.10 / Amends / Joss Whedon / Joss Whedon

3.11 / Gingerbread / Jane Espenson / James Whitmore, Jr.

3.12 / Helpless / David Fury / James A. Contner

3.13 / The Zeppo / Dan Vebber / James Whitmore, Jr.

3.14 / Bad Girls / Douglas Petrie / Michael Lange

3.15 / Consequences / Marti Noxon / Michael Gershman

3.16 / Doppelgängland / Joss Whedon / Joss Whedon

3.17 / Enemies / Douglas Petrie / David Grossman

3.18 / Earshot / Jane Espenson / Regis B. Kimble

3.19 / Choices / David Fury / James A. Contner

3.20 / The Prom / Marti Noxon / David Solomon

3.21 / Graduation Day (Part 1) / Joss Whedon / Joss Whedon
3.22 / Graduation Day (Part 2) / Joss Whedon / Joss Whedon

Season Four

4.1 / The Freshman / Joss Whedon / Joss Whedon
4.2 / Living Conditions / Marti Noxon / David Grossman
4.3 / The Harsh Light of Day / Jane Espenson / James A. Contner
4.4 / Fear, Itself / David Fury / Tucker Gates
4.5 / Beer Bad / Tracey Forbes / David Solomon
4.6 / Wild at Heart / Marti Noxon / David Grossman
4.7 / The Initiative / Douglas Petrie / James A. Contner
4.8 / Pangs / Jane Espenson / Michael Lange
4.9 / Something Blue / Tracey Forbes / Nick Marck
4.10 / Hush / Joss Whedon / Joss Whedon
4.11 / Doomed / Marti Noxon, David Fury, and Jane Espenson / James A. Contner
4.12 / A New Man / Jane Espenson / Michael Gershman
4.13 / The I in Team / David Fury / James A. Contner
4.14 / Goodbye Iowa / Marti Noxon / David Solomon
4.15 / This Year's Girl (Part 1 of 2) / Douglas Petrie / Michael Gershman
4.16 / Who Are You? (Part 2 of 2) / Joss Whedon / Joss Whedon
4.17 / Superstar / Jane Espenson / David Grossman
4.18 / Where the Wild Things Are / Tracey Forbes / David Solomon
4.19 / New Moon Rising / Marti Noxon / James A. Contner
4.20 / The Yoko Factor / Douglas Petrie / David Grossman
4.21 / Primeval / David Fury / James A. Contner
4.22 / Restless / Joss Whedon / Joss Whedon

Season Five

5.1 / Buffy vs. Dracula / Marti Noxon / David Solomon
5.2 / Real Me / David Fury / David Grossman
5.3 / The Replacement / Jane Espenson / James A. Contner
5.4 / Out of My Mind / Rebecca Rand Kirshner / David Grossman
5.5 / No Place Like Home / Douglas Petrie / David Solomon
5.6 / Family / Joss Whedon / Joss Whedon
5.7 / Fool for Love / Douglas Petrie / Nick Marck
5.8 / Shadow / David Fury / Daniel Attias
5.9 / Listening to Fear / Rebecca Rand Kirshner / David Solomon
5.10 / Into the Woods / Marti Noxon / Marti Noxon
5.11 / Triangle / Jane Espenson / Christopher Hibler

5.12 / Checkpoint / Douglas Petrie and Jane Espenson / Nick Marck
5.13 / Blood Ties / Steven DeKnight / Michael Gershman
5.14 / Crush / David Fury / Daniel Attias
5.15 / I Was Made to Love You / Jane Espenson / James A. Contner
5.16 / The Body / Joss Whedon / Joss Whedon
5.17 / Forever / Marti Noxon / Marti Noxon
5.18 / Intervention / Jane Espenson / Michael Gershman
5.19 / Tough Love / Rebecca Rand Kirshner / David Grossman
5.20 / Spiral / Steven DeKnight / James A. Contner
5.21 / The Weight of the World / Douglas Petrie / David Solomon
5.22 / The Gift / Joss Whedon / Joss Whedon

Season Six

6.1 / Bargaining (Part 1) / Marti Noxon / David Grossman
6.2 / Bargaining (Part 2) / David Fury / David Grossman
6.3 / After Life / Jane Espenson / David Solomon
6.4 / Flooded / Douglas Petrie and Jane Espenson / Douglas Petrie
6.5 / Life Serial / David Fury and Jane Espenson / Nick Marck
6.6 / All the Way / Steven S. DeKnight / David Solomon
6.7 / Once More, with Feeling / Joss Whedon / Joss Whedon
6.8 / Tabula Rasa / Rebecca Rand Kirshner / David Grossman
6.9 / Smashed / Drew Z. Greenberg / Turi Meyer
6.10 / Wrecked / Marti Noxon / David Solomon
6.11 / Gone / David Fury / David Fury
6.12 / Doublemeat Palace / Jane Espenson / Nick Marck
6.13 / Dead Things / Steven S. DeKnight / James A. Contner
6.14 / Older and Far Away / Drew Z. Greenberg / Michael Gershman
6.15 / As You Were / Douglas Petrie / Douglas Petrie
6.16 / Hell's Bells / Rebecca Rand Kirshner / David Solomon
6.17 / Normal Again / Diego Gutierrez / Rick Rosenthal
6.18 / Entropy / Drew Z. Greenberg / James A. Contner
6.19 / Seeing Red / Steven S. DeKnight / Michael Gershman
6.20 / Villains / Marti Noxon / David Solomon
6.21 / Two to Go / Douglas Petrie / Bill Norton
6.22 / Grave / David Fury / James A. Contner

Season Seven

7.1 / Lessons / Joss Whedon / David Solomon
7.2 / Beneath You / Douglas Petrie / Nick Marck
7.3 / Same Time, Same Place / Jane Espenson / James A. Contner

7.4 / Help / Rebecca Rand Kirshner / Rick Rosenthal

7.5 / Selfless / Drew Goddard / David Solomon

7.6 / Him / Drew Z. Greenberg / Michael Gershman

7.7 / Conversations with Dead People / Jane Espenson and Drew Goddard / Nick Marck

7.8 / Sleeper / David Fury and Jane Espenson / Alan J. Levi

7.9 / Never Leave Me / Drew Goddard / David Solomon

7.10 / Bring on the Night / Marti Noxon and Douglas Petrie / David Grossman

7.11 / Showtime / David Fury / Michael Grossman

7.12 / Potential / Rebecca Rand Kirshner / James A. Contner

7.13 / The Killer in Me / Drew Z. Greenberg / David Solomon

7.14 / First Date / Jane Espenson / David Grossman

7.15 / Get It Done / Douglas Petrie / Douglas Petrie

7.16 / Storyteller / Jane Espenson / Marita Grabiak

7.17 / Lies My Parents Told Me / David Fury and Drew Goddard / David Fury

7.18 / Dirty Girls / Drew Goddard / Michael Gershman

7.19 / Empty Places / Drew Z. Greenberg / James A. Contner

7.20 / Touched / Rebecca Rand Kirshner / David Solomon

7.21 / End of Days / Douglas Petrie and Jane Espenson / Marita Grabiak

7.22 / Chosen / Joss Whedon / Joss Whedon

Angel *(Number / Title / Writer / Director)*

Season One

1.1 / City Of / David Greenwalt and Joss Whedon / Joss Whedon

1.2 / Lonely Heart / David Fury / James A. Contner

1.3 / In the Dark / Douglas Petrie / Bruce Seth Green

1.4 / I Fall to Pieces / Joss Whedon and David Greenwalt / Vern Gillum

1.5 / Rm w/a Vu / David Greenwalt and Jane Espenson / Scott McGinnis

1.6 / Sense and Sensitivity / Tim Minear / James A. Contner

1.7 / The Bachelor Party / Tracey Stern / David Straiton

1.8 / I Will Remember You / David Greenwalt and Jeannine Renshaw / David Grossman

1.9 / Hero / Howard Gordon and Tim Minear / Tucker Gates

1.10 / Parting Gifts / David Fury and Jeannine Renshaw / James A. Contner

1.11 / Somnambulist / Tim Minear / Winrich Kolbe

1.12 / Expecting / Howard Gordon / David Semel

1.13 / She / David Greenwalt and Marti Noxon / David Greenwalt

1.14 / I've Got You Under My Skin / David Greenwalt and Jeannine Renshaw / R.D. Price
1.15 / The Prodigal / Tim Minear / Bruce Seth Green
1.16 / The Ring / Howard Gordon / Nick Marck
1.17 / Eternity / Tracey Stern / Regis B. Kimble
1.18 / Five by Five / Jim Kouf / James A. Contner
1.19 / Sanctuary / Tim Minear and Joss Whedon / Michael Lange
1.20 / War Zone / Garry Campbell / David Straiton
1.21 / Blind Date / Jeannine Renshaw / Thomas J. Wright
1.22 / To Shanshu in L.A. / David Greenwalt / David Greenwalt

Season Two

2.1 / Judgement[3] / Joss Whedon and David Greenwalt / Michael Lange
2.2 / Are You Now or Have You Ever Been? / Tim Minear / David Semel
2.3 / First Impressions / Shawn Ryan / James A. Contner
2.4 / Untouched / Mere Smith / Joss Whedon
2.5 / Dear Boy / David Greenwalt / David Greenwalt
2.6 / Guise Will Be Guise / Jane Espenson / Krishna Rao
2.7 / Darla / Tim Minear / Tim Minear
2.8 / The Shroud of Rahmon / Jim Kouf / David Grossman
2.9 / The Trial / David Greenwalt / Bruce Seth Green
2.10 / Reunion / Tim Minear and Shawn Ryan / James A. Contner
2.11 / Redefinition / Mere Smith / Michael Grossman
2.12 / Blood Money / Shawn Ryan and Mere Smith / R.D. Price
2.13 / Happy Anniversary / Joss Whedon and David Greenwalt / Bill Norton
2.14 / The Thin Dead Line / Jim Kouf and Shawn Ryan / Scott McGinnis
2.15 / Reprise / Tim Minear / James Whitmore, Jr.
2.16 / Epiphany / Tim Minear / Thomas J. Wright
2.17 / Disharmony / David Fury / Fred Keller
2.18 / Dead End / David Greenwalt / James A. Contner
2.19 / Belonging / Shawn Ryan / Turi Meyer
2.20 / Over the Rainbow / Mere Smith / Fred Keller
2.21 / Through the Looking Glass / Tim Minear / Tim Minear
2.22 / There's No Place Like PLRTZ GLRB / David Greenwalt / David Greenwalt

Season Three

3.1 / Heartthrob / David Greenwalt / David Greenwalt
3.2 / That Vision Thing / Jeffrey Bell / Bill Norton
3.3 / That Old Gang of Mine / Tim Minear / Fred Keller

3.4 / Carpe Noctem / Scott Murphy / James A. Contner
3.5 / Fredless / Mere Smith / Marita Grabiak
3.6 / Billy / Tim Minear and Jeffrey Bell / David Grossman
3.7 / Offspring / David Greenwalt / Turi Meyer
3.8 / Quickening / Jeffrey Bell / Skip Schoolnik
3.9 / Lullaby / Tim Minear / Tim Minear
3.10 / Dad / David H. Goodman / Fred Keller
3.11 / Birthday / Mere Smith / Michael A. Grossman
3.12 / Provider / Scott Murphy / Bill Norton
3.13 / Waiting in the Wings / Joss Whedon / Joss Whedon
3.14 / Couplet / Tim Minear and Jeffrey Bell / Tim Minear
3.15 / Loyalty / Mere Smith / James A. Contner
3.16 / Sleep Tight / David Greenwalt / Terrence O'Hara
3.17 / Forgiving / Jeffrey Bell / Turi Meyer
3.18 / Double or Nothing / David H. Goodman / David Grossman
3.19 / The Price / David Fury / Marita Grabiak
3.20 / A New World / Jeffrey Bell / Tim Minear
3.21 / Benediction / Tim Minear / Tim Minear
3.22 / Tomorrow / David Greenwalt / David Greenwalt

Season Four

4.1 / Deep Down / Steven S. DeKnight / Terrence O'Hara
4.2 / Ground State / Mere Smith / Michael Grossman
4.3 / The House Always Wins / David Fury / Marita Grabiak
4.4 / Slouching Toward Bethlehem / Jeffrey Bell / Skip Schoolnik
4.5 / Supersymmetry / Elizabeth Craft and Sarah Fain / Bill Norton
4.6 / Spin the Bottle / Joss Whedon / Joss Whedon
4.7 / Apocalypse, Nowish / Steven S. DeKnight / Vern Gillum
4.8 / Habeas Corpses / Jeffrey Bell / Skip Schoolnik
4.9 / Long Day's Journey / Mere Smith / Terrence O'Hara
4.10 / Awakening / David Fury and Steven S. DeKnight / James A. Contner
4.11 / Soulless / Sarah Fain and Elizabeth Craft / Sean Astin
4.12 / Calvary / Jeffrey Bell, Steven S. DeKnight, and Mere Smith / Bill Norton
4.13 / Salvage / David Fury / Jefferson Kibbee
4.14 / Release / Steven S. DeKnight, Elizabeth Craft, and Sarah Fain / James A. Contner
4.15 / Orpheus / Mere Smith / Terrence O'Hara
4.16 / Players / Jeffrey Bell, Sarah Fain, and Elizabeth Craft / Michael Grossman

4.17 / Inside Out / Steven S. DeKnight / Steven S. DeKnight
4.18 / Shiny Happy People / Elizabeth Craft and Sarah Fain / Marita Grabiak
4.19 / The Magic Bullet / Jeffrey Bell / Jeffrey Bell
4.20 / Sacrifice / Ben Edlund / David Straiton
4.21 / Peace Out /David Fury / Jefferson Kibbee
4.22 / Home / Tim Minear / Tim Minear

Season Five

5.1 / Conviction / Joss Whedon / Joss Whedon
5.2 / Just Rewards / David Fury and Ben Edlund / James A. Contner
5.3 / Unleashed / Sarah Fain and Elizabeth Craft / Marita Grabiak
5.4 / Hell Bound / Steven S. DeKnight / Steven S. DeKnight
5.5 / Life of the Party / Ben Edlund / Bill Norton
5.6 / The Cautionary Tale of Numero Cinco / Jeffrey Bell / Jeffrey Bell
5.7 / Lineage / Drew Goddard / Jefferson Kibbee
5.8 / Destiny / David Fury and Steven S. DeKnight / Skip Schoolnik
5.9 / Harm's Way / Elizabeth Craft and Sarah Fain / Vern Gillum
5.10 / Soul Purpose / Brent Fletcher / David Boreanaz
5.11 / Damage / Steven S. DeKnight and Drew Goddard / Jefferson Kibbee
5.12 / You're Welcome / David Fury / David Fury
5.13 / Why We Fight / Drew Goddard and Steven S. DeKnight / Terrence
    O'Hara
5.14 / Smile Time / Joss Whedon and Ben Edlund / Ben Edlund
5.15 / A Hole in the World / Joss Whedon / Joss Whedon
5.16 / Shells / Steven S. DeKnight / Steven S. DeKnight
5.17/ Underneath / Sarah Fain and Elizabeth Craft / Skip Schoolnik
5.18 / Origin / Drew Goddard / Terrence O'Hara
5.19 / Time Bomb / Ben Edlund / Vern Gillum
5.20 / The Girl in Question / Steven S. DeKnight and Drew Goddard /
    David Greenwalt
5.21 / Power Play / David Fury / James A. Contner
5.22 / Not Fade Away / Jeffrey Bell and Joss Whedon / Jeffrey Bell

Firefly *(Number / Title / Writer / Director)*

1.1 / Serenity (Parts 1 and 2) / Joss Whedon / Joss Whedon
1.2 / The Train Job / Joss Whedon and Tim Minear / Joss Whedon
1.3 / Bushwhacked / Tim Minear / Tim Minear
1.4 / Shindig / Jane Espenson / Vern Gillum

1.5 / Safe / Drew Z. Greenberg / Michael Grossman
1.6 / Our Mrs. Reynolds / Joss Whedon / Vondie Curtis Hall
1.7 / Jaynestown / Ben Edlund / Marita Grabiak
1.8 / Out of Gas / Tim Minear / David Solomon
1.9 / Ariel / Jose Molina / Allan Kroeker
1.10 / War Stories / Cheryl Cain / James Contner
1.11 / Trash / Ben Edlund and Jose Molina / Vern Gillum
1.12 / The Message / Joss Whedon and Tim Minear / Tim Minear
1.13 / Heart of Gold / Brett Matthews / Thomas J. Wright
1.14 / Objects in Space / Joss Whedon / Joss Whedon
Serenity / Joss Whedon / Joss Whedon

Dollhouse *(Number / Title / Writer / Director)*

Season One

1.1 / Ghost / Joss Whedon / Joss Whedon
1.2 / The Target / Steven S. DeKnight / Steven S. DeKnight
1.3 / Stage Fright / Maurissa Tancharoen and Jed Whedon / David Solomon
1.4 / Gray Hour / Sarah Fain and Elizabeth Craft / Rod Hardy
1.5 / True Believer / Tim Minear / Allan Kroeker
1.6 / Man on the Street / Joss Whedon / David Straiton
1.7 / Echoes / Elizabeth Craft and Sarah Fain / James A. Contner
1.8 / Needs / Tracy Bellomo / Felix E. Alcalá
1.9 / A Spy in the House of Love / Andrew Chambliss / David Solomon
1.10 / Haunted / Jane Espenson, Maurissa Tancharoen and Jed Whedon /
    Elodie Keene
1.11 / Briar Rose / Jane Espenson / Dwight Little
1.12 / Omega / Tim Minear / Tim Minear
1.13 / Epitaph One / Maurissa Tancharoen, and Jed Whedon / David
    Solomon

Season Two

2.1 / Vows / Joss Whedon / Joss Whedon
2.2 / Instinct / Michele Fazekas and Tara Butters / Marita Grabiak
2.3 / Belle Chose / Tim Minear / David Solomon
2.4 / Belonging / Maurissa Tancharoen and Jed Whedon / Jonathan Frakes
2.5 / The Public Eye / Andrew Chambliss / David Solomon
2.6 / The Left Hand / Tracy Bellomo / Wendey Stanzler

2.7 / Meet Jane Doe / Maurissa Tancharoen, Jed Whedon, and Andrew
  Chambliss / Dwight Little
2.8 / A Love Supreme / Jenny DeArmitt / David Straiton
2.9 / Stop-Loss / Andrew Chambliss / Felix E. Alcalá
2.10 / The Attic / Maurissa Tancharoen and Jed Whedon / John Cassaday
2.11 / Getting Closer / Tim Minear / Tim Minear
2.12 / The Hollow Men / Michele Fazekas, Tara Butters, and Tracy Bellomo
  / Terrence O'Hara
2.13 / Epitaph Two: The Return / Maurissa Tancharoen, Jed Whedon, and
  Andrew Chambliss / David Solomon

Chapter Notes

Preface

1. I would like to extend my thanks to Professor Emeritus Mary Alice Money of Gordon College, Barnesville, Georgia, for reading this Preface and for her helpful comments and suggestions.

2. The voice-over spoken by Rupert Giles over the credits of *Buffy* during Season One.

3. Van Helsing was the vampire hunter/slayer in Bram Stoker's 1897 novel *Dracula* and continued his work in both the Universal Studios *Dracula* films as well as the Hammer Studios films. For more discussion of the slayer, see William Patrick Day.

4. Sarah Michele Gellar, who portrays Buffy, is 5 feet, 2.5 inches, and weighs between 97 and 108 pounds. Not only is this tiny, she would actually be considered underweight.

5. *Buffy the Vampire Slayer* the movie was a great disappointment to Joss Whedon, who wrote the original screenplay, not the one that was actually filmed. However, the events that happened in the movie are referred to in the series as part of the back story to explain Buffy's move to Sunnydale.

6. Given Liam's actions prior to being turned into a vampire, I wonder if he even had a soul to begin with. Perhaps that is why Darla finally chooses Liam to turn. Apparently in her 100-odd years of vampireness prior to this time, she has never turned anyone else. For further discussion of the relationship between Darla and Angel see Joy Davidson's essay "There's my boy…" in her book.

7. I really hate the way people write about women and babies. Why must women automatically fall in love with babies? Here is a female vampire who has been the epitome of evil for almost 400 years. She gets pregnant and becomes a mushy idiot. Scully acted the same way on *The X-Files*, as did Aeryn Sun on *Farscape* (I do a little rant on this in my book about women in science-fiction television).

8. This is voice-over for the credits of *Firefly*. Joss Whedon modeled this series loosely after the American Civil War and what happened to the Confederate States and those who fought on the losing side after the war. If *Star Trek*'s mythology states that it was a "Wagon Train to the Stars" then *Firefly*'s is that it is a "Stagecoach" (Alexander; *Firefly* Vol. One).

9. Victor is the one male Active we see regularly. His "real" name is Tony and he apparently joined the Dollhouse after military service. Sierra (Priya) refused the attentions of a wealthy businessman who gave her to the Dollhouse so that he could use her whenever and however he wished. Mellie's primary purpose was to engage Paul Ballard and misdirect his efforts to find Echo. Otherwise, her Active name was November; she had joined the Dollhouse following the death of her child. Dr. Saunders was actually an Active named Whiskey until mutilated by an Active named Alpha (who subsequently escaped). Since Alpha had also killed the Dollhouse's doctor and Whiskey was useless as an Active, she was imprinted

with the knowledge necessary to serve as a physician. She had a psychotic break when she discovered the truth about her past.

Chapter 1

1. Portions of this chapter were presented at the annual meeting of the Popular Culture Association of the South, in October 2009. I would like to extend my thanks to Professor Emeritus Mary Alice Money of Gordon College for reading this chapter and for her helpful comments and suggestions.

2. Definition retrieved March 11, 2011, from www.hypnosis.org.

3. For ease of typing and reading I will use the word *Buffy* (in italics) to denote the series *Buffy the Vampire Slayer*. I will use *BtVS* as well, but generally only when denoting an episode from that series. Likewise, I will use *FFS* to refer to *Firefly/Serenity* and *DH* to refer to *Dollhouse* episodes from those series. When Buffy is not italicized then I am referring to Buffy Summers, the character. *Angel* in italics will refer to the series, and Angel will refer to the character. *Dollhouse* is the title of the series. When I will refer to a specific Dollhouse I will preface the word with the, as in "Actives in the various Dollhouses." Likewise, *Serenity* is the film, but Serenity is the name of Mal's spaceship. Finally I will indicate the title of the episode to which I am referring for each series as well as its location in the series. Thus, the first episode of the third season is 3.1. It is possible to get confused about the episodes when discussing *Buffy* and *Angel*, with their cross-over characters and cross-over episodes. In such a case, I will denote whether the episode is a *Buffy* (e.g., "Fool for Love" *BtVS* 5.7) or an *Angel* ("Dear Boy" *Angel* 2.5). Otherwise, I will assume that the reader understands to which series I am referring by the context of the paragraph. I realize that *Angel* is a spin-off of *Buffy* and thus a continuation of that world. For ease of reference I will designate the world of *Buffy* as the Buffyverse and use that term to refer collectively to the events that occur in the seven seasons of that series. I will use the term Angelverse to refer collectively to the events that occur in the five seasons of that series.

4. Thanks to Mary Alice Money for reminding me that Mal's power is sometimes "more of a mishmash of wit and lucky witlessness than gunpowder and death rays."

5. I definitely include Riley in that group. I disagree with those who think that Riley could cope with Buffy being the Slayer. Despite his many protests, he was too macho to be happy with a girlfriend stronger than he was. I think that the episodes when he is consorting with vampires ("Into the Woods" 5.10), and when he will not get help for his heart condition ("Out of my Mind" 5.4), support my argument. See also Tamy Burnett's comments on this in her essay "Anya as Feminist Model of Positive Female Sexuality," in Waggoner's book.

6. Parenting styles vary along two dimensions, warmth and demandingness, leading to four categories of parents: authoritarian, authoritative, permissive (indulgent), and uninvolved. The latter can be characterized as not demanding very much of their children and, in extreme cases, may be abusive or neglectful. Permissive parents also do not demand much of their children, providing little guidance, although they generally have some degree of warmth for their children. These styles can have long-term consequences for children, with children of permissive parents being immature and unable to accept responsibility. Based upon the few times we saw their parents, Xander and Willow would appear to have parents who ranged from permissive to uninvolved. Willow definitely does not seem to be immature, except when we first meet her and it looks like her mother does dress her. However, Willow's immaturity is readily apparent when Oz leaves her. Her sadness is real, but she does not give her friends (especially Buffy, who had to kill her boyfriend) credit for having experienced that kind of pain before. She is angry with them for not supporting her in her pain. Xander's antics as the class clown do mask his insecurity, and he is immature, taking a long time to accept responsibility for his actions and respecting his friends' decisions.

7. Google the term "soul definition" and note the number received. I liked this one the best as it seemed to reflect exactly what Joss Whedon meant by the term. The source of this

definition was en.wikipedia.org/wiki/Soul. The same is true of the definition I used for conscience. The source was en.wikipedia.org/wiki/Conscience (retrieved March 11, 2011).

8. That does not make what he did right. This act — attempted rape — demonstrated that Spike was dangerous, as both a vampire and as a man. Men are potentially dangerous to women. Although it is doubtful that any real person actually said that "all men are rapists," the sentiment is felt by many women. See Chapter 3.

9. We are angry about it. Everyone was angry about it. But Buffy forgave him for it and I guess we will have to as well.

10. "Let's watch a girl get beaten to death." Posted by Joss Whedon, May 20, 2007, on http://whedonesque.com/comments/13271 (retrieved March 11, 2011).

11. I love all of the *Firefly* episodes, but show "The Train Job" to my students every semester because it is a perfect complement to my lecture on motivation. One of my favorite quotes is by Jayne, spoken to Simon: "You know what the chain of command is? It's the chain I go get and beat you with 'til ya understand who's in ruttin' command here."

12. Thanks to Mary Alice Money for pointing out that in *Dollhouse* the magick of choice is science.

Chapter 2

1. Portions of this chapter were presented at the annual meetings of the Popular Culture Association, St. Louis, Missouri, in April 2010, and the Popular Culture Association of the South, Savannah, Georgia, in October 2010. My special thanks to Dr. K. Dale Koontz for her helpful comments and suggestions on this chapter and all of my other Whedon ideas. I have fabulous friends and colleagues.

2. All quotes in this section are to be found in Robert J. Sternberg's book *Cupid's Arrow*. See Works Cited for the complete citation.

3. The details about how to sire a vampire often contradict one another, depending upon which episode one watches. See Nikki Stafford's *Bite Me!* for a more complete discussion of this issue.

4. Does a moment of pure happiness only occur when you are experiencing an orgasm with someone you love, or does that moment of happiness occur during any orgasm? It must have something to do with true love, as his sexual encounter with Darla does not restore Angelus.

5. Yes, I know that "sleeping with someone" is code for sex, but come on; there was no sleeping going on between Spike and Buffy. They were doing IT (and innocent masonry was being destroyed).

6. I would characterize Spike's relationship with Harmony as infatuated, i.e., it contained only passion, but mostly because she was available. She probably felt romantic love for him, because that was the type of woman she was. He certainly did not like her; his actions and words showed how contemptuous of her he really was.

7. Nikki Stafford speculates in each of her series guides about how vampires can have relationships given that they are dead and have no souls. Well, apparently their brains are still working and love lies in the head, not the heart. And, no one has yet to answer the question of what is a soul and where it resides. But, I say, why shouldn't demons have relationships with each other? Or with humans, for that matter? Mythology, even Christian mythology, is rife with examples of paranormal and supernatural beings mating with humans (see, for example, *Genesis* 6).

8. Another example of infatuation in *Buffy* was displayed by Dawn, who developed crushes on both Xander and Spike.

9. And, of course, Cordy becomes part demon in *Angel* ("Birthday" 3.11) in order to receive the visions from the Powers That Be, which allow Angel Investigations to continue their mission to help the helpless. If Cordy does not consent to becoming part demon, the effects of the visions will eventually cause her a painful, bloody death (see Chapter 5).

10. I think it was very interesting how they aged Connor so quickly, from being approximately 16 years old when he returned from Quor-toth to 18 years old right before he and Cordelia had sex. Perhaps they were trying to prepare for the firestorm of criticism that was sure to arise. I don't know about California, but most states have statutes against adults having sex with those who are underage.

11. Mal is sorely tempted to have sex with Saffron, who is "Our Mrs. Reynolds" (*Firefly* 1.6). Saffron is a con artist who is well-schooled in the arts of seduction. Inara tells the crew that Saffron has had Companion training because Saffron tries to seduce Inara, and Inara recognizes the techniques. Saffron notes that men are easily played and she uses sex as both a lure and a weapon. Her actions and opinions clearly reflect evolutionary theory's tenets about male sexuality.

12. I refer to female and male sex workers as "whores" because that is the way they are referred to in *Firefly*.

13. Could this perhaps be a portent of things to come, given his fate on *Serenity*?

14. Thanks to Dale Koontz for reminding me that Nandi asks Mal if he is "sly" in this episode. In the 'verse, "sly" refers to homosexuality. When Mal acts hesitant about having sex with any of her whores, Nandi asks him if he is sly and reminds him that she has male whores as well as female. Mal replies that he is not "sly," that he "leans toward womenfolk," and he is not offended by the remark.

15. Commander Susan Ivanova is bisexual, enjoying sexual relations with both male and female lovers. Her female lover was the telepath Talia Winters, who was actually a sleeper agent.

16. This is one of my favorite sayings, by Susan Ivanova on *Babylon 5*, one of my top-three favorite science-fiction series of all time (tied for tops with *Farscape* and *Firefly*).

17. Look at any TV series and notice how many of the lead characters are single. If they become involved with anyone, that person is likely to die, the Little Joe Phenomenon as Rhonda V. Wilcox calls it in her essay "'Who Died and Made Her Boss?': Patterns of Mortality in *Buffy*" in Wilcox and Lavery. Just think about poor Samantha Carter on *Stargate SG1*. Oh, there are exceptions, like in my beloved *Babylon 5*. But I was really sweating in *Farscape* that they would kill off Aeryn Sun, or when they did kill her off, that they would not bring her back.

Chapter 3

1. Portions of this chapter were presented at the annual meeting of the Popular Culture Association in San Antonio, Texas, in April 2011. I would like to thank Dr. Linda J. Jencson of Appalachian State University, Boone, North Carolina, and Dr. K. Dale Koontz of Cleveland Community College, Shelby, North Carolina, for reading this chapter and for their helpful comments and suggestions.

2. Definitions of abuse include: to use wrongly or improperly, to misuse; to assault sexually, to rape or molest; to hurt or injure by maltreatment; to insult or revile; and, an unjust or wrongful action. www.thefreedictionary.com (retrieved June 11, 2011).

3. My thanks to Dr. Jencson for pointing out that domestic violence increases in times of crisis or stress, such as economic downturns. Its occurrence is also correlated with certain types of religious beliefs. Statistics for domestic violence are from http://www.ncadv.org/files/DomesticViolenceFactSheet(National).pdf (retrieved June 6, 2011).

4. One of the most chilling characters in the Buffyverse was Caleb, a serial killer who delighted in murdering young women.

5. Adults who wish to engage in sadomasochistic sex play are welcome to do so as far as I am concerned. What consenting adults do with each other is fine by me as long as it does not involve children or animals (neither of which can give consent). Boys who think they can beat up their girlfriends because that is what Spike does to Buffy, need to be reminded that she also beat the crap out of him. I disapprove of violence under any circum-

stance, so I do not think that she should be hurting him either. I know there was a great deal of discussion about the rape scene. People argued that Buffy should not have been so beaten up by the fight earlier in the evening. She should have been able to defend herself against Spike's advances more so than she did. She was always hitting him and he usually did not retaliate against her (even when he could). (See also Tamy Burnett's discussion in her essay "Anya as Feminist Model of Positive Female Sexuality.") I tend to agree with this last argument. Not that I think Spike should have raped her or attempted to rape her, but I do know that a simple content analysis of the number of times she hit him compared to him hitting her, would find that her abuse of him outweighed his abuse of her. *And, that is not a good thing.*

6. I must confess that I did not like *Angel* as much as *Firefly* or *Buffy*. When Heather M. Porter and Tanya R. Cochran interviewed me for their documentary on Joss Whedon, I ranked *Angel* as number 3, with *Firefly* first and *Dollhouse* last. Part of the problem I had with *Angel* was the way in which the producers changed the focus of the series in Season One, from monster-of-the-week to Angel-angst. I understand that Angel has emotional baggage: as I mentioned in the Introduction, he was not a nice man *before* he became a vampire. However, I would have preferred that the series explore the ways in which he protected Los Angelenos from the denizens of the dark rather than continually seeing him facing his past and being all broody and dark. And, frankly, I thought that the plots got silly in places toward the end of the series.

7. Walker proposes that abused women present with Post-Traumatic Stress Disorder. However, women and children who have been sexually or physically abused are not suffering *post*-traumatic stress. I propose that they live the stress and the memories every day.

8. Linda Jencson reminded me of one of the "history" episodes, when Angelus begins to teach Spike about the ways to be a vampire ("Destiny" 5.8). It appears as if he is giving Spike "a tidbit" (a girl) and permission to "use it" as he sees fit. Dr. Jencson says that this scene is "pretty explicit to me that Whedon is showing Angelus training Spike to rape." Angelus tells Spike, that as a vampire, "You take what you want, have what you want." Spike is upset that Angelus is having sex with Drusilla, whom Spike loves. My personal opinion is that one of the ways in which Angelus drove Dru insane was with repeated rapes. Spike does remark that, although it was Drusilla who made him a vampire, it was Angelus who made him a monster.

9. http://www.pbs.org/kued/nosafeplace/studyg/rape.html.

10. I am well aware that at the time Liam lived women did not have many rights.

11. Shepherd Book's refusal to discuss the past suggests that it was unsavory. Unfortunately, the graphic novel about him (*The Shepherd's Tale*) does not completely clear up the mystery, but it does show multiple scenes of extreme violence.

12. Thanks to Tamy Burnett for making that observation at the Popular Culture Association meeting in San Antonio, Texas, in April 2011.

13. Dr. Koontz points out that these qualities would also be true of Inara, and this might be another reason for Mal's verbal barbs.

14. I do not really need to point out that Jayne is a violent man. However, it is clear that Jayne's violence does not steer toward women. Comments that Jayne makes throughout the series and the film indicate that he does not abuse women, nor does he condone such abuse. See also Koontz.

15. Quite a number of people have commented on this aspect of the series. It was very difficult for many Whedon fans to believe that he would produce a series such as *Dollhouse*, with its obvious depiction of sex trafficking. That people seriously engaged with the issue and discussed the reality of sex trafficking in contemporary society was surely his *raison d'être*. See Note 10 in Chapter 1.

16. One wonders how a college professor can afford the Dollhouse's fees. Let's face it; we college professors do not do it for the money. Dale Koontz wonders if he has an endowed chair.

17. Any woman reading this chapter will be able to recall her own experiences with sexual harassment in college, graduate school, or on the job. And, if not her own, then she will likely know someone who did experience this type of abuse. It was pretty rampant in my graduate program, and I also experienced it at one of my former jobs.

18. According to statistics, 75–80 percent of incarcerated women who killed their partners had experienced abuse by that partner; as many as 80 percent of incarcerated women have experienced abuse, either in childhood or as an adult. A large percentage of incarcerated women are convicted of crimes they commit because their partners coerced them into activities such as robbery or drug-related crimes. They may also commit crimes to help them cope with the abuse, such as drug abuse for self-medication. For more information, see http://www.freebatteredwomen.org/resources/incarcerated.html.

19. If you are a victim of domestic violence or know someone who is, referral and support information can be obtained from these sources. The National Victim Center's website is www.ncvc.org, and their telephone number is 1-800-FYI-CALL. The National Domestic Violence Hotline is 1-800-799-7233. The website for the National Coalition Against Domestic Violence is www.ncadv.org.

Chapter 4

1. http://www.adherents.com/Religions_By_Adherents.html (retrieved June 6, 2011).
2. http://www.thefreedictionary.com/pagan (retrieved June 6, 2011).
3. http://www.ecauldron.net/newpagan.php (retrieved June 6, 2011).
4. http://www.wicca.com/celtic/wicca/wicca.htm (retrieved June 6, 2011).
5. http://www.thefreedictionary.com/witchcraft (retrieved June 6, 2011).
6. Many people are unaware of the fact that Satan is a Christian concept; many religions of the world do not having an evil deity. I am aware that J. K. Rowling helped the world of witchcraft with her series of books on the boy wizard Harry Potter. Astute viewers of the Harry Potter films and readers of the books know that the wizards and witches of the Potter world do not disavow Christianity, although one could argue that Rowling included Christian symbols and rituals (e.g., Christmas) to placate critics who condemned the books for their sympathetic portrayal of all things "witchy." As a psychologist, I saw Harry as an unloved boy, looking for a place to belong. In Rowling's world people, whether muggle or not, could be good or evil. I never wavered in my belief that Severus Snape was good.
7. http://www.skepdic.com/magick.html (retrieved June 6, 2011).
8. http://www.thefreedictionary.com/demon (retrieved June 6, 2011).
9. As a number of people have noted, Willow is not Wiccan. For instance, see Christie Golden's argument "Where's the Religion in Willow's Wicca?" in Yeffeth's book on *Buffy*.
10. I really think these Scourge demons look like Reavers. Apparently just as human beings have no compunctions against harming other human beings, demons will harm other demons, another case of us versus them (the in-group versus the out-group [Meyers]).
11. Many records are no longer extant, or are in such poor condition as to be unreadable. In addition, not all notaries or scribes recorded the names of the accused or the executed. For example, in France over 10,000 people were accused of witchcraft, with over 5,000 executed (Barstow 180).
12. Seriously, I could only read so much of Cawthorne's book at a time. His account is based upon the actual records and trial transcripts of the victims. Some of the torturers apparently took really good notes.
13. Jane Espenson says that she "always felt that there was something between those two when they were younger" (Kaveney 112).
14. All bets are off in the Season Eight comics.
15. It is interesting to note that, at least in America, two of the most celebrated cases of witchcraft involved adolescent girls. See Godbeer and Boyer and Nissenbaum for more in-

formation. A goodly number of young girls were killed during the witchcraze in Europe, but so were people of all ages and those from all walks of life. The numbers of the dead are simply staggering.

16. How does any school get away with letting a student teach class, even on a temporary basis? Are there no unions in California? Are the schools not accredited?

17. The issue of whether Willow was or was not an addict was debated, sometimes virulently, in some of the books and essays I read about the Buffyverse. Given that Whedon himself indicated her use of magick is a metaphor for addiction would seem to be the definitive statement on the issue. Having lived with a family member who was an addict for a good number of years, as well as being a psychologist who has studied drugs and addiction, I feel confident in my assessment that Willow's actions with respect to magick are similar to people who are addicted to various types of drugs, gambling, eating, sexing, et cetera.

18. This essay is entitled "Power of Becoming" and can be found in Yeffeth's book on *Buffy*.

19. Whedon has joked many times about the adolescent girls who figure prominently in his works. Adolescence is a time of great physical, emotional, cognitive, and psychological change in youth. All of these make this time of life a perfect metaphor for the attainment of power as well as the sheer destructiveness of power.

20. With a few exceptions (like Clem) demons in the Buffyverse are generally evil; however, this is not true in the Angelverse. Two of Angel's best friends are the demon Lorne and the half-demon Doyle. In addition, many of the demons encountered in the Angelverse are in need of help, just as the humans are. Demons are not necessarily as "sexy" in these two Whedonverses as are (certain of) the vampires, but just as vampires can be redeemed, apparently so too can demons.

21. She has absolutely the best legs of any woman in show business, in my opinion.

22. Obviously this woman has a few problems with her fiancée, given that he is talking with women on-line and then planning to meet them.

23. Given the events that occur at the end of Season Four, when Connor's memory and identity are erased and he is given a new life ("Home"), one can say that the prophecy came true. Connor did die at the hands of his father (and his father's deal with Wolfram and Hart).

24. It is interesting to see how religious doctrine is mistranslated and misused on the various planets visited by Serenity's crew.

25. See both essays by Lorrah. One is "Love Saves the World" in Yeffeth's book on *Buffy*. The other is "A World Without Love: The Failure of Family in *Angel*" in Yeffeth's book on *Angel*.

26. My best friend in high school, Chris, and I used to joke that planet Earth and all of its inhabitants were simply the science project of some kid in the eighth-grade on another planet. I figure the poor kid probably did not win first prize, but the kid's parents were proud just the same. Now that kid has grown up and the project is forgotten in some corner of the attic where it is stored. Not much has changed my mind since then.

Chapter 5

1. Portions of this chapter were presented at the fourth biennial Slayage Conference of the Whedonverses, held at Flagler College, St. Augustine, Florida, in June 2010. Special thanks to Dr. Tanya R. Cochran of Union College for her helpful comments and suggestions. One of those suggestions was to include pictures or diagrams of the various brain structures described in this chapter. I would have loved to include those, but it is quite difficult to find the "perfect" pictures and even more difficult to obtain permission to reproduce them. The interested reader can use any number of search engines to obtain images of the brain. One of the best books ever written about neuroscience is the one by Kandel, Schwartz, and Jessell; it got me through my Ph.D. comprehensive examination. The reference can be found in the Works Cited.

2. The *endocrine system* provides another means of communication in the body; however, instead of using electrical means, the endocrine system utilizes specific chemical compounds called hormones. It is important to know that hormones are produced in various parts of the body, but generally produce their effects far removed from the site of their production. The endocrine system is important for maintaining homeostasis, which is a process that permits an organism to maintain a more or less stable existence in an unstable environment through a variety of adaptive mechanisms. For example, the human body must maintain an internal temperature of 98.6 degrees. If the temperature rises too high, we sweat. If the temperature drops too low, we shiver in order to release heat. The hypothalamus serves as the control center for the endocrine system. It makes its own hormones as well as producing releasing and inhibiting factors which act at the pituitary gland, causing it to release its hormones. The hypothalamus controls the endocrine system through feedback loops. If the circulating levels of a particular hormone drop too low, then receptors in the hypothalamus detect this deficit and release the appropriate releasing factor. The releasing factor will then travel to the pituitary gland, causing it to release the appropriate hormone. When the circulating levels of the hormone reach normal again, the hypothalamus will release an inhibiting factor and the pituitary will stop the release of the hormone in question.

3. Some of the symptoms presented by hebephrenic schizophrenics are: active, but in an aimless and not constructive way; bizarre and inappropriate emotional responses; false, fixed beliefs (delusions); inability to feel pleasure; inappropriate grinning and grimacing; lack of emotion and motivation; seeing or hearing things that aren't there (hallucinations); and silly behavior. Some of these symptoms are also observed in other types of schizophrenia. The main difference is erratic behavior, with speech that is not grammatical or is random-ordered. Dr. Cochran points out that this is characteristic of River, but I think that River's speech makes perfect sense when you realize that the seeming randomness of her speech actually presages future events on the series.

4. The word "amygdala" is singular; the plural is "amygdalae." There are two amygdalae and two hippocampi, one located in each cerebral hemisphere.

5. For information about Klüver-Bucy Syndrome, see Kandel, Schwartz and Jessell. Information can also be found at the following website, http://www.ninds.nih.gov/disorders/kluver_bucy/kluver_bucy.htm (retrieved February 2, 2011).

6. Dr. Cochran suggested that perhaps River is trying to scare Jayne when she tells him that she can kill him with her brain. After all, River realizes that Jayne tried to turn her over to the Alliance. River might well be playing with Jayne, but I think she is dead serious. She is realizing how powerful she is, even if she does not completely understand everything yet.

7. A chakra is a center of energy in the body. For more information see http://heartofhealing.net/energy-healing/human-energy-field/chakras/ (retrieved February 27, 2011).

8. http://www.crystalinks.com/chakras.html (retrieved May 23, 2010).

9. The evil scientist of the story, Crawford Tillinghast, constructs a machine that will allow him to transform the pineal gland into the "psychic third eye." The machine, the Resonator, will allow him to see beyond our world into one that is violent and strange. Tillinghast wishes to enter into this world to more fully explore his deviant and twisted sexuality. Stuart Gordon filmed a loose adaptation of Lovecraft's short story in 1986; it includes one of the most shocking and disgusting (in my opinion, anyway) sex scenes ever filmed. During the course of the film, the machine alters Tillinghast's assistant: his pineal gland grows out of his head, on a stalk, and shows a marked preference for eating brains.

10. One of Nikki Stafford's nitpicks about "Out of My Mind" (*Buffy* 5.4) in *Bite Me!* concerned the attempt to remove Spike's chip without the aid of anesthesia. Sorry, Nikki, but they do brain surgery without anesthesia. It is not necessary. Let me digress for a moment on pain. Pain is a psychological concept, meaning it is entirely subjective. Just like your eyes do not see, your body does not feel pain. Located within your skin and deep tissues are specialized receptors called nociceptors. When these are activated you will respond to their ac-

tivation but you will not necessarily be aware of your response. You constantly make minute adjustments to the position of your body, for example, in order to relieve pressure on various joints. If you do not make those adjustments you will eventually feel the discomfort that you will label as pain. Messages from nociceptors are transmitted to the brain to specialized processing centers that analyze the type of pain, where it is located, what it means, et cetera. However, the brain itself does not contain these nociceptors, hence the ability to do neurosurgery without anesthesia. Any pain in the surgery would result from the nociceptors located in the skin of the head being cut open, and you would receive a local anesthetic for that. Being awake for the surgery would allow the surgeon to more accurately locate the specific area being targeted because the surgeon would be able to talk to the patient. This is very important if the surgeon must operate in any area near the language centers of the brain, which (in the majority of people) are located in the left hemisphere. I am not trying to say that all neurosurgery occurs with the patient awake, but my colleagues (see Note 14) assure me that it still does occur and for the reasons I mention.

11. This is one of the most famous lines of the 1931 film *Frankenstein*, directed by James Whale. Henry Frankenstein declares that a new race of beings will call him God.

12. *CT* stands for computed tomography. It is basically an X-Ray of the interior of the body, with the pictures being compiled by a computer to produce a cross-sectional image. With the CT scan a physician can diagnose various conditions such as tumors, cancer, and musculoskeletal disorders, among others. The scan can determine the exact location and size of the insult, and whether nearby tissue is affected. Like any X-Ray, a CT scan involves radiation.

13. *MRI* stands for magnetic resonance imaging. MRIs are generally preferred to CT scans because of the detail in the image. However, they can be more expensive than CT scans and, thus, most insurance providers prefer a CT scan. Besides the quality of the image, another advantage of an MRI is that it does not use radiation. Rather, the patient is bombarded with radiofrequency waves while lying in a magnetic field.

14. I would like to acknowledge the helpful comments and suggestions of three of my colleagues with respect to the information on Joyce Summers's brain tumor and Spike's chip. The first is Samuel Greenblatt, M.D., Professor of Neurosurgery and Neuroscience at Brown University, Providence, Rhode Island. Next is Peter Koehler, M.D., Ph.D., from the Department of Neurology at the Atrium Medical Center in Heerlen, The Netherlands. Third is Moshe Feinsod, M.D., Head of the Division of Clinical Neurosciences at The Technion Israel Institute of Technology in Haifa, Israel.

15. The definition of an aneurysm is from http://www.webmd.com/heart-disease/understanding-aneurysm-basics (retrieved June 11, 2011).

16. Cordelia received the visions from Doyle, a half-human, half-demon hybrid, before he died (*Angel* 1.9). Given his feelings for her, it is unlikely he realized how dangerous the visions would be when he gave them to her.

Chapter 6

1. Portions of this chapter were presented at the fourth biennial Slayage Conference on the Whedonverses, held at Flagler College in St. Augustine, Florida, in June 2010. A shorter version, examining memory only in *Dollhouse*, was published in a special double issue of *Slayage: The Journal of the Whedon Studies Association*. I would like to extend special thanks to Rhonda V. Wilcox, David Lavery, and Cynthea Masson for their comments and suggestions on the *Slayage* paper, and to David Lavery for his comments on this extended version.

2. We are not completely sure of how information is selected from the sensory memory for further processing, but one could speculate that a lifetime of experience would allow the brain's unconscious processors to make the distinction.

3. Fugue is a rare psychological/psychiatric condition defined as a "dissociative disorder in which a person forgets who they are and leaves home to create a new life. During the

fugue, there is no memory of the former life, and after recovering, there is no memory for events during the dissociative state" (wordnetweb.princeton.edu/perl/webwn). Based upon the preceding discussion, persons experiencing a fugue state would have lost access to their episodic memories. Fugue usually occurs following a traumatic event. Whereas a person with amnesia may also experience a loss of memory of events occurring in their own life, the cause is generally organic; that is, following head trauma, such as an accident, or disease, such as Alzheimer's. Fugue states are reversible in the sense that the patient will often recover from the fugue and memories of events prior to the fugue will be recovered; however, memories of events occurring during the fugue state will not.

4. As I indicated earlier (see Chapter 5) there are no pain receptors in the brain. However, one could argue that the pain that the Actives experience during an imprint occurs as a result of memory blocks being destroyed. In other words the Actives would be feeling psychic, not physical, pain.

5. See the section on *A Short Lesson on the Nervous System* in Chapter 5.

6. Echo will learn later what really happened that night, once again confirming the fallibility of memory. After she and Bennett break into Rossum's headquarters to set the bomb, Caroline discovers that people are still in the building. Trying to delay hers and Bennett's departure so that no one will be harmed, Caroline declares that she will be the only one caught. Unfortunately, Bennett is trapped under the rubble when the explosion occurs. Before leaving her, Caroline tells Bennett to claim she was in the building because she was working late. This ploy apparently works as Bennett is hired for a high-ranking position at Rossum, whereas Caroline is indeed trapped. This event leads to her eventual "service" in the Dollhouse.

7. Psychologists do not believe that humans possess instincts, and they certainly do not believe that there is a maternal instinct. Anyone who does need only look at the statistics on child murder to realize that women murder their children more often than do men.

Chapter 7

1. Portions of this chapter were presented at the annual meeting of the Popular Culture Association, New Orleans, Louisiana, in October 2009. I would like to thank Heather M. Porter, President of Smart Chicks with Super Powers Productions, for her helpful comments and suggestions about this chapter. It was she who reminded me of Giles' excessive use of alcohol during Season Four and Terry's use of drugs to enact his horrible games with his victims on the *Dollhouse* episode "Belle Chose."

2. Students (and sometimes professionals) confuse punishment and negative reinforcement. Reinforcement ALWAYS strengthens a response and increases the probability that a response will reoccur. Both positive and negative reinforcement lead to a satisfying state of affairs for the individual. For example, the student who studies hard for a test and makes an "A" is positively reinforced. The student has gained something positive and will likely continue to engage in the behavior that yielded the positive outcome. The student whose headache disappears after she takes an aspirin has been negatively reinforced. She is likely to take an aspirin in the future when she feels the beginning of a headache. Punishment, on the other hand, is designed to weaken a response and decrease the probability that a response will reoccur. A student who decides to party rather than studying for a test gets an "F." We refer to that as positive punishment: receiving an unpleasant stimulus as a consequence for undesired behavior. The student who received the "F" is not allowed to go to the dance. We refer to that as negative punishment: removing a pleasant stimulus as a consequence for undesired behavior. We hope that the student will not engage in either of those behaviors again.

3. A discussion about the mechanisms through which your brain responds to various drugs of abuse is beyond the scope of this chapter. Suffice it to say that your body does not like it when you mess with it. It compensates, as those of us who yo-yo with our weight are well aware.

4. In other words, soma was negatively reinforcing. If anyone in this *Brave New World* experienced the slightest tinge of discomfort, they simply had to take their soma to relieve those unpleasant feelings. As the drug continued to work, it produced euphoria, which was positively reinforcing. Drugs such as alcohol, caffeine, and nicotine work this way to produce their powerful addictive effects.

5. Okay, this is a digression, but what about other bodily processes? Yes, vampires have sex — apparently a lot of sex. Do vampires have semen? The answer would apparently be "yes," given that Darla got pregnant. On the other hand, considering all of shagging going on, why has no other woman (human or vampire) gotten pregnant by a vampire? If vampires have semen, then why does Buffy casually walk away from a sexual encounter with Spike, as if there is no semen dripping down her legs? Does Spike use condoms? That fact, plus the lack of foreplay (as if women are always "ready" for sex) is why I cannot suspend my disbelief long enough to "enjoy" sex scenes on film: they just look fake. I include the so-called sex scene between Tara and Willow in that assessment ("Once More, with Feeling" 6.7). And do not even get me started on Spike's smoking (vampires aren't supposed to breathe!).

6. Why do we expect Xander to be able to swim fast enough and well enough to make it through the tryouts for the swim team?

7. Why is no one questioning a pub on a college campus? Is one really allowed to have a pub on a college campus in the U.S.? The legal drinking age in the U.S. is 21, and, thus, most college students are not legally able to drink. Many college campuses closed their pubs and bars on campus when the legal drinking age was raised to 21. College administrators did not want to be held responsible for controlling access to alcohol for underage students. That is also why one cannot buy alcohol at sporting events on college campuses. And, why is Xander selling Buffy alcohol? That's a pretty fast way to lose your job — violating the local alcohol control board's rules — and have the pub lose its license to operate.

8. Learn more about paranoid schizophrenia at http://www.mayoclinic.com/health/paranoid-schizophrenia/DS00862/DSECTION=symptoms.

9. Whedon refused a request to tell about the syringe in the *Firefly the Official Companion Volume Two*, stating that he would keep that secret for the future. I think that Inara's comments about not wanting to die ("Out of Gas" 1.8) are what most of us would say in such a situation; I certainly do not want to die (although note to all Vampires: I do not want to live forever either). In addition, Nandi's comment about how Inara hasn't aged a day since they last met ("Heart of Gold") also seems normal. Just go to your high school or college reunion and listen to all of the people tell you that you have not aged a day since then. It is just politeness. However, I must admit that the short story, "Crystal," by Brett Matthews, in *Firefly Still Flying*, made me wonder what question about herself Inara would have asked River. Also, if Simon is such as gifted doctor, wouldn't he have been able to tell that something was wrong with Inara? In any case, the most important question for me with respect to Inara is, *why does she have flash bombs in her boudoir?*

10. If Inara did something really bad that got her expelled from her Training House, then she has apparently been forgiven. After all, they let her come back. I understand that she is at a different house but it stands to reason that there is some type of ruling counsel for the Companion Guild who would control the Guild and enforce Guild Law.

11. See, for example, Barlett and Steele.

12. There are various sites on the web where one can read Timothy Leary's best quotes, and some of them are great. For more, see http://www.brainyquote.com/quotes/authors/t/timothy_leary.html.

13. I haven't got the foggiest notion what would be considered the "sleeping" part of the brain. Yes, there are parts of the brain that control sleeping, but the brain itself never sleeps. I am presuming they are talking about the so-called 10 percent of the brain that we do not use (See Chapter 5).

14. Terry, the psychopathic villain on the episode "Belle Chose" (*Dollhouse* 2.3), uses drugs to incapacitate his victims. He does not need to use ropes to bind his victims because

the drugs are so powerful they render the women helpless, unable to escape or fight back against their abuse.

15. Many people think of cocaine or the various amphetamines when they think of psychomotor stimulants. However, other drugs that fall into this category are caffeine and nicotine, two of the most widely used drugs in the world. People with attention-deficit disorder (ADD) are also treated with stimulant drugs. Sedative-hypnotic drugs can be used to treat epilepsy.

Chapter 8

1. I would like to thank Dr. Alyson R. Buckman of California State University at Sacramento for her helpful comments and suggestions. She responded to my urgent call for help, reading the chapter and replying with her comments within four days. I am extremely grateful to her for making time in her busy schedule for this.

2. Definition of symbol from http://www.thefreedictionary.com/symbol (retrieved May 21, 2011).

3. Jesus of Nazareth is all too frequently referred to as Jesus Christ, as if Christ is his surname. The word Christ is actually a title, meaning Messiah. Using the term Jesus Christ thus implies that the user is Christian, i.e., one who believes that Jesus of Nazareth is the Messiah. The correct way to use the term is Jesus the Christ, which still implies that the user is Christian. People living in the United States are very Christocentric, and do not seem to understand (or care) that the majority of people in the world are not Christians.

4. Whether the myth about the claddagh is true or not, it sounds quite romantic. Google the word "claddagh" and you will get over 5 million hits, most of which will try to sell you a ring or will repeat the legend of its origin. I admit that I own about a dozen or so claddagh rings, earrings, toe rings, necklaces, et cetera. But, then again, my ancestry is Irish. Remember when I said that I did not watch *Buffy* until the last few years? Most of my claddaghs date from before my *Buffy*-watching days. After I finally started watching *Buffy* I understood why so many of my students were wearing claddaghs.

5. The fact that Buffy is able to pull a stake out of seemingly thin air is sometimes mystifying given the skin-tight clothes she wears. That also applies to her cell phone. No wonder Buffy does not drive — where would she put her car keys?

6. Thanks to Alyson Buckman for pointing out the obvious question of how Buffy's body is also resurrected, given that decomposition should have been well underway. Obviously, the spell that Willow casts revitalizes Buffy's body. And, one can only imagine what Joyce would have been like following Dawn's spell to bring her back from the dead ("Forever" 5.17).

7. Frankly, I would think that Zoe is still wearing her boots from the war. Good boots should last for years.

8. I think this is characteristic of the color purple, which was the "royal" color for many centuries; wearing purple by non-royals was punishable by death.

9. Definition of fear from http://www.thefreedictionary.com/Fear (retrieved May 21, 2011).

10. See Note 9, Chapter 7.

11. The first three seasons of *Buffy* occur during the high school years. Buffy and the Scoobies spend an inordinate amount of time in the school library, but apparently none of the other students do. As a matter of fact, the only books we ever see in the library are Giles' books on the occult. Giles also does not seem to have any assistants working for him. I, for one, also wonder why none of the other teachers ever questioned his relationship with Buffy.

12. If these people are supposed to be so media savvy, then why do they not have cell phones? Plus, they absolutely never text each other! How odd is that? It is pretty damned weird for their generation. Alyson Buckman notes that texting was not as ubiquitous in

1997, when Buffy began, as it is nowadays. But the lack of cell phone usage is odd, she says, especially when they were in college. I agree, and sometimes I wish I could zap my students when they grab those annoying devices.

13. This quote has been attributed to both Plato and Sir Francis Bacon. Quote from http://www.brainyquote.com/quotes/quotes/f/francisbac100764.html (retrieved May 31, 2011).

14. I understand that not all of the demons in Buffy's world are evil, just most of them. Certainly Clem was a sweetheart and he was probably Dawn's closest pal. *Angel* was written specifically with the intent of showing that demons also needed help and, like their human counterparts, were just trying to get by.

15. Thanks to Mary Alice Money for reminding me that Giles not only had "book-learning," but practical experience as well. Wesley was much younger than Giles when he arrived in Sunnydale and his inexperience frequently resulted in trouble. By the time he appears on *Angel*, he has much more experience in the field. Unfortunately, by the end of *Angel*, Wesley has become tough and, in some instances, downright brutal.

16. Thanks to Alyson Buckman for also pointing out that Cordelia's computer skills were never at par with Willow's. And, we can never forget that one of the most proficient of the computer "geeks" was Jenny Calendar.

17. According to Tim Minear, Kate Lockley was never meant to be a romantic interest for Angel (*Angel* Season One DVD Special Features: "*Angel* Season One").

18. Both definitions of family from http://www.thefreedictionary.com/family (retrieved May 21, 2011).

19. A discussion of the family in history is beyond the scope of this chapter. However, it is important to note that until the modern-era children were typically considered to be small adults and were not provided the childhood deemed critical in contemporary American society. Very young children worked in times past, and parents were not considered necessary for raising their children beyond the age of weaning. People in the upper socioeconomic strata hired nannies and other persons to care for their children. Women were not considered to be worthy of raising their own children until the latter part of the 19th century and into the present. Unless wealthy, children lived very hard lives and the mortality rate was very high. For a fascinating look, see Prost and Vincent.

20. Frankly, a daughter who is slaying vampires at night should be capable of washing her own clothes, especially if she is trying to keep her secret from her mother.

21. I understand that the *Buffy* family falls apart in the Season Eight comics. I am trying not to think about it.

22. Of course, one could also see Mal as the patriarchal male who makes and enforces the rules aboard his boat. Anyone who disagrees with the patriarch risks being excluded from the group. Mal exerts his authority at various times throughout the series, such as in "Serenity" (1.1), when Mal tells Jayne to leave the table after Jayne makes sexual remarks about Kaylee's attraction to Simon. Mal also asserts his authority in *Serenity* after the crew discovers the massacre on Haven. By the way, considering the way that Inara acts at the end of "Heart of Gold," when she tells Mal she is leaving Serenity, leads me to believe that there is something going on with respect to her family or a family she might have created for herself in the past. She talks about getting too close and getting too comfortable, which makes one never want to leave that safety and comfort. It would appear that she got too close to someone and then lost them at some point in her past. This might explain the mystery of why she left the inner planets and rented a shuttle from Mal. Perhaps one day Whedon will tell us a story about Inara, much as he did for Shepherd Book.

23. It is true that there is some evidence of bonding on the part of the Actives prior to the events occurring after the imprinting technology is used on the general population. For example, Topher notes that the Actives tend to stick together but refers to it simply as herd behavior; however, it is a clear indication that their memories have not been completely wiped (see Chapter 6). They "remember" each other.

Appendix A

1. Character names and descriptions were taken from the companion volumes to the series in question. See Works Cited for the complete citation for each: *Buffy*, Golden and Holder; Holder; Ruditis; Stafford; *Angel*, Holder, Mariotte, and Hart; Ruditis and Gallagher; Stafford; *Firefly, The Official Companion*, Volumes One and Two; *Firefly Still Flying*; *Serenity: The Official Visual Companion*. There are no *Dollhouse* companions (to date). The brief descriptions of the characters are my own. My purpose in providing this list was to aid the reader in keeping characters straight on the various series, as the character lists for each series could be quite long (see Kaveney, for example).

Appendix B

1. The episodes listed herein are those that were filmed and/or broadcast for each of the four series discussed in this book. I have not included the air dates for the various episodes as these dates are readily available from a variety of sources and do not necessarily reflect the order in which they were meant to be seen. This was especially true of *Firefly*. I have listed the episodes in the order in which they are indicated on the respective DVD. All of the information in this list was verified by the DVDs for each series, episode guides in various companions, and a multitude of internet sites. I am indebted to Rhonda V. Wilcox and K. Dale Koontz for giving me copies of their episode lists for *Buffy* and *Angel*, which I then re-verified. Each of the four series is available for purchase from the usual sources.

2. See Note 1 Appendix A. Each of the companion guides also provides a synopsis of the plot for each episode; some are more complete than others. The interested reader is advised to check multiple sources.

3. According to the dictionary I use (*Oxford English Dictionary and Thesaurus*, American Edition, 1997), the word "judgement" can be spelled with the "e." I know there was great debate over the spelling of this episode's title when it originally aired. Some sources spell the title with the "e" and others do not. My DVD collection spells the title with the "e."

Works Cited

The scholarly literature examining the Whedonverses is quite extensive. I have tried to find the works published to date on all things Whedon, and I have tried to read it all. As anyone can see, however, I have not been able to cite everything written, nor have I have included it all in a Bibliography. To do so would have been prohibitive. I apologize to anyone who has written a paper that was not cited specifically. The contribution of all authors and researchers is acknowledged in the collections that contain their work.

Abadinsky, Howard. *Drug Use and Abuse: A Comprehensive Introduction*, 7th ed. Belmont, CA: Wadsworth Cengage Learning, 2011.

Abbott, Stacey. *Angel*. Detroit: Wayne State University Press, 2009.

_____, ed. *Reading* Angel: *The TV Spin-Off with a Soul*. London: I.B. Taurus, 2005.

Aberdein, Andrew. "The Companions and Socrates: Is Inara a hetaera?" In *Investigating Firefly and Serenity: Science Fiction on the Frontier*, edited by Rhonda V. Wilcox and Tanya R. Cochran. London: I.B. Taurus, 2008.

Adam, Charles, and Paul Tannery, eds. *Oeuvres de Descartes*, 2d ed. Paris: Vrin, 1974–1986.

Alabama Coalition Against Domestic Violence. acadv.org/dating.html (accessed May 15, 2011).

Alexander, David. *Star Trek Creator: The Authorized Biography of Gene Roddenberry*. New York: ROC, 1994.

Alzheimer's Association. "Alzheimer's disease facts and figures, 2010." http://www.alz.org/documents_custom/report_alzfactsfigures2010.pdf (accessed January 31, 2011).

American Psychiatric Association. *Diagnostic and Statistical Manual of Mental Disorders*. Revised 4th ed. Washington, DC: APA, 2000.

Bardi, C. Albert, and Sherry Hamby. "Existentialism meets Feminism in *Buffy the Vampire Slayer*." In *The Psychology of Joss Whedon*, edited by Joy Davidson, 105–117. Dallas: BenBella, 2007.

Barlett, Donald L., and James B. Steele. "Deadly Medicine." *Vanity Fair*, January 2011.

Barr, Marleen. *Alien to Femininity: Speculative Fiction and Feminist Theory*. New York: Greenwood, 1987.

_____. *Lost in Space: Probing Feminist Science Fiction and Beyond*. Chapel Hill: University of North Carolina Press, 1993.

Barstow, Anne Llewellyn. *Witchcraze: A New History of the European Witch Hunts*. San Francisco: Pandora, 1974.

Battis, Jes. *Blood Relations: Chosen Families in* Buffy the Vampire Slayer *and* Angel. Jefferson, NC: McFarland, 2005.

Baumeister, Roy F., and Brad J. Bushman. *Social Psychology and Human Nature*, 2d ed. Belmont, CA: Wadsworth Cengage Learning, 2011.

Benokraitis, Nijole V. *Soc*. Belmont, CA: Wadsworth Cengage Learning, 2010.

Bloom, Floyd E., Susan D. Iversen, Robert H. Roth, and Leslie L. Iversen. *Introduction to Neuropsychopharmacology*. London: Oxford University Press, 2008.

Boyer, Paul, and Stephen Nissenbaum. *Salem Possessed: The Social Origins of Witchcraft.* New York: MJF, 1974.

Brannon, Julie Sloan. "'It's About Power': Buffy, Foucault, and the Quest for Power." *Slayage The Online International Journal of Buffy Studies*, 6.4 [24], 2007.

"Break the Cycle: Empowering Youth to End Domestic Violence." www.breakthecycle.org. (accessed 15 May 2011).

Browne, Angela. "Violence Against Women by Male Partners." *American Psychologist* 48 (1993): 1077–1087.

Buckman, Alyson. "Triangulated Desire in *Angel* and *Buffy*." In *Sexual Rhetoric in the Works of Joss Whedon*, edited by Erin Waggoner, 48–92. Jefferson, NC: McFarland, 2010.

Burnett, Tamy. "Anya as Feminist Model of Positive Female Sexuality." In *Sexual Rhetoric in the Works of Joss Whedon*, edited by Erin Waggoner, 117–145. Jefferson, NC: McFarland, 2010.

Buss, David M. *The Evolution of Desire: Strategies of Human Mating*. New York: Basic, 1994.

_____, Randy J. Larsen, Drew Westen, and Jennifer Semmelroth. "Sex Differences in Jealousy: Evolution, Physiology, and Psychology." *Psychological Science* 3 (1992): 251–255.

Bussolini, Jeffrey. "A Geopolitical Interpretation of *Serenity*." In *Investigating Firefly and Serenity: Science Fiction on the Frontier*, edited by Rhonda V. Wilcox and Tanya R. Cochran, 139–152. London: I.B. Taurus, 2008.

Buunk, Bram P., Alois Angleitner, Viktor Oubaid, and David M. Buss. "Sex Differences in Jealousy in Evolutionary and Cultural Perspective: Tests from The Netherlands, Germany, and the United States." *Psychological Science* 7 (1996): 359–363.

Cawthorne, Nigel. *Witches: History of a Persecution*. London: Arcturus, 2004.

Coker, Catherine. "Exploitation of Bodies and Minds in Season One of *Dollhouse*." In *Sexual Rhetoric in the Works of Joss Whedon*, edited by Erin Waggoner, 226–238. Jefferson, NC: McFarland, 2010.

Connor, Ed. "Psychology Bad." In *The Psychology of Joss Whedon*, edited by Joy Davidson, 185–195. Dallas: BenBella, 2007.

Cooper, Jack R., Floyd E. Bloom, and Robert H. Roth. *The Biochemical Basis of Neuropharmacology*, 8th ed. London: Oxford University Press, 2002.

Daniels, Bradley J. "'Stripping' River Tam's Amygdala." In *The Psychology of Joss Whedon*, edited by Joy Davidson, 131–140. Dallas: BenBella, 2007.

Darwin, Charles. *The Descent of Man and Selection in Relation to Sex*. London: Murray, 1871.

_____. *On the Origin of Species by the Means of Natural Selection, or Preservation of Favoured Races in the Struggle for Life*. London: Murray, 1859.

Davidson, Joy, ed. *The Psychology of Joss Whedon*. Dallas: BenBella, 2007.

_____. "Whores and Goddesses." In *Finding Serenity: Anti-heroes, Lost Shepherds and Space Hookers in Joss Whedon's* Firefly, edited by Jane Epenson, 113–129. Dallas: BenBella, 2004.

Day, William Patrick. *Vampire Legends in Contemporary American Culture: What Becomes a Legend Most*. Lexington: University of Kentucky Press, 2002.

Descartes, Rene. *Treatise of Man*. Translation and Commentary by Thomas Steele Hall. Amherst, New York: Prometheus, 2003.

Dick, Philip K. *Do Androids Dream of Electric Sheep?* New York: Del Rey, 1968.

Duffy, K.G., Steven J. Kirsh, and Eastwood Atwater. *Psychology for Living: Adjustment, Growth, and Behavior Today*, 10th ed. Boston: Prentice Hall, 2011.

Early, Frances, and Kathleen Kennedy, eds. *Athena's Daughters: Television's New Women Warriors*. Syracuse, NY: Syracuse University Press, 2003.

Edwards, Lynne Y., Elizabeth L. Rambo, and James B. South. *Buffy Goes Dark: Essays on the Final Two Seasons of* Buffy the Vampire Slayer *on Television.* Jefferson, NC: McFarland, 2009.

Ekman, Paul, ed. *Darwin and Facial Expression.* Cambridge, MA: Malor, 2006.

Erdmann, Terry J. *Star Trek Deep Space Nine* ® *Companion.* New York: Pocket Books, 2000.

Espenson, Jane, Georges Jeanty, and Joss Whedon. *Buffy the Vampire Slayer Season Eight Volume 6: Retreat.* Milwaukie, OR: Dark Horse Comics, 2010.

Firefly Still Flying. London: Titan, 2010.

Firefly the Official Companion Volume One. London: Titan, 2006.

Firefly the Official Companion Volume Two. London: Titan, 2007.

Fuller, Robert C. *Stairways to Heaven: Drugs in American Religious History.* New York: Basic, 2000.

Ginn, Sherry. "Joss' Brains: Memory, Mind and Mayhem." Paper presented at the Slayage 4 Conference on the Whedonverses, St. Augustine, FL, 2010.

_____. "Memory, Mind, and Mayhem: Neurological Tampering and Manipulation in Dollhouse." *Slayage: The Journal of the Whedon Studies Association* 8.2–3 (Summer/Fall 2010). Special Issue: Fantasy Is Not Their Purpose: Joss Whedon's *Dollhouse.* Edited by Cynthea Masson and Rhonda V. Wilcox.

_____. *Our Space, Our Place: Women in the Worlds of Science Fiction Television.* Lanham, MD: University Press of America, 2005.

Godbeer, Richard. *Escaping Salem: The Other Witch Hunt of 1692.* New York: Oxford University Press, 2005.

Goddard, Drew, Georges Jeanty, and Joss Whedon. *Buffy the Vampire Slayer Season Eight Volume 3: Wolves at the Gate.* Milwaukie, OR: Dark Horse Comics, 2008.

Golden, Christopher, and Nancy Holder. *Buffy the Vampire Slayer: The Watcher's Guide,* Vol. 1. New York: Simon Spotlight Entertainment, 1998.

Goodfriend, Wind. "Terror Management Aboard Serenity." In *The Psychology of Joss Whedon,* edited by Joy Davidson, 91–104. Dallas: BenBella, 2007.

Grayling, A.C. *Descartes: the Life and Times of a Genius.* New York: Walker, 2005.

Greco, Nicholas. "The Companion as a Doll: The Female Enigma in *Firefly* and *Dollhouse.*" In *Sexual Rhetoric in the Works of Joss Whedon,* edited by Erin Waggoner, 239–247. Jefferson, NC: McFarland, 2010.

Greenberg, Benjamin D., Donald A. Malone, Gerhard M. Friehs, Ali R. Rezai, Cynthia S. Kubu, Paul F. Malloy, Stephen P. Salloway, Michael S. Okun, Wayne K. Goodman, and Steven A. Rasmussen. "Three-Year Outcomes in Deep Brain Stimulation for Highly Resistant Obsessive-Compulsive Disorder." *Neuropsychopharmacology* 31 (2006): 2384–2393.

Gruenbaum, Ellen. *The Female Circumcision Controversy: An Anthropological Perspective.* Philadelphia: University of Pennsylvania Press, 2001.

Halpern, Sue. *Can't Remember What I Forgot: The Good News from the Front Lines of Memory Research.* New York: Harmony Books, 2008.

Havens, Candace. *Joss Whedon: The Genius Behind Buffy.* Dallas: BenBella, 2003.

Hilts, Philip J. *Memory's Ghost: The Nature of Memory and the Strange Tale of Mr. M.* New York: Simon and Schuster, 1995.

Holder, Nancy. *Buffy the Vampire Slayer: The Watcher's Guide,* Vol. 2. New York: Pocket Books, 2000.

_____, Jeff Mariotte, and Maryelizabeth Hart. *Angel: The Casefiles,* Vol. 1. New York: Simon Pulse, 2002.

Hook, Misty. "Dealing with the F-Word." In *The Psychology of Joss Whedon,* edited by Joy Davidson, 119–129. Dallas: BenBella, 2007.

Humanitas. "Power and personality: Acton's law in *Buffy the Vampire Slayer.*" (April 2, 2002). http://www.atpobtvs.com/existentialscoobies/essays.html (accessed September 21, 2009).

Hunt, R. Reed, and Henry C. Ellis. *Fundamentals of Cognitive Psychology.* 7th ed. Boston: McGraw-Hill, 2004.

Huxley, Aldous. *Brave New World.* New York: Harper Perennial, 2005.

_____. *Brave New World Revisited.* New York: Harper Perennial, 2005.

Jong, Erica. *Witches.* New York: Abradale Press, 1997.

Jowett, Lorna. *Sex and the Slayer: A Gender Studies Primer for the Buffy Fan.* Middletown, CT: Wesleyan University Press, 2005.

Julien, Robert M., Claire D. Advokat, and Joseph E. Comaty. *A Primer of Drug Action*, 11th ed. New York: Worth, 2008.

Kandel, Eric, James H. Schwartz, and Thomas M. Jessell. *Principles of Neural Science*, 4th ed. New York: McGraw-Hill, 2000.

Kaveney, Roz, ed. *Reading the Vampire Slayer: The New, Updated Unofficial Guide to* Buffy *and* Angel. London: Taurus Parke, 2004.

Kent, William. "Demonology." *The Catholic Encyclopedia*, Vol. 4. New York: Robert Appleton Company, 1908. http://www.newadvent.org/cathen/04713a.htm (accessed June 1, 2011).

Keyes, J. Gregory. *Babylon 5 Dark Genesis: The Birth of Psi Corps.* New York: Del Rey, 1995.

Koontz, K. Dale. *Faith and Choice in the Works of Joss Whedon.* Jefferson, NC: McFarland, 2008.

LaBar, Kevin S. "Beyond Fear: Emotional Memory Mechanisms in the Human Brain." *Current Directions in Psychological Science* 16 (2007): 173–177.

LeDoux, Joseph. *The Emotional Brain: The Mysterious Underpinnings of Emotional Life.* New York: Touchstone, 1996.

Lemonick, Michael D. "The Many Flavors of Memory." Edited by Jeffrey Kluger. *Your Brain: A User's Guide.* New York: Time Inc. Home Entertainment, 2009.

Loftus, Elizabeth F. "Creating False Memories." *Scientific American* 277 (1977): 70–75. http://faculty.washington.edu/eloftus/Articles/sciam.htm.

Lovecraft, Howard P. "From Beyond." In *The Lurking Fear and Other Stories*, 59–66. New York: Random House, 1971.

Macmillan, Malcolm. *An Odd Kind of Fame: Stories of Phineas Gage.* Cambridge, MA: The MIT Press, 2002.

Marano, Michael. "River Tam and the Weaponized Women of the Whedonverse." In *Serenity Found: More Unauthorized Essays on Joss Whedon's* Firefly *Universe*, edited by Jane Espenson. Dallas: BenBella, 2007.

Martin, Lois. *The History of Witchcraft.* Edison, NJ: Chartwell, 2007.

Mascetti, Manuela Dunn. *Vampire: The Complete Guide to the World of the Undead.* New York: Viking Studio, 1992.

Mashour, George A., Erin E. Walker, and Robert L. Martuza. "Psychosurgery: Past, Present, and Future." *Brain Research Reviews* 48 (2005): 409–419.

Matthews, Brett. "Crystal." In *Firefly: Still Flying: A Celebration of Joss Whedon's Acclaimed TV Series*, 104–113. London: Titan, 2010.

Mayberg, Helen S., Andres M. Lozano, Valerie Voon, Heather E. McNeely, David Seminowicz, Clement Hamani, Jason M. Schwalb, and Sidney H. Kennedy. "Deep Brain Stimulation for Treatment-Resistant Depression." *Neuron* 45 (2005): 651–660.

Meltzer, Brad, Georges Jeanty, and Joss Whedon. *Buffy the Vampire Slayer Season Eight Volume 7: Twilight.* Milwaukie, OR: Dark Horse Comics, 2010.

Memory (definitions). http://medicaldictionary.thefreedictionary.com/Memory+(psychology) (accessed December 14, 2011).

Mesmer, Franz A. *Mesmerism by Dr. Mesmer* (G. Fankau, ed., V.R. Myers, Trans.). London: Macdonald, 1948.

Meyer, Stephanie. *Twilight.* Boston: Little, Brown, 2006.

Meyers, David. *Exploring Social Psychology*, 5th ed. New York: McGraw-Hill, 2009.

Moldovano, Pnina. "Virtually a Femme Fatale: The Case of *Buffy*'s Faith." In *Sexual Rhetoric in the Works of Joss Whedon*, edited by Erin Waggoner, 194–214. Jefferson, NC: McFarland, 2010.

Naficy, Siamak Tundra, and Karthik Panchanathan. "Buffy the Vampire Dater." In *The Psychology of Joss Whedon*, edited by Joy Davidson, 141–153. Dallas: BenBella, 2007.

National Coalition Against Domestic Violence (NCADV). "The Problem." NCADV.org.learn/the problem-100.html (2005).

National Institute of Mental Health. "Statistics." http://www.nimh.nih.gov/statistics/index.shtml (accessed December 14, 2011).

Prost, Antoine, and Gérard Vincent, eds. *A History of Private Life* (Five Volumes). Translation by Arthur Goldhammer. Cambridge, MA: The Belknap Press, 1991.

Rabb, J. Douglas, and J. Michael Richardson. "Reavers and Redskins: Creating the Frontier Savage." In *Investigating Firefly and Serenity: Science Fiction on the Frontier*, edited by Rhonda V. Wilcox and Tanya R. Cochran, 127–138. London: I.B. Taurus, 2008.

Riess, Jana. *What Would Buffy Do? The Vampire Slayer as Spiritual Guide.* San Francisco: Jossey-Bass, 2004.

Richardson, J. Michael, and J. Douglas Rabb. *The Existential Joss Whedon.* Jefferson, NC: McFarland, 2007.

Rotter, Julian. "Internal-external locus of control scale." John P. Robinson and Phillip R. Shaver, eds. *Measures of Social Psychological Attitudes* (56). Ann Arbor: Institute for Social Research, 1973.

Ruditis, Paul. *Buffy the Vampire Slayer: The Watcher's Guide*, Vol. 3. New York: Simon Spotlight, 2004.

_____, and Diana G. Gallagher. *Angel: The Casefiles*, Vol. 2. New York: Simon Spotlight Entertainment, 2004.

Sacks, Oliver. "The Abyss: Music and Amnesia." *The New Yorker* (January 20, 2010). http://www.newyorker.com/reporting/2007/09/24/070924fa_fact_sacks?currentPage=all.

Schneider, Julie A., Zoe Arvanitakis, Woojeong Bang, and David A. Bennett. "Mixed Brain Pathologies Account for Most Dementia Cases in Community-dwelling Older Persons." *Neurology* 69 (2007): 2197–2204.

Seligman, Martin E.P. "Learned Helplessness." *Annual Review of Medicine, 23,* 407–412, 1972.

Shelley, Mary. *Frankenstein.* 1818, 1831.

Shin, Lisa M., Scott L. Rauch, and Roger K. Pitman. "Amygdala, Medial Prefrontal Cortex, and Hippocampal Function in PTSD." *Annals of the New York Academy of Sciences, 1071* (2006): 67–79.

Silverberg, Robert. *Drug Themes in Science Fiction.* Rockville, MD: National Institute on Drug Abuse. DHEW Publication No. ADM (1974): 75–190.

South, James B. *Buffy the Vampire Slayer and Philosophy: Fear and Trembling in Sunnydale.* Chicago: Open Court, 2003.

SparkNotes Editors. "SparkNote on *Brave New World*." SparkNotes (2002). SparkNotes.com. (accessed May 17, 2011).

Stafford, Nikki. *Bite Me! The Unofficial Guide to* Buffy the Vampire Slayer: *The Chosen Edition.* Toronto, Ontario, Canada: ECW Press, 2007.

_____. *Once Bitten: An Unofficial Guide to the World of* Angel. Toronto, Ontario, Canada: ECW Press, 2004.

Sternberg, Robert J. *Cupid's Arrow: The Course of Love through Time.* Cambridge: Cambridge University Press, 1998.

Stevenson, Robert Louis. *Strange Case of Dr. Jekyll and Mr. Hyde.* London: Longmans, Green, 1886.

Stoker, Bram. *Dracula.* 1897.

Stoy, Jennifer. "Blood and Choice: The Theory and Practice of Family in *Angel*." Roz Kaveney, ed. *Reading the Vampire Slayer: The New, Updated Unofficial Guide to* Buffy *and* Angel. London: Taurus Parke, 2004.

Vaughan, Brian K., Georges Jeanty, and Joss Whedon. *Buffy the Vampire Slayer Season Eight Volume 2: No Future For You*. Milwaukie, OR: Dark Horse Comics, 2008.

Waggoner, Erin. *Sexual Rhetoric in the Works of Joss Whedon*. Jefferson, NC: McFarland, 2010.

Walker, Lenore E. "Post-traumatic Stress Disorder in Women: Diagnosis and Treatment of Battered Women Syndrome." *Psychotherapy* 28 (1991): 21–29.

_____. "Understanding Battered Women Syndrome." *Trial* (February 1995): 30–37.

_____. "Victimology and the Psychological Perspectives of Battered Women." *Victimology: An International Journal* 8 (1983): 82–104.

Weber, Kathryn. "Exploding Sexual Binaries in *Buffy* and *Angel*." In *Sexual Rhetoric in the Works of Joss Whedon*, edited by Erin Waggoner, 248–261. Jefferson, NC: McFarland, 2010.

Whedon, Joss. *Serenity: The Official Visual Companion*. London: Titan, 2005.

_____, Jane Espenson, Steven S. DeKnight, Drew Z. Greenberg, Jim Krueger, Doug Petrie, and Georges Jeanty. *Buffy the Vampire Slayer Season Eight Volume 5: Predators and Prey*. Milwaukie, OR: Dark Horse Comics, 2009.

_____, and Georges Jeanty. *Buffy the Vampire Slayer Season Eight Volume 1: The Long Way Home*. Milwaukie, OR: Dark Horse Comics, 2007.

_____, Brett Matthews, and Will Conrad. *Serenity: Better Days*. Milwaukie, OR: Dark Horse Comics, 2008.

_____, Karl Moline, and Jeph Loeb. *Buffy the Vampire Slayer Season Eight Volume 4: Time of Your Life*. Milwaukie, OR: Dark Horse Comics, 2009.

_____, Karl Moline, and Andy Owens. *Fray*. Milwaukie, OR: Dark Horse Comics, 2003.

_____, Zach Whedon, and Chris Samnee. *Serenity: The Shepherd's Tale*. Milwaukie, OR: Dark Horse Comics, 2010.

Wilcox, Rhonda V. *Why Buffy Matters: The Art of Buffy the Vampire Slayer*. London: I.B. Taurus, 2005.

_____, and David Lavery, eds. *Fighting the Forces: What's at Stake in* Buffy the Vampire Slayer. Lanham, MD: Rowman & Littlefield, 2002.

Yeffeth, Glenn, ed. *Five Seasons of* Angel: *Science Fiction and Fantasy Writers Discuss their Favorite Vampire*. Dallas: BenBella, 2004.

_____. *Seven Seasons of* Buffy: *Science Fiction and Fantasy Writers Discuss their Favorite Television Show*. Dallas: BenBella, 2003.

Zelazny, Roger. *Nine Princes in Amber*. Garden City, NY: Nelson Doubleday, 1970.

Works Consulted but Not Cited

Note that some essays in the collections listed herein are cited in text. Those individual essays are included in the "Works Cited" section.

Abbott, Stacey. "Walking the Fine Line Between Angel and Angelus." *Slayage: The Online International Journal of Buffy Studies*, 3.1 [9] (2003).

Atkins, Thomas R., ed. *Sexuality in the Movies*. Bloomington: Indiana University Press, 1984.

Battis, Jes. "'She's Not All Grown Yet': Willow as Hybrid/Hero in *Buffy the Vampire Slayer*." *Slayage: The Journal of the Whedon Studies Association*, 2.4 [8], (2003).

Berenstein, Rhonda J. *Attack of the Leading Ladies*. New York: Columbia University Press, 1996.

Butler, Ivan. *Horror in the Cinema*. New York: Paperback Library, 1971.

Calvert, Bronwen. "Mind, body, imprint: Cyberpunk echoes in the *Dollhouse*." *Slayage: The Journal of the Whedon Studies Association* 8.2–3 (Summer/Fall 2010). Special Issue: Fantasy

Is Not Their Purpose: Joss Whedon's *Dollhouse*. Edited by Cynthea Masson and Rhonda V. Wilcox.

Campbell, Joseph. *The Hero with a Thousand Faces*. 3rd ed. Novato, CA: New World Library, 2008.

Carroll, Noel. *The Philosophy of Horror or Paradoxes of the Heart*. New York: Routledge, 1990.

deCandido, Keith R.A. *Serenity* (a novel based on the motion picture screenplay by Joss Whedon). New York: Pocket Star Books, 2005.

Durand, Kevin K. Buffy *Meets the Academy: Essays on the Episodes and Scripts as Texts*. Jefferson, NC: McFarland, 2009.

Espenson, Jane, ed. *Finding Serenity: Anti-heroes, Lost Shepherds and Space Hookers in Joss Whedon's* Firefly. Dallas: BenBella, 2004.

_____. *Inside Joss'* Dollhouse: *From Alpha to Rossum*. Dallas: SmartPop, 2010.

_____. *Serenity Found: More Unauthorized Essays on Joss Whedon's* Firefly *Universe*. Dallas: BenBella, 2007.

Everson, William K. *Classics of the Horror Film*. New York: Citadel Press, 1974.

Faludi, Susan. *Backlash: The Undeclared War Against American Women*. New York: Knopf Doubleday, 1992.

Heinecken, Dawn. *The Warrior Women of Television: A Feminist Cultural Analysis of the New Female Body in Popular Media*. New York: Peter Lang, 2003.

Ireland, Andrew, ed. *Illuminating Torchwood: Essays on Narrative, Character and Sexuality in the BBC Series*. Jefferson, NC: McFarland, 2010.

Jowett, Lorna. "'Not like Other Men'?: The Vampire Body in Joss Whedon's *Angel*." *Studies in Popular Culture* 32 (2009): 37–51.

Kendrick, Walter M. *The Thrill of Fear*. New York: Grove Weidenfeld, 1991.

King, Stephen. *Danse Macabre*. New York: Everest House, 1981.

Lee, John A. *The Colors of Love: An Exploration of the Ways of Loving*. Don Mills, Ontario: New Press, 1976.

Levine, Elana, and Lisa Parks. *Undead TV: Essays on* Buffy the Vampire Slayer. Durham, NC: Duke University Press, 2007.

Lovecraft, Howard P. *Supernatural Horror in Literature*. New York: Dover, 1973.

Machiavelli, Niccolò. *The Prince*. Mineola, NY: Dover, 2002.

Magoulick, Mary. "Frustrating Female Heroism: Mixed Messages in *Xena*, *Nikita*, and *Buffy*." *The Journal of Popular Culture* 39 (2006): 729–755.

Marx, Karl, and Friedrich Engels. *The Communist Manifesto*. New York: Barnes and Noble Classics, 2005.

McAvan, Em. "'I Think I'm Kinda Gay': Willow Rosenberg and the Absent/Present Bisexual in *Buffy the Vampire Slayer*." *Slayage: The Journal of the Whedon Studies Association*, 6.4 [24], (2007). Edited by Cynthea Masson and Rhona V. Wilcox.

Ostow, Micol, and Steven Brezenoff. Buffy the Vampire Slayer: *The Quotable Slayer*. New York: Simon Pulse, 2003.

Parkin, Frank. *Max Weber*, rev. ed. London: Routledge, 2002.

Pateman, Matthew. *The Aesthetics of Culture in* Buffy the Vampire Slayer. Jefferson, NC: McFarland, 2006.

Perdigao, Lisa K. "'This One's Broken': Rebuilding Whedonbots and Reprogramming the Whedonverse." *Slayage: The Journal of the Whedon Studies Association* 8.2–3 (Summer/Fall 2010). Special Issue: Fantasy Is Not Their Purpose: Joss Whedon's *Dollhouse*. Edited by Cynthea Masson and Rhonda V. Wilcox.

Puchalski, Steven. "The Continuing Identity Crisis: Man or Machine?" *Sci Fi Entertainment*, August 1996.

_____. "From Brain Enhancement to Brain Damage: SF Films at the Frontier of the Mind." *Sci Fi Entertainment*, June 1996.

Ramachandran, V.S. *The Tell-Tale Brain: A Neuroscientist's Quest for What Makes Us Human*. New York: W.W. Norton, 2011.

Rambo, Elizabeth L. "'Queen C' in Boys' Town: Killing the Angel in Angel's House." *Slayage: The Online International Journal of Buffy Studies*, 6.3 [23] (2007).

Roberts, Adam. *The History of Science Fiction*. Houndmills, UK: Palgrave Macmillan, 2006.

Ruddell, Caroline. "'I Am the Law' 'I Am the Magics': Speech, Power and the Split Identity of Willow in *Buffy the Vampire Slayer*." *Slayage: The Online International Journal of Buffy Studies*, 5.4 [20], (2006).

Sagan, Carl. *The Demon-Haunted World*. New York: Random House, 1995.

Sternberg, Robert J. *The Triarchic Mind: A New Theory of Human Intelligence*. New York: Viking Press, 1988.

_____, and Michael L. Barnes, eds. *The Psychology of Love*. New Haven: Yale University Press, 1988.

Whedon, Joss, Brett Matthews, and Will Conrad. *Serenity: Those Left Behind*. Milwaukie, OR: Dark Horse Books, 2006.

Wilcox, Rhonda V. "Echoes of Complicity: Reflexivity and Identity in Joss Whedon's *Dollhouse*." *Slayage: The Journal of the Whedon Studies Association* 8.2–3 (Summer/Fall 2010). Special Issue: Fantasy Is Not Their Purpose: Joss Whedon's *Dollhouse*. Edited by Cynthea Masson and Rhona V. Wilcox.

_____, and Tanya R. Cochran, eds. *Investigating* Firefly *and* Serenity: *Science Fiction on the Frontier*. London: I.B. Taurus, 2008.

Winslade, J. Lawton. "Teen Witches, Wiccans, and 'Wanna-Blessed-Be's': Pop-Culture Magic in *Buffy the Vampire Slayer*." *Slayage: The Online International Journal of Buffy Studies*, 1.1 [1], (2001).

Videography

Angel

Angel Seasons 1–5. The DVD Collector's Limited Edition Set. Beverly Hills, CA: Twentieth Century–Fox Home Entertainment, 2007.

Buffy the Vampire Slayer

The Complete First Season on DVD. Beverly Hills, CA: Twentieth Century–Fox Home Entertainment, 2001.

Season Two on DVD. Beverly Hills, CA: Twentieth Century–Fox Home Entertainment, 2006.

The Complete Third Season on DVD. Beverly Hills, CA: Twentieth Century–Fox Home Entertainment, 2003.

The Complete Fourth Season on DVD. Beverly Hills, CA: Twentieth Century–Fox Home Entertainment, 2003.

The Complete Fifth Season on DVD. Beverly Hills, CA: Twentieth Century–Fox Home Entertainment, 2003.

The Complete Sixth Season on DVD. Beverly Hills, CA: Twentieth Century–Fox Home Entertainment, 2004.

The Complete Seventh Season on DVD. Beverly Hills, CA: Twentieth Century–Fox Home Entertainment, 2004.

Dollhouse

Joss Whedon's Dollhouse Season One. Beverly Hills, CA: Twentieth Century–Fox Home Entertainment, 2009. DVD.

Joss Whedon's Dollhouse The Complete Season Two. Beverly Hills, CA: Twentieth Century–Fox Home Entertainment, 2010. DVD.

Firefly

Joss Whedon's Firefly The Complete Series. Beverly Hills, CA: Twentieth Century–Fox Home Entertainment, 2003. DVD.
Serenity Collector's Edition. Universal City, CA: Universal, 2007. DVD.

Fringe

"Jacksonville." *Fringe.* Executive Producer: J.J. Abrams. Director: Charles Beeson. Writers: Jack Stentz and Ashley Miller. Beverly Hills, CA: Fox Broadcasting Co., 2010. DVD.
"Olivia." *Fringe.* Executive Producer: J.J. Abrams. Director: Joe Chappelle. Writers: J.H. Wyman and Jeff Pinkner. Beverly Hills, CA: Fox Broadcasting Co., 2010. DVD.
"Over There, Part 2 of 2." *Fringe.* Executive Producer: J.J. Abrams. Director: Akiva Goldsman. Writers: Jeff Pinkner, J.H. Wyman, and Akiva Goldsman. Beverly Hills, CA: Fox Broadcasting Co., 2010. DVD.
"The Plateau." *Fringe.* Executive Producer: J.J. Abrams. Director: Brad Anderson. Writers: Alison Schapker and Monica Breen. Beverly Hills, CA: Fox Broadcasting Co., 2010. DVD.

Other Film and Video Sources

American Gothic. Creator: Shaun Cassidy. Universal City, CA: Universal, 1995. DVD.
Buffy the Vampire Slayer. Director: Fran Rubel Kuzui. Beverly Hills, CA: Twentieth Century–Fox, 1992. DVD.
Dark City. Director: Alex Proyas. Burbank, CA: New Line Cinema, 1998. DVD.
Dr. Horrible's Sing-Along Blog. Director: Joss Whedon. New York: New Video, 2009. DVD.
The Day the Earth Stood Still. Director: Robert Wise. Beverly Hills, CA: Twentieth Century–Fox, 1951. DVD.
Dracula. Director: Tod Browning. Universal City, CA: Universal, 1931. DVD.
Horror of Dracula. Director: Terence Fisher. (Hammer Film Productions, 1958.) Warner Home Video, 2002. DVD.
Dracula 2000. Director: Patrick Lussier. New York: Dimension Films, 2000. DVD.
Frankenstein. Director: James Whale. Universal City, CA: Universal Studios, 1931. DVD.
From Beyond. Director: Stuart Gordon. New York: Orion Pictures, 1986. DVD.
Independence Day. Director: Roland Emmerich. Beverly Hills, CA: Twentieth Century–Fox, 1996. DVD.
The Island. Director: Michael Bay. Universal City, CA: Dreamworks Video, 2005. DVD.
The Matrix. Directors: Andy Wachowski and Larry Wachowski. Burbank, CA: Warner Home Video, 2007. DVD.
Memento. Director: Christopher Nolan. Los Angeles: Newmarket Capital Group, 2001. DVD.
Moonlight: the Complete Series. Creators: Ron Koslow and Trevor Munson. Burbank, CA: Warner Home Video, 2011. DVD.
"Passing Through Gethsemane." *Babylon 5.* Executive Producers: David Netter and J. Michael Straczynski. Director: Adam Nimoy. Writer: J. Michael Straczynski. Burbank, CA: Warner Home Video, 1995. DVD.
The Puppetmasters. Director: Stuart Orme. Burbank, CA: Walt Disney Video, 1994. DVD.
True Blood, Season One. Creator and Producer: Alan Ball. New York: HBO Home Video, 2009. DVD.0

Index

Alzheimer's disease 88, 95, 98, 99, 106, 111, 168*n*3
amnesia 101, 102, 111, 168*n*3; anterograde 88, 100, 102, 108
amygdala(e) 87, 88, 89, 108, 109, 166*n*4
aneurysm 94, 167*n*15
Angel 2, 3, 4, 11, 13, 15, 16, 17, 21, 22, 27, 28, 30, 31, 34, 42, 48, 49, 50, 51, 52, 53, 54, 63, 64, 69, 71, 73, 74, 75, 76, 77, 78, 80, 95, 112, 113, 122, 123, 132, 134, 136, 137, 138, 141, 143, 159*n*6, 160*n*3, 161*n*9, 163*n*6, 171*n*17
Angel (series) 1, 3, 9, 13, 16, 21, 34, 49, 53, 54, 62, 74, 75, 76, 91, 95, 96, 128, 131, 132, 134, 137, 160*n*3, 171*n*14, 171*n*15; Angelus 2, 3, 4, 17, 18, 27, 29, 30, 49, 53, 54, 71, 74, 76, 141, 161*n*4, 163*n*8; Charles Gunn 4, 35, 42, 51, 53, 64, 75, 76, 77, 78, 123, 141, 143; Connor 4, 16, 17, 34, 75, 76, 77, 78, 112, 113, 162*n*10, 165*n*25; Darla 3, 4, 17, 27, 34, 42, 76, 132, 141, 159*n*6, 161*n*4, 169*n*5; Doyle 3, 4, 34, 50, 53, 74, 77, 95, 137, 165*n*20, 167*n*16; Fred (Winifred) Burkle 4, 35, 42, 51, 53, 75, 76, 77, 78, 141; Groosalugg (Groo) 75, 77; Holtz 4, 17, 75, 76 ; Illyria 78, 143; Jasmine 50, 75, 77, 78; Justine 34; Kate Lockley 34, 122, 123, 137, 171*n*17; Liam 3, 17, 53, 74, 132, 141, 159*n*6, 163*n*10; Lilah Morgan 35, 42, 50, 51, 52, 53; Lorne (The Host) 4, 75, 76, 112, 165*n*20; Oracles, Brother and Sister 76, 137; Powers That Be 3, 4, 16, 34, 74, 75, 76, 113, 123, 137, 161*n*9; Pylea 35, 53, 75, 77, 78; Wolfram & Hart 4, 50, 51, 76, 165*n*25
Angel Investigations 2, 4, 34, 51, 52, 76, 77, 78, 123, 136, 137, 141, 161*n*9

Angelverse 18, 21, 63, 64, 77, 79, 80, 123, 131, 132, 136, 141, 142, 143, 160*n*3, 165*n*20
apocalypse 4

Babylon 5 38, 89, 98, 119, 162*n*16
Battered Women Syndrome 52; *see also* domestic violence; interpersonal violence
Brave New World 118, 169*n*4
Browncoats 19
Buffy Summers 2, 9, 11, 13, 14, 16, 18, 21, 22, 27, 28, 29, 30, 31, 32, 34, 42, 45, 46, 48, 49, 63, 64, 67, 68, 69, 70, 71, 72, 73, 74, 79, 80, 91, 93, 94, 98, 112, 113, 120, 121, 131, 134, 136, 137, 140, 141, 143, 159*n*4, 159*n*5, 160*n*3, 161*n*9, 161*n*5, 162*n*5, 163*n*5, 169*n*5, 169*n*7, 170*n*5, 170*n*6, 170*n*11
Buffy the Vampire Slayer (film) 140
Buffy the Vampire Slayer (series) 1, 2, 9, 11, 12, 13, 21, 27, 28, 29, 31, 32, 34, 40, 43, 45, 47, 49, 53, 62, 65, 67, 74, 75, 76, 79, 81, 91, 96, 98, 111, 112, 119, 120, 128, 131, 132, 134, 137, 141, 143, 144, 159*n*2, 160*n*3, 163*n*6, 170*n*4, 170*n*11, 171*n*21; Adam 71, 81, 91, 92, 93, 95; Amy Madison 33, 67, 68, 71, 79; Andrew 47, 68, 69; Anya/Anyanka 2, 14, 32, 34, 42, 46, 68, 70, 79; Buffybot 69; Dark Willow 72, 73; Dawn Summers 3, 13, 14, 54, 67, 69, 70, 79, 93, 98, 112, 134, 140, 170*n*6, 171*n*14; Drusilla (Dru) 17, 18, 27, 29, 31, 42, 119, 120, 163*n*8; Ethan Rayne 15, 68, 120, 121; Faith 15, 16, 42, 46; Glory 71; Harmony Kendall 92, 161*n*2; Initiative 3, 31, 68, 69, 91, 92, 119, 120; Jenny Cal-

endar 53, 71, 171n16; Jonathan Levinson 47, 68, 69, 79; Joyce Summers 2, 48, 69, 81, 91, 93, 94, 96, 112, 113, 121, 140, 141, 167n14, 170n6; Kendra 73; Kennedy 3, 31, 33, 72; Maggie Walsh, Professor 92, 93, 95, 120, 121; Oz (Daniel Osbourne) 2, 14, 15, 16, 32, 42, 48, 68, 70, 160n6; Potential(s) 2, 14, 31, 72, 73, 143; Riley Finn 3, 30, 31, 42, 70, 91, 92, 120, 121, 159n2, 160n5; Rupert Giles 2, 14, 16, 31, 33, 64, 67, 68, 73, 74, 112, 120, 121, 122, 128, 136, 137, 140, 168n1, 170n11, 171n15; Scooby/Scoobies 14, 16, 31, 32, 45, 46, 49, 64, 69, 70, 75, 91, 92, 93, 98, 112, 113, 136, 140, 143, 170n11; Sunnydale, California 2, 3, 12, 32, 45, 67, 68, 69, 70, 91, 119, 121, 131, 136, 140, 159n5, 171n15; Sunnydale High School 15, 67, 70, 71, 120, 136; Tara Maclay 2, 15, 33, 42, 47, 48, 66, 69, 70, 71, 72, 73, 112, 134, 141, 169n5; The Troika/Trio 47, 68, 69; University of California–Sunnydale 14, 91; Vamp Willow, 33; Veruca 16, 32; Warren Mears 33, 40, 47, 68, 69, 72; Watcher 2, 16, 137, 140; Watchers' Council 16, 120, 140; William (the Bloody) 18, 29, 31; Xander Harris 2, 12, 13, 14, 15, 31, 32, 34, 42, 46, 64, 67, 68, 70, 72, 79, 120, 121, 134, 140, 160n6, 161n8, 169n6, 169n7

Buffy Season Eight comics 1, 68, 69, 72, 164n14, 171n21

Buffyverse 4, 18, 21, 63, 69, 72, 79, 119, 122, 132, 136, 140, 141, 142, 143, 160n3, 162n4, 165n17, 165n20

chip (neurological) 29, 31, 81, 91, 92, 93, 96, 119, 166n10, 167n14

Chosen One 2, 11, 14

claddagh 132, 170n4

conscience 17, 78, 122, 161n7

Cordelia Chase 2, 4, 14, 15, 16, 17, 21, 32, 34, 42, 46, 49, 50, 51, 53, 64, 67, 68, 70, 75, 77, 78, 81, 91, 95, 112, 113, 123, 137, 141, 161n9, 167n16, 171n16

Cordy see Cordelia Chase

demon(s) 2, 4, 10, 18, 29, 32, 34, 46, 48, 49, 50, 53, 63, 64, 65, 66, 67, 68, 69, 70, 74, 75, 77, 78, 80, 91, 92, 93, 95, 119, 120, 122, 131, 132, 136, 137, 139, 161n7, 164n10, 165n20, 167n16, 171n14

Descartes, René 89, 90

Devil 65; see also Satan

Dollhouse (series) 1, 6, 9, 13, 19, 20, 21, 27, 38, 41, 42, 58, 62, 81, 97, 98, 103, 104, 105, 106, 107, 111, 113, 119, 126, 127, 128, 135, 142, 160n3, 161n12, 163n6, 163n15, 167n1, 168n1; Active(s) 6, 13, 19, 22, 27, 38, 39, 40, 41, 58, 59, 60, 103, 105, 106, 107, 108, 109, 110, 111, 126, 127, 135, 142, 159n9, 160n3, 168n4, 171n23; Adelle DeWitt 6, 40, 61, 135; Alpha 59, 105, 107, 108, 110, 111, 135, 142, 159n9; Bennett Halverson 107, 110, 168n6; Boyd Langton 6, 39, 108; Caroline 6, 7, 38, 106, 108, 109, 110, 111, 113, 135, 142, 144, 168n6; Claire Saunders 6, 59, 111, 159n9; Dollhouse(s) 6, 7, 38, 39, 40, 59, 60, 98, 103, 104, 105, 106, 107, 108, 111, 127, 135, 143, 159n9, 160n3, 163n16, 168n6; Echo 6, 7, 38, 39, 40, 41, 42, 58, 59, 60, 103, 104, 105, 106, 107, 108, 109, 110, 111, 113, 126, 127, 128, 135, 142, 143, 144, 159n9, 168n6; Joe Hearn 39, 60, 103; Laurence Dominic 108; Mellie 6, 39; November 6, 39, 58, 111, 159n9; Paul Ballard 7, 38, 39, 42, 59, 104, 109, 142, 159n9; Priya Tsetsang 42, 60, 61, 127, 142, 159n9; Rossum Corporation 6, 7, 19, 21, 27, 38, 103, 106, 109, 110, 111, 127, 135, 142, 168n6; Sierra 6, 38, 39, 42, 58, 60, 61, 103, 105, 111, 127, 159n9; Tony 42, 142, 159n9; Topher Brink 6, 38, 60, 81, 104, 105, 106, 107, 108, 109, 110, 127, 135, 171n23; Victor 6, 38, 39, 40, 42, 58, 60, 103, 107, 108, 159n9; Whiskey 58, 59, 104, 110, 111, 135, 159n9

domestic violence 43, 44, 45, 47, 162n3, 164n19; see also interpersonal violence

dopamine 115, 117, 124

Dracula (book and character) 2, 11, 131, 159n3

Dracula 2000 131

drugs 19, 22, 95, 96, 102, 106, 107, 109, 114, 115, 116, 117, 118, 119, 120, 121, 122, 123, 124, 126, 127, 128, 129, 130, 138, 144, 165n17, 168n3, 169n4, 169n14, 170n14; antianxiety (anxiolytic) 116, 117, 118, 124, 128; antidepressant 116, 124, 125, 126, 128

female genital circumcision 52

Firefly (series) 1, 5, 9, 11, 13, 19, 21, 22, 27, 35, 36, 40, 41, 43, 55, 57, 62, 78, 81, 96, 112, 119, 123, 124, 125, 128, 132, 134, 135,

138, 141, 159n8, 160n3, 161n11, 162n16, 163n6; Adelai Niska 54, 57, 90; Alliance 5, 19, 20, 21, 22, 54, 56, 58, 79, 87, 88, 89, 90, 95, 112, 124, 125, 135, 138, 139; Companion 5, 35, 37, 40, 55, 57, 133, 162n11, 169n10; Hoban "Wash" Washburne 5, 35, 36, 42, 54, 55, 56; Inara Serra 5, 35, 37, 41, 42, 55, 56, 57, 124, 125, 133, 135, 162n11, 163n13, 169n9, 169n10, 171n22; Jayne Cobb 1, 5, 19, 20, 37, 55, 56, 57, 58, 79, 87, 89, 128, 130, 141, 161n11, 163n14, 166n6, 171n22; Kaylee Frye 5, 20, 36, 42, 55, 56, 57, 91, 171n22; Mal(colm) Reynolds, Captain 5, 13, 19, 21, 22, 35, 37, 42, 54, 55, 56, 57, 58, 79, 89, 125, 132, 133, 135, 138, 139, 141, 142, 143, 160n4, 162n11, 162n14, 163n13, 171n22; Miranda 124, 125, 138, 139, 143; Nandi 35, 36, 37, 57, 162n14, 169n9; Operative 58, 89, 90; Reavers 54, 57, 58, 125, 130, 134, 135, 138, 164n10; River Tam 5, 19, 20, 21, 56, 58, 79, 81, 87, 88, 89, 90, 91, 95, 97, 112, 123, 124, 128, 138, 142, 166n6, 169n9; Shepherd Book 5, 35, 56, 79, 163n1, 171n22; Simon Tam, Doctor 5, 20, 36, 42, 56, 79, 87, 88, 89, 123, 124, 142, 161n11, 169n9, 171n22; Zoe Alleyne Washburne 5, 35, 36, 37, 55, 57, 79, 130, 132, 133, 170n7

Frankenstein 92, 167n11
Fringe 102, 119

Gypsy 2, 3, 71

Henry M. 100, 102, 109
hippocampus 87, 88, 100, 106, 108, 109, 127, 166n4
hostile aggression 44, 57
Huxley, Aldous 118
hypnosis 10, 117

instrumental (proactive) aggression 44, 58
interpersonal violence 45; *see also* domestic violence

Jesus of Nazareth 131, 170n3

Klüver-Bucy Syndrome 88, 166n5

magick 3, 11, 15, 21, 31, 33, 47, 48, 62, 63, 64, 66, 67, 68, 69 71, 72, 73, 74, 76, 77,

78, 79, 80, 112, 120, 122, 130, 144, 161n11, 165n17
memory 6, 19, 21, 33, 38, 58, 76, 77, 81, 86, 87, 88, 97, 98, 99, 100, 101, 102, 104, 105, 106, 107, 108, 110, 111, 112, 113, 114, 117, 126, 127, 130, 139, 144, 165n23, 168n3, 168n4, 171n23; autobiographical 6, 97, 101; episodic 97, 101, 103, 104, 113, 168n3; long-term 88, 99, 100, 108; procedural 39, 60, 97, 101, 103; semantic 97, 101, 104, 113; short-term working 88, 99, 108

oligodendroglioma 93

pagan 62, 63
Pax 125, 138
Paxil 125, 126
pharmaceuticals *see* drugs
pineal gland 89, 90, 166n9
post-traumatic stress/disorder (PTSD) 53, 88, 124, 163n7

relational aggression/violence 45

Satan 63, 65, 90, 164n6
schizophrenia(c) 87, 95, 110, 116, 123, 124, 127, 166n3, 169n8
Serenity (film) 1, 9, 11, 19, 22, 36, 42, 54, 57, 58, 81, 89, 112, 123, 128, 133, 134, 138, 160n3, 162n13, 171n22
Serenity (spaceship) 5, 19, 21, 37, 55, 56, 57, 78, 112, 125, 135, 138, 141, 143, 160n3, 165n24, 171n22
Shelley, Mary 92, 117
Silverberg, Robert 117, 118, 119, 128
Slayage 144, 167n1
Slayer 2, 3, 9, 11, 13, 14, 15, 16, 29, 30, 31, 45, 49, 63, 64, 69, 70, 71, 73, 80, 98, 111, 122, 140, 141, 160n5
soma 118, 126, 169n4
soul 17, 18, 30, 49, 65, 71, 74, 78, 90, 95, 122, 132, 141, 159n6, 160n7, 161n7
Spike 3, 4, 11, 18, 23, 27, 28, 29, 30, 31, 34, 42, 46, 48, 49, 53, 54, 68, 69, 72, 73, 81, 91, 92, 93, 95, 96, 114, 119, 120, 128, 132, 134, 141, 143, 161n8, 161n5, 161n8, 162n5, 163n5, 163n8, 166n10, 167n14, 169n5
Star Trek Deep Space Nine 28
Stoker, Bram 2, 131, 159n13
Straczynski, J. Michael 38, 97

third eye 89, 166n9
Triangular Theory of Love 23, 33

True Blood 28

vampire 2, 4, 11, 13, 14, 17, 18, 21, 27, 28, 29, 49, 50, 53, 54, 64, 67, 70, 74, 77, 78, 80, 91, 119, 122, 123, 131, 132, 135, 136, 139, 159n6, 160n5, 161n8, 161n3, 163n6, 165n20, 169n5, 169n9
'verse 5, 21, 37, 54, 57, 78, 87, 91, 123, 125, 134, 138, 143, 162n14

Wearing, Clive 100, 109
werewolf 16, 32
Wesley Wyndam-Pryce 4, 16, 35, 42, 43, 51, 53, 64, 75, 76, 78, 123, 137, 141, 171n15
Whedon, Joss 1, 6, 9, 10, 11, 13, 19, 20, 21, 23, 27, 29, 30, 32, 34, 37, 41, 43, 47, 54, 57, 61, 63, 74, 78, 81, 95, 96, 97, 98, 102, 105, 106, 107, 111, 113, 114, 117, 122, 125, 126, 127, 128, 129, 130, 131, 133, 136, 137, 139, 143, 144, 159n5, 160n7, 161n10, 163n6, 163n8, 163n15, 165n17, 169n5, 171n22
Whedon Studies Association 144, 167n1
Whedonverse(s) 1, 9, 13, 17, 20, 21, 22, 25, 26, 41, 42, 87, 91, 130, 132, 133, 139, 140, 141, 144, 165n20
Wicca(n) 63, 64, 66, 71, 72, 164n9
Will *see* Willow Rosenberg
Willow Rosenberg 2, 12, 13, 14, 15, 31, 32, 33, 34, 42, 46, 47, 48, 63, 64, 66, 67, 68, 70, 71, 72, 73, 74, 79, 112, 119, 122, 134, 136, 137, 140, 160n6, 164n9, 165n17, 169n5, 170n6, 171n16
witch 10, 15, 33, 56, 62, 63, 64, 65, 66, 70, 72, 77, 79
witchcraft 11, 12, 21, 62, 63, 64, 65, 66, 67, 71, 73, 76, 144, 164n15
witchcraze 64, 65, 66